Empathetic Marketing

Empathetic Marketing

How to Satisfy the 6 Core Emotional Needs of Your Customers

Mark Ingwer

First published in 2012 by
PALGRAVE MACMILLAN®
in the United States—a division of St. Martin's Press LLC,
175 Fifth Avenue, New York, NY 10010.

Where this book is distributed in the UK, Europe and the rest of the world,
this is by Palgrave Macmillan, a division of Macmillan Publishers Limited,
registered in England, company number 785998, of Houndmills,
Basingstoke, Hampshire RG21 6XS.

Palgrave Macmillan is the global academic imprint of the above companies
and has companies and representatives throughout the world.

Palgrave® and Macmillan® are registered trademarks in the United States,
the United Kingdom, Europe and other countries.

ISBN: 978–0–230–34027–5

Library of Congress Cataloging-in-Publication Data

Ingwer, Mark.
    Empathetic marketing : how to satisfy the 6 core emotional needs of
your customers / Mark Ingwer.
       p. cm.
    ISBN 978–0–230–34027–5 (hardback)
       1. Customer relations—Psychological aspects. 2. Consumer
satisfaction. 3. Consumer behavior. I. Title.
HF5415.5.I544 2012
658.8'343—dc23   2011041705

A catalogue record of the book is available from the British Library.

Design by Newgen Imaging Systems (P) Ltd., Chennai, India.

First edition: May 2012

10 9 8 7 6 5 4 3 2 1

Printed in the United States of America.

To Jake, who glows in his father's eye
And to the memory of Lisa

We are continually faced with great opportunities which are brilliantly disguised as unsolvable problems

—MARGARET MEAD

Contents

List of Figures and Tables   ix

Foreword   xi
Chip Conley

Acknowledgments   xiii

Introduction   1

Chapter 1   The Hidden Emotional Needs behind
             Our Decisions   7

Chapter 2   The Needs Continuum   25

Chapter 3   The Need for Control   45

Chapter 4   The Need for Self-Expression   69

Chapter 5   The Need for Growth   99

Chapter 6   The Need for Recognition   125

Chapter 7   The Need for Belonging   151

Chapter 8   The Need for Care   185

Epilogue   207

Notes   225

Index   231

Figures and Tables

Figures

2.1	Merriam-Webster Definition of "Need"	25
2.2	Maslow's Hierarchy of Needs	31
2.3	The Needs Continuum	34
2.4	(p. 40) The Needs Continuum	39
2.4	(p. 45) The Needs Continuum	44
3.1	The Control Need	45
3.2	Potential Messaging Strategies for United	62
3.3	Potential Taglines for United	63
4.1	The Self-Expression Need	69
4.2	Needs/Company Connection Triangle—Cingular	83
4.3	Needs/Company Connection Triangle—Corona	84
5.1	The Growth Need	99
6.1	The Recognition Need	125
7.1	The Belonging Need	151
7.2	Asch Conformity Study Example Comparison Lines	156
8.1	The Care Need	185

Tables

2.1	Comparison American vs. South Korean Emotional Need Rankings	28
7.1	Evolution of American Social Values	158
7.2	Psychodynamics of Shame	179
7.3	Psychodynamics of Fear	180

Foreword

Increasingly, businesses have come to appreciate the potential value in utilizing universal human needs and emotions to connect with their customers. Despite this, they still have not found a way to identify, understand, and capitalize on the deeper needs and wants of many of their customers. As a result they tend to strictly utilize metrics and base the lion's share of their strategy and tactics on assumptions that their customers are inherently rational. This book expands on our existing knowledge base and challenges these assumptions. It provides an extremely creative and thought provoking new approach to understand and satisfy consumers' core, emotional needs.

Though there is a potential wealth of knowledge that social, clinical, and consumer psychology offers business, very few companies have figured out how to embrace and leverage this wisdom. In *Empathetic Marketing*, Dr. Ingwer does a remarkable job of translating psychological theories and studies to make them tangible. He astutely brings the key learnings down from the ivory tower so they can benefit marketers and business leaders across a wide variety of industries. Mark offers not only theory, but also provides concrete tactics that demonstrate the incredible effectiveness of unleashing the power of deeper needs and emotions for success in the marketplace. He thoughtfully and cogently brings it all together to distill the lofty theories to provide manageable, accessible ways to help sustain and propel a business into the future.

Throughout the book, Dr. Ingwer offers a fascinating behind-the-scenes look at a number of different companies that have successfully and unsuccessfully attempted to utilize emotions and needs to deepen relationships with customers and grow their business. He gives new meaning to the meaning that customers take away from their decision-making and brand interaction. Reading this book reaffirmed for me the ultimate power and value that deeper needs can have, now and in the future. At Joie de Vivre, we incorporate many of these ideas into our business plan and day to day practices, and have seen first-hand how effective they can be in helping us to sustain and grow our valued customer base.

Empathetic Marketing provides an updated, easy to understand model of human needs that will help readers to make sense of seemingly enigmatic consumer decision making and to effectively grow their business by satisfying consumers' needs. Dr. Ingwer provides an invaluable framework for organizing and understanding these needs and successfully applying these concepts to your own marketing and brand strategies. Whether you are a start up entrepreneur or run a Fortune 500 company, I am confident that the theory and practices highlighted in *Empathetic Marketing* will provide untold value and wisdom for you and your customers.

Chip Conley
Founder & CEO of Joie de Vivre Hotels
Author of *Peak* and *Emotional Equations*

Acknowledgments

This is a book that is built upon the wisdom and personal experiences of many. I am enormously grateful to them. A wide range of people have influenced the thinking behind this book.

The ideas put forth in this book have been influenced by the writings of Carl Jung, Sigmund Freud, Marshall McLuhan, Harry Levinson, Abraham Maslow, David Ogilvy, and Malcolm Gladwell. Their insight and understanding of psychology, behavior, and business in many ways is timeless. Each of these thinkers and writers has played no small part in helping me craft a broad-reaching business model based on their theoretical contributions. As I began to write this book, I attempted to bridge the thinking of psychology with that of business in the twenty-first century. I only hope to have done justice to these groundbreaking theorists and journalists and hope that their ideas will drive the successful performance of businesses from start-up companies to those that are mature, and for those both small and large.

Importantly, I am also indebted to both the patients and consumers who have shared their lives—their struggles, decisions, hopes, fears, dreams, disappointments, and aspirations—with my colleagues and me at Insight Consulting Group (ICG). I truly appreciate the trust they placed in me and the risks that they take while in the process of defining themselves and forging both an inner and outer identity. They have provided an invaluable source of experiences, rich with contradictions, as to why they do what they do and why they feel the way they do, while ultimately striving to make sense of the two.

Too often consumers' personal lives have been considered to be separate, irrelevant, and distinct from their public business lives. Hopefully, this book will lead to some changes by closing some of this gap so that the firewall that business creates can begin to be dissolved. Perhaps this book will open the door and lead to deeper and more satisfying experiences for both customers and business leaders who make key decisions for their customers.

I am extremely privileged to have the benefit of the intellectual firepower and thoughtfulness of my colleagues and friends. My thanks to Jeff Kiel at Draft FCB, Michael Durange at HBO, Szilvia Kovari-Krecsmary at Mcgarrybowen, Stephen Hersh at Leo Burnett, Debbie Silverman at Digitas, and Roberta Borst at Allstate. I'd also like to thank ICG's business partners, who enabled me to incorporate and evolve some of the ideas of *Empathetic Marketing* in their work with ICG. These include David Budner, Steve Anthony, Jonathan Daly, Linda Krauss, and Marylin Franck.

This book would literally not have been written without the dedication, patience, and thoughtfulness of Ryan Hunt. We spent many hours bantering about how to convey the concepts and how best to structure *Empathetic Marketing*. Also, during the early stages, Brett Ommen played a significant role as sounding board and provided highly useful and incisive comments. Chris Murray offered valuable advice and final editing and commentary.

Additionally, I'd like to thank Aakash Gupta, Bill Hooper, and Matt Nabavian, and Josh Richman—whom we were fortunate to have as part of our research team. I'd like to also offer my gratitude to Sara Block, whose continuous energy, dedication, and talent helped get *Empathic Marketing* to the point of completion. Lloyd Roin also provided his "mild-mannered" support and understood the value of *Empathetic Marketing* for the business community. I would also like to thank my partner at ICG, Nathan Hoffberg, without whose encouragement, business smarts, and urging, this book never would have been written. I could not ask for a better business partner.

I'd like to thank my editor, Laurie Harting, who enthusiastically prodded, challenged, and ultimately championed the idea of *Empathetic Marketing*.

Lastly I'd like to acknowledge the "never in doubt" love and support of my mom and dad.

Introduction

For nearly two decades, much of the business world has increasingly embraced the value of emotion in selling products and services. Countless books and articles deftly describe how emotion factors into human decision making and helps people form bonds with brands, products, services, advertising, and other people. More and more business leaders, strategists, product developers, marketers, innovation specialists, advertisers, and salespeople have come to see the value of appealing not merely to consumers' reason and logic but to their heartstrings as well. There is little doubt that emotions offer buried treasure for businesses. Companies must invest exceptional resources to unearth them and guide them to the surface in order to harness their business value. Emotions can be powerful economic tools if understood and excavated properly. But without the benefit of a proven psychological theory to tell us where, when, and how to extract emotional insights, opportunities are lost and business resources wasted.

The word "emotion" is derived from the Latin word *movere* for "to move," suggesting that emotions literally take us to another place or compel us to act in certain ways. Businesses surely try "to move" their customers, but it's crucial to ask: where are they moving them? The logical answer is "to the sale." But that's the short view we've come to know. It misses the deeper role and the potential value of emotion and risks alienating or misdirecting the audience. Google, a company that since its founding had shown a brilliant understanding of the needs of customers, launched its social media answer to Twitter and Facebook in February 2010 with a new product called Google Buzz. There was no doubt that millions of people were (and still are) ready and willing to share posts, pictures, and other information with friends over the Internet. Google, however, vastly underestimated consumers' deep concern with privacy. The launch of Buzz immediately led to an angry outcry over privacy issues connected to the service. For example, Buzz made all of a user's email contacts public. Personal email addresses were easily accessible. The application made connections to other Google services such as Picasa automatically, making more personal information accessible to Internet surfers. A class-action suit concerning these and other privacy issues was filed, resulting in a $8.5 million settlement—surely a token amount for Google but a move that potentially reinforced the damage to Google's image. Despite addressing the privacy issues, Buzz never caught the imagination of the Internet consumer, and in October 2011, Google announced they were discontinuing the service.

I contend that emotions and resulting behaviors are the foundation for satisfying complex psychological needs. Our individual well-being—self-esteem, success, relationships, and happiness—is a result of our meeting emotional needs. An individual's needs are satisfied when he or she is connected meaningfully to others, and through those connections comes to find his or her own unique value and identity. It is a ceaseless, evolving, lifelong endeavor. Needs are at the root of our triumphs and setbacks in our personal lives, and as we'll see time and time again, they also affect many of the consumer decisions that fuel commerce.

The central premise of this book is that businesses must have an intimate and conceptual framework for understanding these emotional needs and a passion for meeting them at every step of the way. For example, Facebook succeeds because it satisfies both an internal yearning for connectivity to a group, and a need to celebrates one's individuality through creative self-expression. Most businesses leaders claim they care about their consumers' needs, and yet they lack a conceptual framework for understanding the way in which these needs dovetail with their business. In this book we'll introduce a framework that will help business executives to comprehend the science of vital emotional needs and incorporate this perspective into their own strategy.

But first, in order for this to occur, business leaders must acquire a broader, more humanistic perspective rooted in the experience of people's personal and economic behavior.

As a research psychologist and clinician, I've witnessed how inner emotional experiences move people through the complexities of daily life—through their relationships with spouse, friends, and family, through their career and life aspirations, and through their evolving self-images. By listening to people describe their inner emotional lives through the years—their hopes and yearnings, their fears and anxieties, their best and worst selves—I've come to see what matters most to people at every life stage and have helped many come to peace with achieving personal and professional goals.

And as a consumer and a clinical psychologist, and a market researcher and marketing consultant, I've had the privilege of working with thousands of consumers and business professionals face to face, from underprivileged city children, to chief executive officers, to stay-at-home moms (and dads), to patients and medical doctors, to salespeople selling everything from pharmaceuticals to high-tech equipment. These interviews often take place in front of a two-way mirror. Our clients observe from the other side. At the end of the evening, they will typically state what they heard in the discussion. Frequently, I have a different perception or interpretation. When I report this, the client sometimes counters, "That's not what they said." But I listen with what psychologists call "the third ear," a trained lens that helps me see beyond the surface of what people say and toward a deeper empathic understanding of their emotional needs, the hidden meaning behind many conscious thoughts, feelings, and behaviors. What I do is not magic; in a way it is a lot like the finely honed listening skills top executives use to skillfully navigate corporate politics or manage tense situations in business meetings. But as a business psychologist, I specialize in listening to and understanding a much larger, more diverse and complex group of people—your customers.

Many highly successful business leaders have spent their entire professional lives focused on one discipline or one market. Their specialization, after all, gave rise to their success. However, the breadth of my experience in addressing diverse client issues has enabled me to identify universal tenets in human behavior, regardless of industry or discipline: no matter the situation and differences in gender, economic status, or age, and no matter the changes in technology, trends, and behaviors, we all act to satisfy the same core needs. The more things change, the more they stay the same.

Despite the business culture's growing embrace of emotion, and thereby the presence of needs, this awareness is often the first thing people shut out of their professional mindsets. Too often, we build a firewall that helps us rely on our logic and reason skills to solve business problems. We follow a well-structured playbook. We stick to what works or what is perceived to be the safest method of satisfying our business challenges. The sciences, including psychology, are not immune from this either, as they attempt to create a fact-based, quantified approach that ultimately tends to sanitize or reify people. In this effort we forget about the humanity of consumers. We filter out the raw emotion underlying the needs. This book is an invitation to take down that firewall, an invitation to adopt a holistic looking glass into the human mind. In the chapters that follow, we offer not a formula but rather a strategic philosophy of the guiding needs shared by us all.

Solving business problems and generating insights is more about connecting the dots than drawing new ones. Oftentimes, the answer is found when we widen the scope. We can learn about the needs (the contents of which we'll explore in the upcoming chapters) by peering inside the dynamics of human relationships. We can learn about the needs by observing the psychological underpinnings of how and why people use products and services. We can learn by listening to others through an empathic understanding of their emotional lives.

In short, understanding how human needs manifest in the marketplace requires businesses to learn from disciplines that are often overlooked in boardrooms and on the ground floor. Drawing from the perspectives of sociology, ethnography, and psychology—neurological, behavioral, clinical, and psychodynamic—blended together with traditional consumer insights, this book makes the bold case for an emotional needs-based paradigm shift in the business community. These perspectives result in better way to listen to, talk to, observe, and understand where people are in life and where they are going. It's about stepping away from the spreadsheet and into family kitchens, local bars, and doctor's offices.

Bringing together decades of research in these fields, this book introduces a vantage point that will help leaders in any discipline reconnect with audiences that are always on the move. In part 1, I lay out the impetus behind the shift toward a needs-based approach and discuss the impact of needs on our own well-being. Then, I lay out a model of needs that represents the balancing act required of a psychologically healthy life.

In part 2, I focus on each of these core needs individually. In these chapters, we'll see how needs emerge in daily life through the stories of a manager, a middle school teacher, an unemployed job seeker, a salesperson, a husband, and a retiree. Then, each need's historic context is discussed, as well as contemporary business challenges and opportunities related to the need. Finally, in each chapter, we review a business case study and the tools that can be used to connect the presence of a need to a tangible solution.

CHAPTER 1

The Hidden Emotional Needs behind Our Decisions

One of the country's largest meat producers exhausted considerable resources researching and developing a breakthrough pork product lean enough to earn its title as the "other white meat." Because of the product's unique composition, this pork only needed to be cooked for 3 to 4 minutes, unlike other cuts. Sales expectations were high due to the fact that the product scored extremely well in controlled taste tests. However, once the preproduct launch testing moved from the plant to volunteers cooking the meat for themselves in their homes, the previously positive results did not hold. The research participants—"caregiver" consumers who regularly served pork to their families—reported back with negative reviews, stating that the pork was dry and bland. But self-reports indicated that almost all participants cooked the meat for 7 to 8 minutes, ignoring the explicit instructions about the shorter cooking time. This confounding behavior was poised to derail the product's acceptance.

A leading discount shoe store wanted to increase sales to middle-class audiences. To this end, they had made steady inroads in changing their merchandise and shopping experience. They wanted female shoe shoppers to know that they needn't sacrifice style for a lower price. Researchers observed participants from the target audience as they browsed and shopped at the store. Many of the women, despite finding several appealing, stylish pairs of shoes at attractive prices, reported that the store was still a place they were unlikely to shop at in the future. They couldn't articulate why at the time, but research ultimately discovered that their reluctance was due to the store's subtle scent of synthetic leather (also known as "pleather"), which acted as a strong unconscious inhibitor.

An iconic breakfast cereal brand already very popular with children sought to expand its market share among adults. Traditionally a kids' brand, the cereal aspired to position itself in a way that appealed to older audiences without deterring its primary audience. At the same time, a trend was prompting more Americans to embrace healthier lifestyles. The cereal was whole-grain and was rich with soluble and dietary fibers, known to be a factor in lowering cholesterol. To signal potential benefits, the company focused first and foremost on designing a simple heart logo and health-benefit statement to place front and center on its yellow box. Their sales soared, and their box became a symbol of heart-healthy consumer food products.

*   *   *

AT FIRST GLANCE, there's nothing remarkable about these anecdotes. Stories and discoveries like these appear in the business pages every day. People notoriously don't follow directions. Researchers have known for a century that background aesthetics (music, smell, floor design) are subliminally persuasive. Corporations have always used basic package design and benefit claims as part of broader marketing campaigns to change perception and increase sales. So it's all too easy to treat the stories described above in isolation, arrive at a logical conclusion for each, and turn the page.

While they lack logical kinship on the surface, these stories do share one trait: each reflects the importance of uncovering and satisfying emotional human needs. In identifying the deeper emotion-based needs of specific audiences, the business community can discover and fine-tune insights that transcend standard marketing practices. It can learn to look beyond the logical explanations of consumer behavior associated with the stories above. Let's see how.

My consulting firm conducted the research for each example. Much of our research for the pork producer took place in the South, a region where culinary traditions have existed for generations. People had been cooking meat the same way for decades, and admittedly, were quite good at it. When I, a complete stranger, came into their homes and asked them to set aside their routines, we immediately saw they had trouble making the mental leap toward the short cooking time. They lived true to their mothers' ways. To them, pork really isn't pork if it's ready in three minutes. People naturally fear consuming undercooked meat. So even though the instructions on the package reiterated the shorter, but safe, cooking time as boldly as possible, it didn't matter. Their cooking habits, rooted in all-important ancestral traditions, were far more persuasive than the directions. They ignored them and followed their instincts, not risking undercooked meat and a sick family.

People need control, a baseline, a secure feeling that next week isn't going to be all that different from this one or the last. Some of us are able to live spontaneously and cope with change more quickly than others, but in a world that appears as random as ours, we're ingrained with a drive to achieve balance and normalcy. At the very least, we want to establish control over facets of our life that we know we can control—such as making simple household repairs, fixing a nasty slice on the driving range, or in this case, playing the family caretaking role by not undercooking meat. We develop internal, instinctive road maps that guide behavior.

The consumers' insistence on cooking the pork "the best way" reflects this deeper need for control. It helped the participants sustain their identities as family caregivers. The manufacturers, in contrast, had identified a need for healthier and better-tasting pork and devoted a lot of resources to developing it. But the product, even though it was a breakthrough innovation, could not satisfy the arguably more deep-set, emotional need of caring for one's family. The manufacturer first had to master the art of empathy—penetrate the hearts and minds of this audience, what we termed the "caring-segment"—and align its approach with the identified emotional need. This means that to change behavior and decision making, the manufacturer first had to observe the lives of the audience, listen to their fears, and experience the routines of their kitchen at dinner time, including how they read instructions, or whether they read them at all. The manufacturer would have learned that cooking instructions on a package don't easily overrule long-held culinary habits and traditions, such as cooking pork for at least 7 to 8 minutes to avoid food poisoning and for a better tasting and healthier meal. The standard "faster food" marketing approach, that is, simply informing the consumer that the product cooks faster, such as on Minute Rice packages, is not enough to push consumers to "take a risk" on undercooked pork. Realizing this, the manufacturer would have seen the need to emphasize in its marketing and outreach efforts the *safety* of the quick-cooking pork, as well as the *benefit* of spending less time in the kitchen and more time with the family. Both of these attributes speak to the nurturing or caregiving emotional drive of its customers and change their perspective: customers see the quicker cooking as an opportunity in their role as caregiver, not a risk.

Oddly enough, this unforeseen impediment is why my firm's experience with pleather is not much different from our work with the pork. The term "pleather" was coined in the '70s by a New York fashion designer attempting to market the new material. Leather was in vogue at the time—pants, jackets, suits, and boots. So when the cheaper, polyurethane alternative showed up for the masses, the term was used derogatorily. Pleather signified that its wearer couldn't afford genuine leather. The term kept its tongue-in-cheek connotation straight through the hairband days and the '90s, into the new millennium. And for the women participating in our shoe store research, the nearly subliminal pleather scent symbolized a deeply held fear. They felt that by changing how and where they shopped for shoes, they were altering how they were viewed and how they expressed themselves. The need for self-expression is a constant drive to convey who we are to ourselves and others. So many decisions in the marketplace are based on how a product or service matches one's sense of self. Fashion has always been one of the most prominent arenas for this process. The women in our research were genuinely willing to trim their budget by trading higher-ticket designer brands for an equally attractive and stylish, but less prestigious label; however, that didn't matter. The store's atmosphere became an unconscious symbol that undermined how the women sought to express themselves. The subtle scent stood in the way of their normal, cathartic shoe-shopping experience.

As a direct result of the researchers making this determination, the store began to enhance its perception through the combination of redesigned sales floors, a celebrity fashion diva spokesperson, and a product line that was even more stylish and less "pleathery." But this lesson carries over to countless other marketplace examples. It is often not easy to identify deeper emotional needs in what people say or do, because our needs drive us in ways that operate beyond the bounds of conscious awareness.

Yet timing is everything. Ironically, had our research taken place a few years later, pleather might not have been a problem at all. Due to the oddly cyclical nature of fashion trends, a solution arrived by way of the phenomenon known as "vegan" or "eco" fashion, a niche that is still growing exponentially by the year. A Web search for "vegan footwear" yields thousands of stores, designers, and blogs that all embrace pleather, which is now often called "vegan," "vegetarian," or "eco-vegan" leather. In fact, in a sign that they've embraced the emerging trend, our client is among the first options listed in the search engine. The once-deterring scent is now a facilitator for product adoption—a lower-cost way to look good, feel good, and commit oneself to an emerging cause.

As we saw with pleather, a long-existing product attribute can become highly relevant to consumers as trends change. This turned out to be a major opportunity for the iconic cereal brand. The heart on the cereal box is a straightforward appeal to the universal human need to care for others and oneself. Our interest in the health of loved ones is an integral facet of this need. But why was the box such an effective vehicle? To answer that, we have to understand how important symbols are to a person's process of creating meaning. A compelling symbol is as effective as written, verbal, or body language in communicating a complex message. The heart is the universal symbol for the vitality of both life and love. To shoppers in the cereal aisle, it addressed legitimate rational desires to live healthily—an innate impulse to care for themselves or whomever they are shopping for. With one exceedingly simple element serving as a marketing foundation, and imposing minimal additional costs, the manufacturers communicated a rich symbol and extended their core market beyond children.

The company considered launching the initiative through traditional advertising channels—digital, television, print—but decided against it for the early stages. The box was the cornerstone of their strategy. This turned out to be an ideal tactic, because the cereal box, and the way people use it, proved to be the most effective advertisement of all. This is a simple case of behavioral psychology. The "heart" would speak to people in the cereal aisle, but more importantly, it would reinforce the symbol to those eating it every morning. When one actually has time to sit down for breakfast, what is the most common routine? We sit down with our bowl, flip open the newspaper, and set the box in front of us. As our attention wanders from the bowl and the news, our eyes latch onto the back of the box, which instantly becomes a billboard that reinforces the message we discovered at the purchasing point. And because people reading the box at breakfast aren't always the ones buying the cereal initially, it's a message that resonates with children who may even ask their parents about the meaning of cholesterol (causing parents to consider their own cholesterol levels). But it also resonates with adults without children, who perhaps feel they've outgrown kids' cereal but now have a practical, health-related reason to buy the product. The company later expanded the promotion and reach of their "heart-healthy" message by making cholesterol the focus of future television advertisements.

Of course, none of this matters if the cereal can't actually satisfy the established need. At a much later phase of the campaign, the box claims were considered to have overstated their health benefits according to the Food and Drug Administration (FDA), but then the cereal was proven to lower cholesterol marginally if balanced with a regular diet. Now virtually every cereal brand, whether it's healthy or not, claims to contain some redeeming nutritional value. This either makes the consumer work harder to find a truly healthy selection, or on the other hand, makes it easier for them to return to a brand they trust and enjoy—which our client's product delivered on.

In both the pork and the pleather research, the companies focused on valid surface needs (lean and better-tasting meat; affordable and stylish shoes in hard times) while overlooking seemingly small details that would affect their audiences' behavior more than any other factor. In the cereal research, the company addressed and satisfied a need with minute expenditures. The lesson in each case: no matter the situation or the industry, the successes, failures, and challenges of business can most always be traced to a core set of human needs applicable to specific audiences. With a humanistic, emotional, needs-based approach, businesses can make more sense of their customers' enigmatic behavior.

They will see how and why a shorter cooking time can be an unwelcome impediment for consumers, and how and why a barely noticeable and seemingly innocuous background smell can have an impact on how shoppers see themselves.

It's important to note that the customer needs that business must address will be both emotional and rational. The lesson to be drawn from the examples described above is that businesses must take into consideration the emotional needs of their customers. However, if the pork is tasteless, if the shoes fall apart, or if the cereal is proven to be less healthy than described, no amount of effort to address emotional needs will win over the rational side of the consumer's brain that says to reject the product.

In short, there must be a balance. If a company focuses solely on rational, logical decision making, they will make mistakes and lose customers. If they focus only on emotions, they may be able to attract customers initially, but those customers are not likely to stay loyal. To be effective, they need to engage consumers emotionally and to direct them rationally.

The Psychology behind Unconscious Needs

The motivation and emotion behind our quest for needs satisfaction and identity fulfillment all too often are not always consciously available to us. Our behavior fluctuates in seemingly enigmatic ways. Every day we walk, breathe, and complete countless other actions without consciously telling ourselves we are doing so. Similarly, we're not aware of how we use marketplace symbols—products, services, activities—to form our sense of identity, and of how these symbols have an impact on us.

Carl Jung spent his career in psychiatry questioning how people form limitlessly diverse personalities. He introduced the idea of the human "persona," which is the social face we show to the world that conceals our true nature. As we grow older, we adjust our behaviors and personality traits based on the social expectations and rules governing our lives, and constantly shed our personas, or retool aspects of our identity to arrive at a desirable sense of self.

The challenging aspect of this process is that much of persona formation, that is, who we become and how we create our selves, occurs beyond our consciousness. Thus, the challenge of anticipating and satisfying needs is summed up in this verse from psychologist and author Daniel Goleman:

> *The range of what we think and do*
> *is limited by what we fail to notice.*
> *And because we fail to notice*
> *that we fail to notice*
> *there is little we can do*
> *to change*
> *until we notice*
> *how failing to notice*
> *shapes our thoughts and deeds.*[1]

"What we fail to notice" is the powerful effect of our unconscious on behavior and personalities. Our thoughts, actions, opinions, and expressions are anchored to hidden ideas buried below our conscious awareness. The words that sway us, the people who touch us, and the products that make us salivate with desire are all related to this unseen force that is instrumental in creating meaning.

This unconcious side of our psyche is what Jung calls the "shadow." The shadow is our unseen self. It represents the repressed elements of our identity that do not fit with our conscious self-image. According to Connie Zweig and Jeremiah Abrams, it's a psychological filter for identity: "The shadow acts like a psychic immune system, defining what is self and what is not-self."[2] Often, the shadow consists of negative or taboo feelings: sexual urges, shame, guilt, anger, selfishness. But throughout our lives, we also repress positive traits that are uncomfortable for us to accept, like imagination, vulnerability, intimacy, and sensitivity. When these traits are locked away in our shadow, then in spite of our attempts to hide them, they still emerge prominently in our emotions, thoughts, and behavior.

The role of the unconscious yields an important opportunity for business. To truly understand why people say what they say and do what they do, we must look at the psychodynamic context surrounding consumer decisions. In the marketplace, consumers often rationalize or project onto products or brands to reduce cognitive dissonance (buyer's remorse). But the initial satisfaction, as we'll see in a bit, is hardly an indicator of whether their affection for the product or service will last. Although this too changes depending upon the segment we fall into, it is driven by our emotional needs.

The "Wisdom" of Emotions

As shown in the examples above, emotions often silently play a major role in guiding our purchasing decisions and behavioral actions. It may seem unwise to let emotions drive our decisions, but as the ground-breaking work of neuroscientist Antonio Damasio has shown, without emotional anchors, we would be unable to make decisions.

In 1982, Damasio began seeing a brain tumor patient named Elliot, who had recently undergone surgery on his frontal lobe. Damasio noted that at first glance, the patient appeared to have made a full recovery. Elliot was intelligent, had a great management job, and was active in his church and with his family. But shortly after the operation, his life fell through the floor boards. Doctors had excised tissue in the frontal cortex associated with feeling and emotion, along with the tumor. Elliot's ability to make simple decisions was permanently impaired as a result. He became a dispassionate observer of his own life. Every decision became an insufferably tedious act. He found himself weighing every pro and con, every variable of the most mundane decisions. Damasio noted: "I never saw a tinge of emotion in him: no sadness, no impatience, no frustration."[3]

Thinking without feeling, as patients like Elliot unfortunately teach us, is undesirable, if not impossible. Later research from Damasio shows that we make nearly 85 percent of our decisions automatically and unconsciously through the emotional area of the brain. Reason alone cannot help us identify and satisfy our personal, emotional needs. Not unlike our relationship habits, when faced with many options and advertisements filling the marketplace, we often decide what's best for us by gravitating toward what *feels* right (or frequently away from what feels wrong).

So if it were just a matter of paying attention to emotion, businesses and marketers would have it easy. It's just that, unfortunately, however, emotions are not easy to identify and calibrate, let alone parse.

Consider a hapless husband wishing his wife would tell him what she wants, and the frustrated wife insisting he should "just know." This is the stuff we see in every romantic comedy and sitcom. Pop culture jokes about it, but the truth is few people possess the experience and introspective skills needed to dissect what their own needs are, let alone the needs of others.

Our brains are designed to perform myriad complex tasks, but using reasoning skills to evaluate lightning-quick gut feelings and emotions does not come naturally to us. Emotions are mostly ineffable. They're the hulking, continental mass underneath the iceberg's tip. We sometimes see them in a person's body language. Every now and then we can strain them out of a conversational tone. But mostly, they float beneath the surface of our awareness. There's currently a massive amount of pop psychology literature touting emotions as essential to healthy decision making when balanced with rational thought processes. Perhaps the most profound finding in this area is the speed (and scary accuracy) at which emotions operate. It's been documented that veteran truck drivers, traveling at 75 mph, who pass hitchhikers know within a split second if it's a good idea to give them a ride. How in this situation can they make a snap judgment, the consequences of which could either make their next several hours unbearable or ease the boredom of life alone on the road? Although instant decision making can be mistaken for reckless guessing, it's anything but. Persuasive feelings are in effect the result of the brain's culling our memories for emotional patterns. Over a lifetime, our brains store a near-infinite database of information—memories, emotional triumphs and wounds, characteristics of past relationships. The cortices of the brain responsible for thought and reason don't have access to everything in the unconscious warehouse. It's all still in there, pushing and pulling us in certain directions in the present, whether we're looking for someone to date or shopping for the right car. And in most instances, as several groundbreaking studies in neuropsychology illustrate, these "gut feelings" lead us in the right direction more often than not for in-the-moment decisions.

This is one reason that the business community, as we will see in the next section, is increasingly viewing customer interactions through the analog of personal relationships. People in healthy relationships will often intuit what their partner needs via similar patterns. Others commit themselves to clear and direct communication. The lesson for a business looking to satisfy customers and meet their needs: explore what's unseen; embrace the emotion underlying the audience's needs.

Needs and Relationships

Many companies talk about the need to establish strong "relationships" with their customers. Some compile complex Customer Relationship Management algorithms and systems to develop and maintain these relationships. These companies say that the transactional interactions of the past are ineffective in creating loyal customers—and they are right.

The concept of customer relationships makes sense in the context of meeting needs. Where else but in interpersonal relationships do we bump up against the emotional needs we've been discussing? As in all interpersonal relationships, from friendships, to marriage, to company and client, trust and the promise of mutual benefits are the foundation for future growth and development. When we put others' needs first in relationships, we're more likely to make those relationships work.

After decades of formally documenting the stages of successful and failed interpersonal and business-customer relationships, we've learned that many companies become complacent in their endeavor to understand, satisfy, and embrace the deeper emotion-based needs of consumers. Companies understand the meaning of "relationships," but they rarely consider what it takes to make their audiences' needs a priority. They seemingly cross their fingers hoping that what brought customers to their company will be the same factor that causes them to stay. Just as in most human romantic relationships, business-to-consumer relationships fall apart when one party (the business) fails to track the evolving needs of the partner (the consumer). The challenge of sustaining lifetime or long-term value naturally pushes businesses toward considering short-term, fling-like relationships as the easiest route to profits.

Indeed, if a department attracts new customers, it wins the lion's share of the marketing budget, but it is well documented that it costs some companies five to ten times more to attract new customers than to retain an existing one. On the other hand, if companies sustain relationships with existing customers, a mere 5 percent decrease in annual defections can lead to anywhere between a 25 percent to 125 percent rise in profits.[4] Another way of crystallizing these figures lies in a social reality of the Internet era. When we are satisfied with a product or service, we may tell three of our friends, but when we are dissatisfied, we're often inclined to tell (or Tweet) it to three thousand. Yet, this "tried and true" business-as-usual approach too often sacrifices long-term viability by overlooking human needs.

Even when they claim to desire lifetime relationships with their clients and customers, many businesses tactically distance themselves from the humanity of their interactions. The systemic nature of marketing and business strategy inadvertently depersonalizes their audience by using language that groups customers into market segments and targets. People are commonly referred to as "buyers," "shoppers," "payers," "nonresponders," "early adopters," and "eyeballs." But too often what is lost is the nuance that makes them *human*. The routine marketing logic seems to follow a self-sustaining, albeit not always sufficient, strategy: measure category and purchasing behaviors, shoot a thoughtful and creative mix of emotionally salient messages and rational pleas at the targets, place all bets on marketing science, and presume the targets can't help but consume. But if we truly view consumers through the lens of relationship dynamics, we'll learn that, whether we are working, shopping, or engaging with friends and family, our foundational psychological needs are a constant driving force. Understanding and putting this into practice (both strategically and executionally) will eliminate the artificial two-way mirror (or more commonly, brick wall) between daily life experiences and the ways businesses communicate with their customers.

The Powerful Role of Trust

Customer relationships, like interpersonal relationships, are built on trust. And if that trust is lost, the relationship is lost as well.

Marketing scholars Jennifer Aaker and Susan Fournier reveal just how closely business relationships and interpersonal relationships mirrored each other in a clever, Internet-based consumer psychology test.[5] Over a two-month period, the researchers measured the evolving strength of their relationship with customers as they were introduced to an online film-processing and digital library business. The participants were told they had been selected for a pilot program before the business was to be opened to the general public. They were told to take pictures and use the website's services at their pleasure, evaluating the experience along the way. Some participants interacted with a version of the website that used exciting, amped-up marketing language in its copy and personal communication. Other participants engaged with a company that was more down to earth, personalized, and directed at forging sincere dialogue.

Aaker and Fournier found, unsurprisingly, that relationships with the "exciting" company had the trajectory of a short-term fling, while those involved with the "sincere" company developed a relationship that deepened over time. The sincere, relationship-oriented business likely raised consumer expectations of the service quality and built loyalty to the website. If the company delivers the services as promised, there is no question that the personal relationship touch will keep customers invested in the experience for a long period of time.

Yet there is one caveat to the research that speaks to the irony and complexity of consumer decision making. When the researchers imposed an unexpected service failure within the experiment—e.g., "Sorry, but we lost all your film!"—the relationships with the users interacting with the sincere business were harmed the most. Why? Because when a business promotes itself as an earnest, personable entity that truly cares about its customers, and then fails to deliver on those expectations, it is doing more harm than simply *not delivering*. This is similar to a husband telling his wife how much he's looking forward to their anniversary and then forgetting the date when it arrives. Sorry, but an apology and flowers aren't going to get him in the clear. "Trust is much heralded in marketing, but it has a downside," said Aaker in an interview for Stanford Graduate School of Business (GSB) News. "What needs to be understood and managed are the contracts, norms and rules that underlie the relationship between a consumer and brand, and how a brand's actions fit or violate those norms."[6]

Businesses must reestablish the emotional trust that is destroyed when they engage in transgressions, be committed to following through on promises, and be prepared to stand by that attitude when crisis strikes. In the days following the British Petroleum (BP) oil spill, how many times did we hear executives tell the public, in more than enough words, not to worry about it? While then-CEO Tony Hayward haplessly expressed how much he'd "like his life back," BP was writing a 187-page legal report that pointed fingers at third-party contractors, seemingly tacking an asterisk to every apology. Perhaps they should have known that what won't work with a friend or loved one probably won't work for an angry general public either. BP's defensive public relations strategy may cost them long after the media turned off their cameras in the Gulf.

The Deceit of Satisfaction

On the surface, one might think that meeting needs is purely about satisfying the consumer. It's hard to deny that sentiment. But this book, skewed one way, is largely about realigning the definition of satisfaction with what makes us truly, deeply, madly satisfied.

Of course, companies are at least trying to interpret and meet emotional needs. But it is questionable whether traditional methods of consumer research are capable of accurately measuring true need satisfaction. Consider these two points:

- Roughly 80 percent to 90 percent of new products and services fail or drastically fall short of sales expectations in their first year.
- Customer satisfaction is used by 90 percent of companies as a benchmark for success. Overwhelmingly, most companies report that their customers like their products just fine.

So what's at play with this apparent contradiction? One reading of the product failure data is that there are just too many products in the marketplace. Not all goods can be tried and adopted en masse by the public. And in most cases of failure, advertising and marketing efforts aren't successfully connecting emotionally with consumers. But the customer satisfaction benchmark is wholly confounding. If everyone says they are satisfied, why are new products failing upon introduction into the market?

As it turns out, positive consumer satisfaction surveys are neither a predictor of repurchase nor an indicator of whether more important emotional needs are met. So most companies ask whether their clientele is satisfied with their experience, and most customers say "yes." The marketers congratulate themselves, only to find later that the same satisfied customers went elsewhere the next go-round. Again, the mental process that occurs during a customer satisfaction survey is typically a rationalization of a past experience. The brain quickly evaluates what the individual's expectations of the product were at the time, and if they were in the ballpark when the product was actually used, great. The product is checked "satisfactory." A one-time purchaser of an electronics brand may never tell a researcher, "It worked well enough. I was satisfied. But the design and overall feel just didn't enhance my crucial and deep-seated feelings of identity and autonomy the way I hoped." These thoughts are most always inaccessible to standard language and reason.

The consumer may have appreciated the product, but if he or she formed no relationship with it, if his or her unarticulated emotional needs went unmet, the appreciation means virtually nothing for a business trying to form a cohesive base of loyal buyers. Their customers will have no problem moving on to another brand.

This is a problem for businesses using a *logical*, traditional process to study the *emotional* issue of satisfaction—an approach that cannot readily deliver the accurate emotional insights required. It's a problem of perspective. If a business is going to learn about an emotional issue, it needs to study the issue with a method that is sensitive to emotion. At the end of the day, businesses must see their customers as individuals always striving for a healthy sense of self-identity.

When people find a product or service that transcends the generic "satisfaction" benchmark, it's gratifying for the consumer, and in turn, a positive for the company that provided it. Yet when a company fails to respond to the needs buried in the consumer psyche—or worse yet, decides for the consumer what he or she needs—the product, service, or brand can be a disappointment instead of a delight, frustrating the consumer and impeding his or her achievement of the ideal sense of self. And just as when we bicker with a partner or confront a rude friend, we can have a need derailed by a negative shopping experience or a poor encounter with a service or sales representative. A need can just as easily be subverted by a bad product design.

But businesses, unlike friends and loved ones, don't often get the luxury of a second chance if they mishandle a situation. From the very first ad, to the policies regulating the company's customer service, to the tone of their chief executive officer's talking points, the business must constantly identify how emotional and rational needs evolve and build their business around meeting them.

This does not mean businesses should give up broad, systemic business and marketing strategies entirely in exchange for an intimate, interpersonal approach. Businesses use quantifiable systems for efficiency and prediction, but if that is where the strategy stops, meaningful, intimate insights into the true drivers of behavior will be lost.

Understanding the "Why"

When business understand consumers' needs more fully, they will see that behavior in the marketplace is rarely simply about the exchange. It is not merely impersonal economic activity. Rather, those functional considerations are interwoven with a deeper, emotional inner dialogue within consumers that asks not, *"What does this product do?"* but rather, *"What will this product do for my emotional self and identity? What does it mean to me? Does it align with how I want to be seen?"* Too often, this inner dialogue, a negotiation of our psychological needs, eludes standard market research tactics.

The late Sidney Levy, of Northwestern University's Kellogg School (where I've lectured), challenged the business community to consider the psychological processes underlying behavior. The marketplace is hardly as rational as Econ 101 would have us believe. "The ideal market is like a Heaven—perfect but dull," he said. "The real one is the human one on earth, fraught with emotion, striving, and the symbolic investments that make us care about what and how we market to and from others."[7] Price, convenience, service delivery, and overall quality are, of course, essential factors. These metrics are the conscious side of what marketers call the *consumer value calculus*; they are the process by which we evaluate the expected utility of a purchase.

But because much of our decision making deals in the realm of the emotional unconscious, this book lays out a challenge that many businesses may be reluctant to take on: paying attention to the wants of an audience implies the audience is conscious of the "why" behind their behavior. It assumes customers know why they want Product A rather than Product B. Certainly in some cases, we absolutely do know why. But other times, customers use a host of rational explanations they make retroactively to describe an immediate, intuitive, emotional response. The rationalizations often obscure the true, deeply embedded reasons for one's marketplace decisions. Wants are merely our conscious expressions connected to largely unconscious emotional needs. This unconscious side of the consumer value calculus contains insights that, if discovered, can allow businesses to hurdle over the competition, not to mention, help their audience feel and live better. In this book, we will learn how brands like National Public Radio (NPR), Universal Studios, Nivea, and Gilead Pharmaceuticals harness psychological insights to deliver at all levels of their business models.

We all strive to become emotionally satisfied, and while simple interactions and transactions in the world of commerce cannot get us all the way there, they matter considerably more than is generally recognized.

Identifying Driving Emotional Needs

In this chapter, we explored the often hidden psychological and emotional needs that drive consumer decisions, and that all business must address to acquire and keep today's customers.

Chapter 1 Summary: Why Business Doesn't Understand Its Customers

- Much of the way in which people act on the surface is driven by subconscious emotions of which they are not aware, or which they may want to repress.
- Decision making is driven by both conscious rational logic and subconscious emotional needs. Often, when faced with too many choices, people will gravitate toward the products or services that "feel" right. In a crowded marketplace, emotional drivers trump rational reflection.
- Businesses are adept at addressing the rational, logical element of the customer decision-making process, but not its emotional

element. Many ignore the core human needs that influence customer decisions, and are then baffled by their failure to reach and keep customers.

- Businesses often talk about "relationships" with their customers, but they make little attempt to understand and respond to the evolving emotional needs of customers, thereby dooming any relationship that they hope to build.

- Business marketing and strategy often dehumanize and depersonalize people—customers are buyers, early adopters, even "eyeballs"—which further undermines businesses' attempts to address the emotional needs driving their customers and prospects.

- Businesses can also be misled by customer satisfaction measures that do not measure whether or not the emotional needs of the customers have been met. As a result, customers may on the surface express satisfaction with a product or service, and yet, subconsciously, they do not have the desire to repeat the experience, deciding instead to go to another product or company.

- Businesses should balance quantifiable marketing strategies for efficiency and production, but then take the further step to understand the "meaningful, intimate insights into the true drivers of behavior."

- Businesses need to understand the "why." They must not only ask, "What will this product do for the customer?" but also, "What will this product do for the customer's emotional self and identity?"

- While a business must address the emotional needs of its customers, it must at the same time respond to their rational needs. There must be a balance. If a business focuses only on the rational drivers of decisions, it will make mistakes. If it focuses only on emotions, and fails to fulfill rational needs tied to the product or service, it will not win the loyalty of customers.

- Understanding the emotional needs that influence and guide customer actions and behaviors begins with EMPATHY on the part of a business—a concerted effort to understand the emotional motivations and needs of customers, and to align the business's approach to customers and prospects with those needs.

CHAPTER 2

The Needs Continuum

Need: n.– a physiological or psychological requirement for the well-being of an organism

Figure 2.1   Merriam-Webster Definition of "Need"

CHAPTER 2

The Needs Continuum

What constitutes a psychologically healthy, meaningful life?

British actor and comedian Michael Palin offers one answer to this philosophical question in the final minutes of Monty Python's 1983 feature film *The Meaning of Life*. He pulls a card from an ostentatiously large gold envelope marked "the meaning of life" and, after an exaggeratedly bored look, reads, "Try and be nice to people, avoid eating fat, read a good book every now and then, get some walking in, and try and live together in peace and harmony with people of all creeds and nations."[1]

Wouldn't it be nice if it were at all that simple? "Meaning" after all, is largely what individuals make of circumstances, decisions, and defining life events. We know from the last chapter that the commercial marketplace is one important arena where this personal quest takes place. We're not just looking for a good and fair deal, but are searching oftentimes for something more. But now let's pinpoint exactly what that "more" is.

No matter what we take life to *mean*, we can be a bit more certain of what factors make life *meaningful*. For centuries, philosophers, scientists, and academics have been trying to identify why we do what we do and what exactly we need in order to function, both physically and mentally. A physical need is more or less easy to understand. Food. Sleep. Sex. Safety. These base requisites for life itself aren't the focus here, however. Physical needs create life and *keep us living*, whereas the emotional needs alluded to earlier are what make life *worth living*. This chapter explores what those emotional needs are, how they operate, and how businesses can do a better job to empathize with the needs of their audience to create superior products and experiences.

We can start this process by thinking about our own experiences and behavior. What drives us through life? What compels us to act in the way we act? Over the course of a day, week, month, year, and lifetime, what are the psychological, emotional needs we attempt to fulfill for our own personal betterment?

Human Needs Are Universal

One of the most revealing studies on needs was conducted by psychologist Kennon M. Sheldon of the University of Missouri Columbia in 2001. Sheldon surveyed volunteers from America and South Korea in order to identify any differences between the needs of starkly individualistic and collectivist cultures. It makes sense that different cultures would have different needs sets. But to his surprise, the same needs existed in each culture, despite an emphasis on different values.

Sheldon and his colleagues ranked needs by analyzing memories. In one of the experiments, participants were asked to share their most satisfying event from the past week. In a second study, new participants explained their most satisfying event from the prior month. In another, they were asked to look back a few months. The participants in each experiment then evaluated and paired their stories with statements

Table 2.1   Comparison American vs. South Korean Emotional Need Rankings[2]

	America	South Korea
1	Self-esteem	Relatedness
2	Relatedness	Self-esteem
3	Autonomy	Autonomy
4	Competence	Pleasure
5	Pleasure	Competence
6	Physical Thriving	Influence/Popularity
7	Self-Actualization	Security
8	Security	Self-Actualization
9	Influence/Popularity	Physical Thriving
10	Luxury/Money	Luxury/Money

Ken Sheldon, "What is satisfying about satisfying events? Testing 10 candidate psychological needs."

connected to a set of values that many psychologists contend are among our most prominent emotional needs. His results yielded a comparative ranking of ten high-value emotional needs.

The most important finding from Sheldon and his collaborators, supported by my own research of routine consumer decision making, is that over the course of a lifetime, diverse peoples are motivated by essentially the same set of needs. The needs from the list exist in us all—across generations and cultures—and when we recognize that very point, we can begin to tailor our personal lives as well as business models around them. It is important to note, though, that the needs differ by segment, which will be discussed more fully later on.

In addition to the "universality" of needs, Sheldon's study offers three other key lessons about needs:

1. **The potential "big three" of emotional needs—relatedness, autonomy, and competence—drive human behavior.**

We simultaneously need to be closely connected to others, maintain our uniqueness and individual control over events, and feel like we have our wits about us to make things happen. Those three needs satisfied together typically result in the list-topping need: higher self-esteem. Sheldon's findings support other studies suggesting a big three of needs.

2. **Money does not buy happiness.**

Luxury and money rank at the bottom of both the American and the South Korean lists. The week-to-week needs of average Americans are not dictated by the idealized pursuit of becoming a billionaire. In fact, a recent study by Princeton University researchers showed that once Americans hit the $75,000 salary level, there are no discernible gains in average happiness for individuals with higher salaries. Other factors, focused on the big three needs mentioned above, are more important to our general contentment and mental well-being over the short term than health, money, and social status. This insight supports studies from around the world that show that cultures with poorer health, that work for less, and that place less emphasis on material acquisitions are often "happier" than the American culture.

3. We ignore some needs until they're gone.

Sheldon's study indicates that we feel some needs the most, such as security (ranked low on both lists), when we're deprived of them. When life is humming by smoothly, we don't actively pay attention to some of our needs. For instance, while the housing bubble was ballooning to its imminent explosion, the nation collectively threw caution to the wind. Only when chaos struck did American families, a sleeping government, and a runaway finance and banking industry think twice about risky loans, massive debts, and stagnant income growth. The need for control and security were activated only when we had little choice but to attend to them.

The business implications of these lessons are varied. The fact that money and material possessions do not translate into happiness should push businesses to utilize more sophisticated marketing strategies beyond the unconvincing "buy this and you'll be happy" television ads. The companies that succeed will be those that offer guidance, inspiration, support, or other benefits beyond and independent of their products—such as Nike's running club, which provides guidance, motivation, and community for runners whether or not they purchase Nike's shoes. The fact that we ignore important needs, such as security, for the sake of other pursuits also creates opportunities for businesses that can anticipate consumers' dormant needs and head them off before an audience is seriously deprived.

The most important implication, however, is found in the big three needs that reveal the tension between two opposite emotions: the need to be autonomous and competent, and the need to be connected. This tension is the foundation of the needs framework that we will present in this book. But no discussion of human needs would be complete without first considering the best-known model of needs—Maslow's hierarchy.

Climbing Mt. Maslow

Abraham Maslow is one of the fathers of humanistic psychology. Before his ideas became popular, psychology as a philosophy and a science was primarily focused on the mentally ill, or how human behavior was

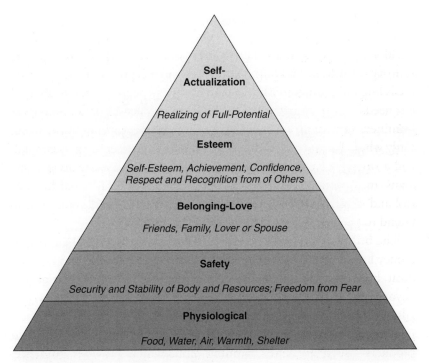

Figure 2.2 Maslow's Hierarchy of Needs

conditioned by external events. In short, positive psychology and emotion weren't hot topics, or even accepted, in the field. Maslow was motivated to understand the inverse. How do successful and happy people become successful and happy? How do we access our inner resources to achieve sustained personal growth? He studied some of America's most famed and brilliant icons like Albert Einstein and Eleanor Roosevelt, and kept close tabs on what made his brightest college students stand above the crowd. He posited that every person holds a strong internal desire to reach his or her full potential. Maslow, a professor at Brandeis University for most of his academic career, sparked the self-empowerment movement that remains influential today. The legacy of Maslow lives on primarily through his hierarchy of needs theory, famously represented by a pyramid listing the progression of the individual's most important needs.[3]

Discussed in most psychology, general marketing, and management textbooks, the pyramid positions needs in five layers. Maslow's theory contends that in order for the individual to pursue a higher need, the needs below it must be firmly met. The first level comprises our basic physiological needs. Safety and security is the second level—a job, good health, property, and so on. Once the basics are secured, we're free to pursue the higher order needs of belonging and love, and further, esteem, influence, and respect. Only when we've got our stomachs filled, our bills paid, our relationships in check, and our career goals on track are we able to arrive at the summit of the mountain and attain our potential. Maslow said only 1 percent of humans are able to reach this healthiest psychological state.

It's important to note that academic psychologists don't treat Maslow's hierarchy as gospel. That's not to say it can't help an individual assess his or her personal journey, but Maslow positions emotional needs like a game show—the $1 million round is experienced by only the most skilled players. The needs in the hierarchy are valuable and very real. But his model is contradicted by most human behavior. Needs satisfaction is not hierarchical but rather latitudinal.

In reality, we oftentimes skip around—meet a higher level need before a lower level need or simultaneously attempt to manage them all at once. For example, a successful businesswoman might be the most talented person in her field, but that doesn't mean she's yet fulfilled the third level of love and belonging. A brilliant moral scholar can be creative, spiritual, wise and nonbiased, but according to Maslow, that must also mean he is secure, has found deep human connection, and achieved what his goals are professionally. The reality: these individuals might not have accomplished any of these things. Happiness studies like the one referenced above routinely prove that families in poverty are able to satisfy higher-level emotional needs even without so much as a consistent income or a solid roof over their heads.

And once met, needs don't simply disappear. We don't fulfill a need and then check it off a list. Needs overlap, interact, coexist, evolve, and resurface over time. In short, "working up the pyramid" makes sense in theory, but those who follow that path precisely are psychological outliers.

Meeting needs is not like climbing a mountain. It's more akin, as we are about to find out, to a lifelong game of tug-of-war.

The Needs Continuum

The model of human needs put forth in this book is rooted in developmental psychology—the scientific study of changes that occur in individuals over a life span. One of the fundamental characteristics of our early years, from the toddler years through youth up to adulthood, is a continuous tension between wanting to be independent and wanting to be connected to others. We can see this in the typical behavior of toddlers. Imagine a little girl, about 20 months old, sitting on her mother's lap. She's engrossed in a storybook. There are vibrant colors, bold words, friendly characters—her imagination soars. This time with her mother each night before bed is a routine she cannot do without. But the phone starts ringing. "Uh oh," says her mother, closing the book and setting it on the coffee table. "Why don't you go play while Mommy says hi to her friend?" The child scurries off the recliner. This is my time, the child thinks to herself. She wanders around the room, picking up and setting down toys while her mother chats and chats. The child is uninterested in diverting her attention from storytime to anything else. After a minute or so, she's had it. The child leaves the room, begging for her mother to notice her. But the mother doesn't. To the child, her mother has checked out. While physically only a few feet away, the mother is mentally in another place. Her daughter knows this. Unable to wait a moment longer, the child plays the ace up her sleeve: A tantrum with an intensity comparable only to a tropical storm. Just as the child planned, the mother wraps it up, runs to the crying child, and storytime resumes as if nothing had ever happened.

There's a reason why all parents are likely familiar with this scenario. Between 15 and 24 months, a child enters a tumultuous phase of development called rapprochement, a term coined by pioneering Hungarian physician Margaret Mahler. During the rapprochement phrase, the world is just becoming known and discoverable to the young mind. A child's newfound curiosity and mobility motivate the desire to explore—so long as the mother is present to share the experience. The child is torn between an emerging sense of independence and the comfort of dependence. The same tension between the desire for independence and the fear of being disconnected from loved ones is

Figure 2.3   The Needs Continuum

reflected in the surly moodiness of teenagers as they seek to break away from their parents but still hunger for love and acceptance.

So what's this got to do with commerce? How is this connected to marketing, innovation and strategy?

Even in adulthood, satisfying needs is a back and forth between the extremes that we originally experienced in our younger years. Throughout life's stages, we balance our primary needs for **individuality** and **connectedness**, which are similar to what Sheldon labels "autonomy" and "relatedness" above. These two needs underlie most all human motivation and serve as the polar forces of a needs satisfaction model, which I call the Needs Continuum. At times, we'll do anything to carve a niche to stand out from the crowd. At other times, we seek the care of another person or the embrace of a community. But in most cases, any individual action is rooted in one of these two fundamental drives.

Satisfying individuality (you) and connectedness (your relationship to others) is a never-ending game of tug-of-war for human beings. When one side dominates, the other pulls harder to inch the rope back to the middle. For the most satisfied individuals, neither need is strong enough to outpull the other. We see this dynamic inch its way into marketplace decisions all the time.

For instance, a spouse may attempt to maintain space from his or her partner. This accounts for the reason why some men use their dens or garages as sanctuaries—they're comfort blankets of individuality, defenses against having their entire world inhabited by their partner. These men fill the room with mementos of self-identity—objects and products that reflect who they are as an individual, not as a connected couple. The flat-screen television with the complicated, blow-the-windows-out sounds system, golf clubs mounted on the wall, pictures from his college years, a bookcase highlighting his intellectual identity, and so forth. His spouse very likely has her own haven of individuality. The rest of the home, then, represents their shared space, their connectedness. We all need this balance, and often use marketplace decisions to facilitate it.

Individuality and connectedness are the core dimensions of the needs-based approach for business strategy. We often rely on products and services to help us play a role that casts us as the unique, autonomous individual, and other times, we consume as a way to connect and relate to others. To successfully employ empathetic marketing, businesses must understand the tap dance between these two poles and the unique value of both individuality and connectedness in our lives. Let's define and explore each in tandem.

Individuality: Standing Out and Controlling Outcomes

This book's road to publication followed much the same path that Miguel Cervantes's novel *Don Quixote* followed when it was published more than four hundred years ago. Both were accepted for publication by an established book publisher (Palgrave in our case, and Juan de la Cuesta in Cervantes's case), who took on the printing and selling costs in exchange for compensation to the authors. In the past few years, however, the centuries-old practices of the publishing industry are being challenged by new print-on-demand and sophisticated self-publishing companies that put all of the publishing decisions, including distribution and marketing, into the hands of the authors. Authors, for example, decide how many books they want printed, what the covers will look like, and at what price the book will be sold. Traditional publishing still dominates the industry, and customers are more likely to buy a book that has gone through the quality-control screening process of a publisher. But sales of print-on-demand and self-published books are growing exponentially. Who knows? Today, Cervantes might have published his classic ode to individuality himself.

Sitting on the left-hand side of the continuum, our need for individuality finds a way to sneak into almost all of our behavior. Western society values the stalwart, self-reliant person. The self-made man or woman. The rugged individualist. The eccentric leader. The rags-to-riches hero. John Wayne is arguably one of America's iconic actors because his characters embodied the individualistic, rule-breaking, risk-taking, do-what-you-gotta-do personality that Americans often see—or hope to see—in themselves and their leaders. Wayne himself, of course, was an actor who never left the comfort of California, even in a time of world war. No matter. It is Wayne the symbol of individualism who continues to be revered. In more recent times, former General Electric (GE) Chairman and Chief Executive Officer (CEO) Jack Welch is one of the new batches of superstar CEOs because he, too, reflects the individual who is not afraid to break rules and ruffle feathers to do what is best, in this case, what is best for the company. Welch was once known as Neutron Jack because his tough policies— selling off businesses that were not number one or two in their markets, firing employees who did not meet strict performance standards—had the impact of a neutron bomb: the buildings were still standing but the people were gone. Today, he is a best-selling author and speaker who enthralls packed business audiences with his take-no-prisoners approach to business. Perhaps one of the most intriguing examples of the nonconformist individualistic business leader is Richard Branson, the long-haired flamboyant founder of the Virgin Group, who built an empire of more than two hundred companies bearing the Virgin brand. His no-holds-barred individuality ranges from his promotional antics (for example, appearing in a $10,000 white wedding gown to promote a new chain of Virgin Bridal shops), to fearlessly plunging into the world of transatlantic airlines by challenging British Airways head-on.

American pop culture consistently reaffirms its attachment to the individualism ideal in literature and mass media. Most contemporary dramas on network television revolve around a central, mesmerizing character leagues ahead of his or her colleagues. In the world of prime time, it pays to be different, even if the cost is breaking all the rules to do what needs to be done. As just one example, the globally successful show *24*, which just finished its run on television, features a character named Jack Bauer, a maverick terror-fighting machine who defends the fabric of liberty by any means necessary, who is sometimes wrong but never in doubt.

We've been primed to value self-reliance and uniqueness. Conformity to the group holds us back, so the ideal goes. Eastern cultures traditionally trend the other way. It is the individual's subordination to the family or the larger group that takes precedent.

But in the West, it's all about being different, not just in appearance or style, but in attitude and behavior. It's about being one's own agent.

Autonomy is an individual's ability to make decisions unhindered by external influence. We've all been around colleagues or friends who can't make up their minds about anything. These individuals are afraid that a self-reliant decision will have a negative impact on someone in their group. They depend on others and avoid making the call so as to steer clear of conflict, hurt feelings, or experiencing failure. But the autonomous individual is capable of reasoning his or her way to a solution—right or wrong.

However, the needs continuum tells us clearly that one's identity is not equal to one's individuality. We subconsciously take and borrow from every one of our relationships and connections in the world to arrive at better sense of self.

Connectedness: Everyone Needs a Tap Code

Now consider Janet's grocery-shopping behavior. When Janet's buying yogurt for herself, she'll buy the store brand—the cheap stuff in the ugly container. It gets the job done. But when she's buying pudding for her daughter, it's the branded Jello-O® kind. What explains this discrepancy? Why does she trade up to higher quality for her kids?

Sitting at the other pole of the continuum, the need for connectedness moves hand in hand with individuality: as a sneaky, unconscious motivator. The need for connectedness motivates us to prioritize friends and family. We often want to buy higher-quality goods and services (or things we perceive as being higher quality) for them than we do for ourselves.

Connectedness, distilled simply, defines our role as social beings. It's impossible to live our lives without others with whom to share it. We must be cared for, loved, nurtured. We must be recognized. We must belong to something larger than ourselves. Connectedness crystallizes the reason why, in moments of crisis, the human spirit shines the brightest. We embrace each other and work to overcome disaster, not just to survive but to ride out the emotional pain of loss and grief through the support and empathy of others. When America was attacked by al-Qaeda on September 11, 2001, the slogan "United We Stand" began to appear everywhere, reflecting the sense that to survive and overcome the devastation of the attack, all Americans had to come together.

We need to seek and achieve connectedness in order to thrive and truly know ourselves. Other people are the mirrors through which we develop and sustain identity. Whether it's achieved through working on a relationship or joining a church choir, to be connected to others is to open the door to sustained personal growth and happiness. Beyond gathering at the stadium, for example, fans of sports teams typically find different ways of watching their favorite athletes in groups—at the local sports bar or at the homes of friends. In July 2011, thousands of fans packed a stadium in Japan to watch their national soccer team win the Women's World Cup in Germany live on a big screen. They wanted to share their joy—or their disappointment, if the team had lost—together.

The importance of connection is so essential to our well-being that the extended isolation of prisoners is considered to be psychological torture. Prisoners of war (POWs) have been kept in solitary confinement for months or years in efforts to "break them," and large numbers literally go mad as a result of this lack of human connection. One former Vietnam POW, Bob Shumaker, attributes his very survival to his ability to break through the imposed isolation and connect with other prisoners. He and the other prisoners went to great lengths to develop a "tap code" alphabet and secretly converse with prisoners in the neighboring cells, enabling them to maintain their sense of connectedness to the world and to reality.

Social support is a key factor in coping with stress and becoming a resilient individual. As Dennis Charney, professor of psychiatry at the Mt. Sinai Hospital, said in an interview with Public Broadcasting Service (PBS) regarding Shumaker's journey. "We can't do it alone. You need other people...Everyone needs a tap code."[4]

The Cast of Needs on the Continuum

It's true: we must be in touch with our individuality to truly connect. But we must also know others in order truly to develop a sense of self. Meeting our needs is somewhat of a paradox for this reason. Devote too much time to individuality, and suddenly, we find ourselves growing distant from our relationships and community. Depend fully on relationships with others to color and define our self-image, and suddenly

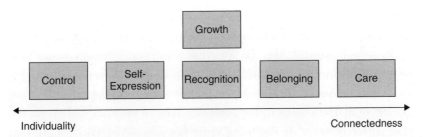

Figure 2.4 (p. 40) The Needs Continuum

we feel we're losing control of our ability to seal our own fates. Striking a balance, however, is a challenge. In fact, we never can figure out the perfect balance or path along the continuum. We can only manage it.

This makes relationships a trick and a half to sustain. It also means businesses must do a better job of treating their customers according to the place they occupy on the continuum. We are beings in conflict, individuals attempting to engage with our many needs outwardly and subconsciously.

Each chapter in this book examines the dynamics of the balancing act, focusing on the marketplace applications of a specific emotional need positioned along the continuum between individuality and connectedness.

The Continuum and the Marketplace

In consumer business strategy, whether branding, advertising, public relations, or product development and design, the process is not as simple as choosing a need and force-fitting it with your product and message.

Years ago, my firm conducted research at Universal Studios Florida and Walt Disney World, both in Orlando. At the time, Universal was searching for new ways to distinguish itself from its giant competitor. We conducted consumer deep-dive research with 14 families with children of varying ages, selected to provide us with a diverse participant mix representing the typical park visitor population. We followed these families around the park, observing their moods and behaviors, and discussing with them their thoughts and impressions as they experienced the parks. Essentially, we wanted to know what was really at play during a family vacation. We all go on vacation to escape daily life or to reconnect with loved ones. To experience thrills and adventure different from everyday life. To see children experience new sights and sounds that they'll take with them into adulthood. To leave our routine responsibilities behind. Some people find it hard to detach from the world of work (Smartphone addicts, raise your hands). But we tell ourselves, if only for a couple days or weeks, that we have to.

Vacations satisfy our need for pleasure, which is a commodity in a culture that refuses to slow down and smile every once in awhile. Just look at Americans' overall attitudes toward downtime. Vacation days in America are miniscule in number compared to our European friends. So what happens in these few weeks of the year when we supposedly escape and let work pile up mercilessly in our inbox?

In the context of emotional needs, a destination theme park can mean a lot more to its patrons than they can readily articulate. It's not about the fun they experience, but rather the function of the fun for the family's growth and sustenance.

One might think that the two parks are locked in a win-lose competition for Sunshine State vacationers and their children, but that's not necessarily true. Many families, especially with children of different ages, go to both parks. At one time, however, the theme parks offered discernibly different experiences. One of our interview vacationers at the time put it best: "Disney is like sitting by a stream. Universal is like going rock climbing. Both are enjoyable, both are nature, but with one, you've got more of that nervous adrenaline rush." My researchers and I spent days observing how this participant's analogy was on the money. The polarity of experiences is perhaps why some vacationers visit both parks. Who doesn't enjoy a little relaxation (sitting by a stream) mixed in with action (rock climbing) on their vacations?

At the time, Universal and Disney mirrored the needs continuum. However, this has changed. They aren't merely high-end amusement resorts that offer different sets of thrills for families. They're helping families access and satisfy different psychological needs for their children. Remember that young people, from toddlers to teens, have conflicting sentiments, with a desire for the security of connectedness pulling them in one direction and a desire for the adventure of independence pulling them in another. At the time of our research, the Walt Disney World experience appealed to their desires for security, safety, and closeness. It is a child's and a family's rite of passage. It has always offered an undeniably fantastic experience that feeds children's imaginations. But generally speaking, its essence nurtures a younger child's connection in a safe, soft, and fantastic world. Disney was the quintessential "mother" archetype.

We found that Universal Studios, on the other hand, appealed to older children and their families' desire to explore, to be curious, and to interact with the world around them, through which they gain a sense of mastery and accomplishment. By developing and solidifying this sense of autonomy, children develop a sense of self-esteem and understanding of personal agency. Universal Studios Florida was rough-edged. It was perceived as edgier and more adventurous—generally more stimulating and intellectually challenging.

No longer was Universal just the more exciting cousin of Disney. Instead, it was an amusement park that satisfied its visitors' needs for individuality and independence in ways Disney wasn't designed to do. Recognizing this fundamental difference between itself and Disney in fulfilling the needs of its visitors, Universal changed its marketing efforts from ham-handed attempts at promoting what it wanted its consumers to experience to a testimonial to what the experience was already providing for its clientele. No longer focusing on their long-standing marketing platform of "ride the movies," they built a new strategy around the platform "Experience an extraordinary escape at Universal." Slowly and steadily, Universal made gains in gate entries.

Of course, this dynamic has changed in recent years. The Disney of the past is not the Disney we find today. Their parks are now much more "Universal" in their feel, entertainment offerings, rides, and attractions. That said, the dynamic illustrates the profound opportunities that arise when a needs-based approach is applied to existing business models.

The process, however, is not simply one of a business matching its product to a customer's psychological needs. A single product category can potentially satisfy different emotional needs for different people. To harness the value of human needs, one must understand where people are in their life cycle. Some emotional needs are more pressing at different ages and milestones, and for different genders and personality types.

Take cell phones as a prime example. Beyond placing calls, sending texts, and checking emails, what is the emotional value of the twenty-first century's most pervasive and influential device? A cell phone can simultaneously satisfy a person's need for control, security, connection, growth, and expression. To be sure, the device can't do all things for all people, and cell-phone providers would be mistaken to try to persuade people otherwise. A company's promoting access to 100,000 apps will appeal to the individual addicted to customization and control, all the while alienating an older audience intimidated by the concept of a smartphone.

For many segments of the population (mainly the nontexters and Tweeters among us), believe it or not, a phone is still primarily used to talk to other people! Parents like the peace of mind that comes from always being connected to their children, but the child may just be after the status symbol or unlimited contact with his or her tightest social circles. These issues raise important questions and challenges for marketers, who must decide where and to whom to direct their resources, what needs are most relevant for a specific segment and audience, and importantly, what communication tone and style work best to appeal to and satisfy a need.

It's also important to note that we see the push and pull between connectedness and individuality at each point on the continuum. In other words, not one of the needs is owned entirely by the individuality or the connectedness side of the continuum. For instance, consider the *need for belonging*. Belonging is essentially connectedness within a community. So much of our daily routine consists of participating in groups. We join groups for closeness, and sometimes, just to know we "fit in." To a great extent, though, the need for belonging is not wholly consumed by the connectedness space. What we belong to is a stamp on our individual identity. Consider how we routinely categorize informal acquaintances. It's not *Dave, the guy with a unique perspective on financial markets*, but rather it's *Dave, the guy from Rutgers, the big Mets fan, the one who volunteers with Habitat for Humanity*. Certainly, we are not the church, synagogue, or mosque to which we belong. We are not the political party we vote for (and on behalf of which we argue with friends and family). We are not the company we work for. Or the brand of shoes we wear and the grocery store we shop at. But each group we "belong" to is a distinct piece of our identity.

The Needs Continuum can best be put into action when matched with a psychological perspective that helps businesses identify their consumers' unmet needs. With the right lens and a clear focus, meeting unmet emotional needs can be much more than a token statement issued in press releases. It can be the very challenge all businesses organize around.

Chapter 2 Summary: The Core Emotional Needs That Drive the Actions, Behaviors, and Thoughts of Consumers

- The needs that motivate and influence people are universal, spanning cultures and generations. No matter what age, nationality, or background, people are driven by essentially the same set of core needs.
- The top three emotional needs that drive human behavior are relatedness, autonomy, and competence. People want to be connected to others while maintaining their individuality, and they want to feel that they are able to have some control over what happens. The three emotional needs converge in the top core need that drives people's behavior and thinking: self-esteem.
- These top three emotional needs reveal a fundamental tension between two opposite emotions: the need to be independent and competent, and the need to be connected to others. This tension between individuality and connectedness is the foundation of the needs framework in this book.
- All emotional needs exist on a continuum that connects the two opposite emotions of individuality and connectedness.
- On this continuum between individuality and connectedness are the following six core emotional needs: control, self-expression, growth, recognition, belonging, and care.
- Depending on their placement on the continuum, individuality has more influence in some needs, while connectedness is more prevalent in others. Every need, however, will have some element of both.

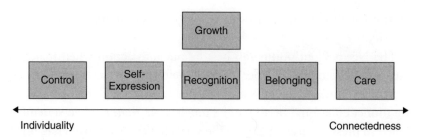

Figure 2.4   (p. 45) The Needs Continuum

- Emotional needs are not items to be checked off a list. People don't achieve one need, cross it off, and move to the next need. This is the fundamental flaw of Maslow's hierarchy of needs. Throughout life, people are constantly moving among different needs.
- When approaching customers or prospects, a business must understand which of the six core needs its product or service addresses, and then tailor its marketing and product development to best address that core need.

CHAPTER 3

The Need for Control

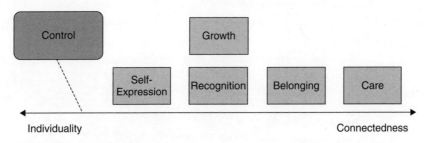

Figure 3.1   The Control Need

CHAPTER 3

The Need for Control

Historically, music lovers had little control over the music that they listened to. They could turn on the radio and choose a radio station, but would have to listen to whatever that station decided to broadcast. Or they could choose a record (later a cassette or compact disc [CD]), but would have to listen to the songs that the artist and the record label had decided to group together. And in most cases, they could only listen to one artist at a time. The Sony Walkman was a revolution in mobility, but the listener's control over the choice of music changed very little. Today, the idea of being forced to listen to a set of songs designed by others is becoming as obsolete as using a typewriter. Technically savvy teens and adults now find it perfectly natural to have thousands of their favorite pieces of music stored in their iPods. The music they store in that device is only the music they want to listen to. With the advent of iTunes, they no longer need to buy an entire collection of songs just to get the two or three that they really like. iPod users can put together their own "playlists" or wait for the end of the current song they are playing before deciding which song they will listen to next. Consumers of all ages have taken advantage of the revolutionary ability to control their personal entertainment—control that was impossible before the technological development of the iPod. Innovators' understanding of the deeply felt desire to be in control played a key role in the success of this powerful technology, which has served as a platform to revolutionize the world of music and technology.

The Psychology of Control

The inability to take the reins and influence the outcome of an event to our liking is deeply unsettling. Standing by as the wrath of nature wrecks communities and economies. Raising a child through the tumultuous adolescent years. Cheering from the stands as a favorite team chokes while on the verge of victory. Watching one's family investments, accumulated over a lifetime, dwindle in a sputtering economic market. Finding oneself at the mercy of a traffic jam, sitting two hours from the exit that's a mere 20 miles away.

The need for control fuels our motivation in every aspect of our lives. Positioned near the individuality pole of the needs continuum, control is essential to our daily functioning. We see how this need influences our lives most profoundly when we're not in control. Some of life's worst and most stressful predicaments are colored by feelings of helplessness—events in which we are unable to prevent or alter the inevitable.

Many situations that fall outside the purview of personal agency hit us in the gut. We feel insecure. We feel small. We fear losing control. And we strive to regain that control. Not only does a loss of control prevent us from achieving specific outcomes, but it is also often wrenching evidence that signifies our relative insignificance in a large (and largely random) universe. When we feel in control of external events, in control of ourselves, and in control of our core relationships, we have a broader and more satisfying feeling of contentment and confidence. Like all the needs on the continuum, we can't grow as individuals without attending properly to this need.

Sometimes we may compensate for the lack of control in one area of life by reasserting control in another. This behavior manifests itself positively or negatively depending upon the person or circumstance. For example, consider the ways in which a person can respond to an untimely and unforeseen job loss. It's a moment millions of Americans have had to experience in recent years. Without the feeling of security afforded by two paychecks a month, an individual may address this setback by bouncing right back, hopeful she'll find a new opportunity in due time. While fending off the anxiety typical of a job search, this individual may choose to fill the gap by paying attention to her physical health, something she hadn't been able to do while working full-time and balancing a social life. She joins a gym, alters her diet, tones up, and loses weight—all through her concerted diligence and self-motivation.

Such behavior is part of an ongoing process of this individual's ego filling the control void that opened after she was laid off. She has discovered a way to address her need for control positively while riding out a period of stressful transition. But she could have easily attended to this need differently. Instead of her making health a priority, she could have let the control need emerge in her personal relationships. She could have become defensive or manipulative toward friends in an effort to defend her autonomy, or become despondent and helpless if she chose to ignore her need for control altogether.

Have It Your Way: Consumers and the Need for Control

For decades, we've witnessed myriad examples of the need for control expressed in traditional marketing. In the 1950s, and for several decades thereafter, Hertz, a leading rental car company, harped on this need relentlessly: "Hertz puts you in the driver's seat." This slogan is a direct appeal to our desire for control. We also see this theme play out in 2010 National Car Rental ads that show how the company allows you to register online, avoid the counter, and pick any car in the lot. The campaign features tennis brat John McEnroe, famous for his mid-match breakdowns of self-control. When told he can select any car he wants, McEnroe shouts, "Choose any car? You cannot be serious!" He's pleasantly surprised that it's true. And why not? The American road represents the essence of freedom and autonomy.

Successful rental car companies position themselves as mere facilitators of the driver's autonomy. We will help you get to where *you* want to go. Most car rental companies already gave drivers some control over the rental process, letting them chose the size of car or request specific models. National has now given even more control to consumers by letting them choose *any car they want*, in much the same way that the iPod lets consumers choose the song they want. A highly successful series of ads for the iPod featured artists, such as Eminem and Lady Gaga, who are known for their individuality and nonconformism. The ads have no marketing pitch—only silhouettes of the artists dancing wildly. The ads let the personality of the artists or the featured song make the point: be who *you* want to be.

At the outset of this book, I proposed that a company naturally tends to its own wants—mainly the desire for profit—all too often at the expense of consumer or employee needs. Corporations also thrive on carefully plotted structural organization to control and replicate outcomes as closely as possible. But when large companies give some degree of ownership to the consumers in the process, that is, when they cede control and empower, it can easily become another support beam on the bridge connecting the consumer and the company. A company's giving control, simply put, is among the best ways to foster consumers' intrinsic motivation to support its product or service, as proven by studies in consumer, social, and clinical psychology.

For example, self-determination theory, developed and tested in great detail by psychologists Richard Ryan and Edward Deci, presumes that positive behavior is a result, in part, of intrinsic motivation. In other words, when a company provides individuals with *greater control* over their purchasing decisions, they experience their behavior as self-determined and internally motivated. Online shopping, for example, gives consumers much greater control over the process. When looking for a specific item, they don't have to shop in the stores that are located nearby, but instead, they can shop in any store in the country or the world. They also have a broader selection, since the selections are not constrained by the walls of a physical store. They can scan through the whole gamut of colors for a blouse, for example, without worrying that some customer just bought the last green one that they really wanted. By providing independence and control to consumers, a company enhances their interest, performance, self-esteem, and general well-being.

When a company allows consumers to play a part in deciding an outcome, and when the consumers internalize a decision—that is, the consumers feel that the outcome is self-directed—they will not only find a greater sense of achievement or satisfaction in the purchase, but they will also hold themselves accountable for the success or failure of the product. But why would consumers ever take the blame when they have a less-than-perfect experience with a product?

- **When perceiving themselves as in control, consumers are more likely to be satisfied with the purchasing experience itself,** regardless of whether they later decide the purchase wasn't worth it.

- When perceiving themselves as in control, consumers are more likely to purchase out of intrinsic motivation, buying something purely for the satisfaction or sense of growth it gives them.
- When perceiving themselves as in control, consumers are more likely to take risks or try new services with a company that empowered them to begin with.

For these reasons, satisfying the control needs of the consumer, more than any individual need discussed in this book, holds the most potential for a company to build loyalty to a brand, product, or service through intrinsic motivation, which is the internal sense of satisfaction with the purchasing process and the resulting purchase. The difference between intrinsic and extrinsic motivation can be illustrated through the example of cleaning the house. Teenagers will begrudgingly vacuum the living room because they are told to do so. They don't really care whether the house is clean or not, as they have no control over the decision. Adults will vacuum the living room for the pure satisfaction of having a clean house, because they are intrinsically motivated to have a clean house.

If enough consumers interact and buy into a brand or service out of intrinsic motivation, the company is bound to thrive.

Buying a new car is a pleasurable purchasing process for many consumers because they have some sense of control over the process itself. They choose which car dealer's lot to visit. They wander through the cars on the lot, looking at style, colors, features, and price. They are allowed to test drive the cars that interest them. And they can even negotiate the price.

In the past, the process of buying a used car was in many ways similar to the process of buying a new car, yet there was one key area in which consumers did not feel in control of the situation: the quality of the car. Although buyers of used cars could assess certain criteria, such as the state of the car's exterior, a used-car dealership could hide the true quality (or lack thereof) of the machine. Used-car buyers had no choice but to trust the dealership. Hence, the famous question: would you buy a used car from this man?

When car dealers began to recognize that used-car buyers wanted more control over the process, they responded by creating the "certified preowned" concept that formalizes the dealer's guarantee of the quality of the car. The "carfax," which tracks the history of used cars, is an additional tool that helps consumers feel as if they have control over the quality of the car they are buying. In sum, a big smile and the words "Trust me!" are no longer enough. Consumers still want and expect something in writing before they will buy.

Without the fear factor, buying a used car today is a more satisfactory experience for consumers than in the past. They are less at the mercy of the used-car salesman, and feel a greater degree of control.

From drugstores to car deals to most other industries, companies have found that the best way to build and keep a loyal customer base is to relinquish control, not hoard it. The more customers are given control, the happier they are with the transaction and their overall relationship with the company.

Customer Service and Proxy Control

Nothing reveals the power of control—and the destructive power of lack of control—than customer service situations.

Companies that sell services or routinely interact with their customers in service settings must pay special attention to a customer's sense of control. When consumers talk to service representatives in a transactional situation or a problem-resolution situation, they know that in order to reach the desired outcome, they must work with the service representative to achieve it. This is what is known as "proxy" control, as opposed to "direct" control. A self-service buffet, for example, is a platform that offers consumers direct control. Proxy control, on the other hand, is when an intermediary facilitates an outcome that the consumer cannot control directly. For example, flagging a waiter down for a check. The diner cannot leave until she has paid, but can still control the behavior of her waiter, the proxy, to reach this end.

Poor customer service results when proxy control is ineffective. If the proxy does not behave as the customer desires, the customer has lost control of the situation. For example, the customer might try to flag a waiter, but the waiter does not come. If a customer stands at a counter in a department store and no clerk comes to assist her, there is nothing she can do but continue to stand there, literally helpless. If the customer service representative on the phone says the company will not accept a return, the customer is again helpless. There is no recourse. The customer does not have control. On the other hand, if the customer gets satisfaction—the waiter comes immediately, a clerk hurries to help the customer at the counter, the customer service person assures the customer that the product can be returned—then he or she feels in control and is much more likely to return to that business.

Customer service is all about control. Without a satisfactory level of either proxy or direct control in a situation, consumers feel manipulated and frustrated, reducing the odds they'll ever seek to do business with the establishment again.

Innovation through Changing Control

In 1916, Clarence Saunders revolutionized the grocery industry by opening Piggly Wiggly as the first self-serve grocery store, which led to a major paradigm shift as other stores quickly followed suit. In essence, Saunders's innovation boiled down to a switch from proxy control to direct control. Instead of having a clerk pull the items off the shelves, the customers did the task directly themselves.

Nearly a century later, Ingvar Kamprad of Sweden revolutionized his industry—the furniture store business—with a similar innovation based on moving customers from proxy control to direct control. In his IKEA stores (the name comes from his initials and the initials of his region in Sweden), Kamprad eliminated the proxy steps in the purchasing process. In the past, furniture buyers would pick out a model and then wait for it to be delivered at their homes. The store itself had the responsibility for taking the actual furniture from its inventory and shipping it to customers. Instead, IKEA gave direct control of the process to its customers: they were now responsible for pulling the items from the shelves and bringing them home. Not only that, since customers did not have the moving vans required to move assembled furniture, IKEA had to sell its furniture disassembled, to be reassembled by customers once they were home.

The international success of IKEA stores proves that moving customers from proxy control to direct control is a powerful way to build a fiercely loyal customer base.

However, it would be a mistake to assume that customers will always prefer direct control to proxy control. Just ask Paul Orfalea. While a student at the University of Southern California (USC), Orfalea noticed that college students spent an inordinate amount of time xeroxing papers. He had an idea for a store that would copy papers for its customers, in essence, taking over direct control of a customer process. Known for his wild curly red hair, Orfalea named his first store after his own nickname: Kinko's. Today, Kinko's (recently renamed FedEx Office after it was acquired by FedEx in 2004) has sixteen thousand employees working in two thousand stores spread across eight countries.

Kinko's is a success because its business model, built on proxy control, helps customers achieve their goals. In other situations, proxy control might be preferable to direct control simply because of customers' habits or comfort. For instance, McDonald's fast-food revolution was based on the idea that people would prefer not to be waited on in restaurants, but in exchange get their food faster. Yet when McDonald's spread to Europe, a wealthy Frenchwoman in Bordeaux, who ate at a restaurant every day, decided to give the newfangled American restaurant a try. She sat down at the new McDonald's and waited for the waiter to take her order. Unhappy with the slow service, she quickly left the restaurant. McDonald's and other fast food franchises have been successfully exported to countries throughout Europe. But just as in the United States, they have complemented but never replaced traditional restaurants. There are times when people are ready to hand over control of certain situations to proxies.

Appealing to Control When Consumers Need Guidance

Renowned psychologist Julian Rotter captivated researchers and the general public alike in the 1950s and '60s with the development of his social learning theory (SLT). Rotter proposed that an individual's behaviors can be evaluated on the basis of exploring the dual function of a) the level of a person's expectation that a decision or action can lead to an outcome and b) the value of the outcome to the person. For example, if I believe that by choosing to purchase Ax Body Spray I'll be more attractive and apt to have girls more attracted to me, I might be persuaded to buy the product. The decision will be all the more easier if the end result—the female sex magnetically drawn to my new, arousing scent—is something I particularly desire. The ads in question are farcical in nature, but the appeal might work on a single, young man in need of both a confidence boost and a partner. Consciously, consumers of Ax Body Spray don't expect the end result to pan out. But on some level, they hope the product will at least make them feel like the end result could pan out. By purchasing the body spray, they take control of their self-image.

These types of ads generally appeal to personalities that believe that outcomes are a consequence of a personal action or inaction. Rotter developed as a component of SLT a now widely used system for gauging peoples' personal sense of agency. Called the "locus of control," Rotter's continuum, shown below, spans two broad character traits. People who largely feel they have no control over their destiny occupy an external locus. They are often fatalistic, feeling nothing they do will affect the random forces that ultimately decide one's fate. These types of people are reticent to take action, passive, and tend to get weighed down by the randomness of life. In contrast, people who occupy an internal locus feel they have complete command over their destiny. They place great weight on fulfilling their individuality needs and express their autonomy in the actions they take. Traditionally, the world of self-help psychology, propelled by the American ideal of self-determination, finds an internal focus superior to an external focus. There's much truth to this sentiment. But as with all continuums, there's a downside toward going too far one in one direction. Internally focused individuals can be unwilling to accept random misfortune as an explanation for success or failure. Luck (or randomness) plays a huge role in even the most successful person's fate—regardless of intelligence or ambition.

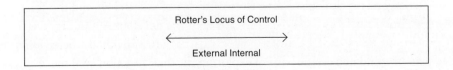

Rotter's Locus of Control

External Internal

The "External" Danger: Forget the Butterflies

As demonstrated by the Ax commercial described above, companies have traditionally appealed through their marketing and business models to the psyche of internally focused customers. Even industries that seemed inherently to be based on the external side of Rotter's locus of control have been moving towards the internal side.

The financial services industry is one example. Because so many factors can impact the financial markets, investing is to a certain extent an externally focused activity: there will be a good measure of luck in any success. In addition, investors hand over their money to money managers, such as investment bankers and stockbrokers, who make all of the decisions on how to invest these clients' funds. And while some research into the track records of money managers might be undertaken, in truth most investors have to *trust* that their financial advisors are skilled and reputable. Whenever trust is involved, there is by definition some measure of luck, depending on how well an individual knows the person in whom he or she is placing trust. In sum, because of the unpredictability of the stock market, customers of financial investment firms have had to adopt a more external, fatalistic approach to the purchase of financial services, instead of the more proactive, take-charge internal attitude related to other purchasing decisions.

However, fatalism only goes so far. Customers who feel that companies are poor stewards of responsibility will rebel.

Before the financial crisis of 2008 struck, one of the most affected firms, American International Group (AIG), was singing a different, highly arrogant tune in its marketing and advertising. In one television spot, a father and his daughter are sitting under a tree. When the father tells the daughter that, like her, he is thinking about butterflies, she asks him, in the language of a financial advisor, whether he isn't worried about his finances. He replies that he doesn't have to worry, he's with AIG.

We can only imagine the father wasn't thinking about butterflies after AIG imperiled his investments in the liquidity crisis, after AIG took a massive federal bailout, after AIG lost 95 percent of its stock value, and after AIG paid $128 million in bonuses to executives.

The ad is laughable now. The AIG campaign expressed the need on the part of the consumer to be dependent upon experts who knew what was best. It wasn't even a stopgap in the continuum. AIG said a client didn't need control, that working with them was the very act of control. That's all well and good, so long as a company backs up its very specious claim. When the wheels come off, however, a marketing message juxtaposed with a contradictory reality will send consumers into a rage.

Today, once naïve consumers in the financial markets are looking to companies that offer control, because losing control of one's finances is damaging psychologically.

Businesses can in fact satisfy a key ego need by appealing to consumer autonomy. But too often companies behave in ways that result in taking away consumer control. Or worse yet, a company will offer no means for coproduction—working hand in hand with the company for the good of the customer. Frequently they launch services that leave consumers helpless, setting the company up for failure down the line. The psychology of zero autonomy is an infringement upon customers' potential growth and satisfaction.

Companies such as E*Trade and Charles Schwab have an attitude that is the polar opposite of AIG's "just leave it to us" approach. These two companies pioneered financial-services business models in which the customer is given control and autonomy; the companies themselves are only the supporting cast.

Going Internal: Talk to Chuck

With the deregulation of the financial services industry in 1975, a new kind of brokerage was born, pioneered by Charles Schwab. "Discount brokerage," as it was known, allowed self-directed customers to take on more of the responsibility for the investment decisions related to their investment funds. The general concept of a discount broker like Schwab is that investors, with support from the company, become the educated deciders in the process while Schwab becomes a partner and implementer. Although Schwab investors are still subject to the vicissitudes of the financial markets, to some degree these self-directed investors acquire a sense of control over the outcomes of their investments they did not enjoy before. In other words, investing travels on the locus of control away from the external end and toward the internal end. Investors acquire the autonomy that was denied to them in the earlier financial-services business model.

One of the key factors in the success of the discount brokerage industry is the amount of support that the company offers its customers. In many ways, the situation is similar to the big-box home improvement industry and its do-it-yourself (DIY) customers. One of the big selling points for companies such as Home Depot and Lowe's is that their sales associates will help customers find the right tools and materials for the job at hand. These associates are, in essence, consultants. Similarly, the discount financial services industry provides "tools" to help do-it-yourself investors do it themselves.

The issue here is known in psychological circles as "self-efficacy." Companies catering to customers interested in directing their own financial decisions must convince those customers that they have the skills, the will, and the tools to get the job done.

Finding a healthy internal locus of control is important when trying to satisfy the need for control. But without self-efficacy, we become shackled by low self-confidence and let opportunities to control outcomes pass by in order to avoid failure. We only spend energy on controlling outcomes proportional to our belief that we can succeed. Albert Bandura, a seminal researcher on the subject of self-efficacy, outlines its importance.

> A strong sense of efficacy enhances human accomplishment and personal well-being in many ways. People with high assurance in their capabilities approach difficult tasks as challenges to be mastered rather than as threats to be avoided. Such an efficacious outlook fosters intrinsic interest and deep engrossment in activities. They set themselves challenging goals and maintain strong commitment to them. They heighten and sustain their efforts in the face of failure... Such an efficacious outlook produces personal accomplishments, reduces stress and lowers vulnerability to depression.[1]

Thus, marketing messages can't just convince people that it is possible to take the reins. That message doesn't reach the millions of listeners who don't believe they are personally capable of doing a task. Therefore, enhancing consumers' cognitive control—the control of what we know—through education can positively affect self-efficacy, increasing the chance that consumers will adopt a brand and be loyal to it.

Boost Cognitive Control: Even a Baby Can Do It!

A breakthrough experiment in the 1970s studied patients undergoing major surgery. The researchers found that the patients most educated about the surgery and its effects afterward recovered faster than those who were not as well informed. The educated patients experienced less stress before and after the operation and requested fewer painkillers during recovery. Knowledge, we can say, is a form of control.

Cognitive control is critical in a marketing context, as well. The more complex a product or service, the more discomfort a consumer may experience. A 2001 study of 103 undergraduate participants measured their need for cognitive control while the students used a new online banking program. College students are good at discretionary spending, but not always competent in the financial management realm. They were asked to imagine that it was one year after graduation, and that they were employed, doing fairly well, and hoping to manage their finances more effectively.

Participants learned about the online service and responded to a survey measuring their perceived cognitive control and their interest in and satisfaction with the service. Analysis showed that the cognitive control scale developed in the experiment was positively correlated with levels of satisfaction and the likelihood of adopting the online banking service. Students with high ratings of perceived cognitive control expressed little trepidation towards the technology. They also expressed significantly higher levels of satisfaction and interest in this new service. In contrast, students who felt they had no cognitive control over the new product were dissatisfied with the service and significantly less likely to adopt it. High levels of cognitive control were also positively correlated with participants' perceptions of how innovative the product was perceived to be.[2] Therefore, when introducing complex, multifunctional technologies, like an iPad for instance, marketers and designers must be certain the complexity is mitigated by clear instructions and intuitive functioning.

Even in service situations where consumers rely on a professional, successful control is more of a state of mind, a feeling, than it is a direct action. For example, our firm researched the pilot program of a new financial planning software suite developed by a large financial advising firm. The software was designed to make the experts' job easy—better and quicker forecasting, simpler data analysis. But after dissecting the dynamics of how the advisors used its tools, my firm discovered that the benefits turned out to be much greater for the client. By providing graphics of a client's assets and showing a variety of options in real time, the firm created a higher degree of trust between the planner and the client. The technology boosted the clients' sense of cognitive control over a subject difficult for many to understand. In the past, providing clients with this type of financial information required an expert who crunched numbers that clients often had to rely on with little understanding of where they came from.

The online brokerage E*Trade has been successful because it has convinced its customers that, with the help of their proprietary tools, investors will have the knowledge they need to make the right investment decisions themselves. E*Trade has successfully dismantled investors' reluctance to take charge of the financial decision-making process that would have kept customers who were unsure of their skills and aptitude from trying the service. Helped by witty advertisement campaigns such as the talking baby, they have demystified the financial services industry.

Fieldwork

The Different Degrees of Control

Airline Travelers and the Need for Control

In early 2010, in a rare moment of unanimous bipartisanship, Congress passed a law prohibiting airlines from holding passengers on the tarmac for more than one hour without taking off. The new regulation tied the knot on a nightmare that had grown disturbingly familiar for airline passengers.

This problem underscores why air travel is routinely among the most stress-inducing activities for Americans. Loss of control is at the heart of this frustration. Long security lines, packed overhead storage bins, delayed and canceled flights, crowded and noisy terminals, crying children in the cabin, lost or damaged luggage, and, of course, the incessant, seemingly arbitrary fees. Inherently, air travel is a mode of transportation where arrival times, security, and the overall quality of the experience are out of the passenger's control. There are more rules in an airport and on an airplane than there are for perhaps any other consumer experience. Many regulations ensure security and safety, of course. This is one of the reasons why air travel is by far the safest way to travel. But all the red tape takes a mental toll on airline passengers. The jumping through hoops and the sacrifice of comfort is unsettling for time-pressed, over-stressed travelers paying top bill for quick transport. Whereas the interstate highway system is a representation of American independence, control, and liberation, airline travel is more akin to a prison.

The fact that airlines can no longer literally lock passengers on the tarmac for an indefinite amount time is surely a victory for travelers, but for the struggling band of airline companies, attending to the control needs of passengers will continue to be front and center. Let's be clear: airline companies will never be able to make flying an easy experience. But making the process and the experience feel less constricted by rigid policies and dreaded routines is worth the product development and marketing dollars. When airline travelers feel they are more in control, whether they are in economy class or first class, are frequent fliers or vacationers, the experience becomes a little bit easier on the ego. Airlines can even mitigate the stress of rising prices and superfluous charges if the consumer experience is more control oriented.

Some airlines now allow the average passenger to select his or her own seat, have a few more inches of legroom for a small extra charge, pick their on-board entertainment, board first and sit wherever he or she likes, bring one extra bag, and choose a compensation package in the event of cancellation of the flight. The goal of these new services is obviously to make passengers feel in control of their travel experience, which is in general hardly deemed pleasurable by the average flier.

The more options found in a rule-bound, routine-anchored experience, the more likely a passenger will associate flying with an experience they can shape and alter.

The trick is for airlines to do so without alienating passengers who aren't willing to pay for the extra charge to receive the perks. Airline travel can be largely seen as a class-based process. Frequent fliers get the upgrades, first priority, better service, higher-quality food, and comfortable seats. Most economy passengers or infrequent fliers are fine with this if they are at least given the option of enhancing their experience for a reasonable cost. This means, even if they feel they have some control, whether or not they utilize the options, their need will be satisfied to a degree. If they feel completely powerless, on the other hand, economy passengers will look with resentment at the elites comfortably dozing at the front of plane. In order to fulfill this need, the passengers must be offered assurance that can create a sense of control. Sure, they can't be the captain, but there must be a host of affordable options that prevent the violation of autonomy while they are traveling in the blue skies.

So a need for control exists in airline travel? That's not too revelatory. But satisfying the need and successfully communicating the need to a diverse range of travelers is a trickier game.

We learned this lesson clearly while interviewing air travelers on behalf of United Airlines in 2008. United was about to launch a new merchandising program. Essentially, it was a suite of travel options created to

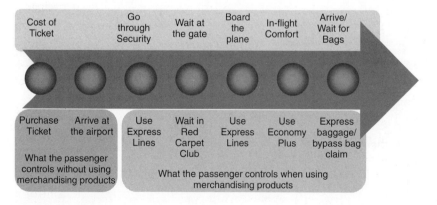

Figure 3.2 Potential Messaging Strategies for United

Customize your trip.
Every traveler is unique and every journey different. That's why United is introducing enhancements you can purchase to customize your trip and travel the way you want.
Be in control.
We understand that you like to be more in control of your travel experience. That's why United is introducing trip enhancements you can purchase. You choose how you want to travel.
Reward yourself.
You work hard and deserve to live a little when you travel. That's why United is introducing enhancements you can purchase to treat yourself and make your trip more rewarding.
Travel smart.
You know what you need when you travel. That's why United is introducing trip enhancements you can purchase. Pay only for what you want and get everything you need.
Enjoy a better experience.
Many airlines make it impossible for infrequent fliers to access some of the benefits of more frequent fliers. That's why United is introducing enhancements you can purchase to make your trip a little more special.

Figure 3.3 Potential Taglines for United

help passengers design the fine details of their experience at each stage. My firm was charged with helping create and explore a number of different messaging strategies to introduce the program to market.

The palette of strategies included the potential marketing taglines and statements listed above.

We introduced these messages to dozens of fliers in in-depth interviews and dyads (interviews in pairs). The profile of the participants was a mix of elite-status frequent fliers, nonelite frequent fliers, business travelers, leisure travelers, and very infrequent fliers. The merchandising program would be offered to all of these groups. Thus, the appeal had to be a hybrid composite of all the needs, fears, and expectations contained within the subgroups.

The results yielded a number of lessons on both the power and the limitations of control. Through these five lessons, listed below, we learned that different "degrees" of control are acceptable and even expected by consumers. In some cases, customers want to be in complete control; in other situations, they realize that complete control is neither possible, nor even desirable.

Here are the five lessons learned from the United Airlines project:

1. **Don't oversell control. Customers know when they are not in control.** We learned that a direct appeal to control was sure to backfire. "Feel in control" is a classic marketing false promise. Sure, the point of the program was to offer options to travelers throughout their trip, but the tagline is a totalizing statement. In other words, the juxtaposition of United telling a passenger, "You're in control," while surrounded by a thousand factors the passenger can't affect produced a countereffective disharmony. One frequent flier threw water on the message immediately: "But being in control is like the one thing I learned about flying: you're not in control. Actually, you relinquish a lot of control because some things are out of your control." Seeing the word "control" elicits an unintended ironic response from the majority of travelers who know anything about air travel. Intended to give peace of mind to the stressful, chained-by-rules traveler, "Be in control" served only to mock the traveler who knew the airline was selling them a need that it could not deliver.

   In some situations, reassurance is all the control that customers want. Our work for United showed that infrequent travelers were consistently unsure of and unsettled by the "control" idea. Thrown into a loud, unfamiliar, crowded, and stressful environment, and wracked by fears of losing baggage, navigating cavernous terminals, and missing the flight, infrequent travelers don't feel they can be in control. What they need is assurance that their experience will be easier than expected. Their control needs are assuaged not through affirmations that they can seize control over the trip, but through messages that appeal to "cognitive" control—the traveler's awareness that the trip will be manageable.

2. **While the idea of "control" elicited concern among some respondents, the idea of "choice" was more acceptable.** The phrase "You choose how you want to travel" did not elicit any negative reactions. You can't be in control, but you have the choice to alter the experience to your benefit—if you so choose. The presence of options raises the perception of control, as we learned from the consumer psychology experiments. Importantly , it also positively

affects even the travelers who decide not to act on those options. This point illustrates the relative strengths of the "customize your trip" platform.

3. **Choice is a virtue; unpredictability is not.** Make sure your message is a message of choice, and not of the unknown. Business travelers and frequent fliers stick with an airline because of its predictability and proximity. A successful trip should be just like the last smooth trip they experienced. If "every journey is different" what sense of control and security is gained?

   Communication is a crucial lever of control. While businesses can rarely give customers complete control, they can allow customers to acquire varying degrees of control through "levers" of control, such as reassurance, choice, and communication. In an experience that's left highly to the winds of fate, travelers want to feel some sense of control and recognition or importance. One simple action that is rarely taken that reaps significant return on investment (ROI) is to continuously communicate with customers to let them know what's going on, and to set up expectations. Airlines should rarely keep customers stuck in one place or delayed indefinitely without conveying the reason. Being informed can provide travelers with the needed sense of control. Services/policies such as texting/emailing people about flight-status updates and delays, allowing them to listen to air traffic control on the flight, and being proactive about communicating expected delays, reasons for delays, and anticipated departure times help fliers to understand, feel valued, and be less frustrated with their lack of control over the experience.

By avoiding polarizing language and not overselling the notion of control, United found they could successfully appeal to and satisfy travelers' need for control by downplaying "control" since it spotlighted an issue travelers were anxious about and had little recourse to change. The lesson for United and for all companies who think they can empower a consumer via control is clear: don't emphasize control when consumers are astute enough to know you can't give them the control and autonomy they yearn for. At the same, offer the three credible levers of control that consumers can use according to the situation: reassurance that the experience is predictable and manageable; products and services with incremental costs that enable them to excercise them some control over the process; and ongoing communication so that consumers are not left in the dark. Not knowing what is happening is the ultimate lack of control.

Chapter 3 Summary: Helping Customers Take Charge

There is little we find more unnerving than the feeling of helplessness associated with the loss of control. Customers want greater control in many aspects of their business transactions, and oftentimes that means having the competence to address new and uncertain situations. At the same time, customers are willing to cede some control to others when they realize that others are more competent or better positioned to resolve a particular challenge or task.

Below are a few key steps businesses can take to effectively respond to consumers' need for control:

Suggested Follow-Up Steps

1. **Review your core marketing message. It should say to customers: you can be in the driver's seat. (assuming products and services can deliver)**

Customers will respond to marketing that empowers them. Choose words carefully. Messaging must never give the impression that someone is *helpless*. Instead, marketing must emphasize that the customer is in control—and will acquire even greater control over his or her life through valued products or services. "Together, let's get it done" is the theme of one Home Depot series of commercials. The commercials end with: "More Savings. More Doing. That's the Power of Home Depot." One of National Car Rental's "Go Like a Pro" commercials says: "You are a business pro. The princess of PowerPoint. Your core competency is competence. And you rent from National." The concept of internal locus means that some valuable customer segments aren't exactly looking for companies to do things *for* them.

They are looking for companies that will enable them to do things themselves. Is there an opportunity to address a segment motivated by this need in your business?

2. **Examine customers' experience. Are prospects and customers in control throughout the path to the final sale and afterwards?**

Below are some ideas as to how businesses can engage with and provide greater control:

Internet. Online selling is perhaps the ultimate in customer control. However, a poorly designed website will undermine a customer's or prospect's sense of control—and can quickly lead to the loss of the sale. How easy is your website to navigate? Are all products easy to find? Are they fully described? Can customers easily order products directly from the website? Is customer support available throughout the web process so customers don't get lost? Too often this is the exception and not the rule.

Retail experience. Start with the store design. This may seem quite obvious. The location of products must be clearly marked. Customers don't want to be frustrated by circling around a store unable to find a product that they know is available. Operational processes are next. Are shelves continuously stocked? Are there enough cash registers open to accommodate customers in the store? Another focus area is sales staff. Train sales staff to be visible and knowledgeable, but without being intrusive. If the customer has a question, he or she wants someone to be nearby with answers. However, hovering over a customer who does not need help can be seen as a bid for control: the sales clerk wants to take control of the transaction.

From start to finish, customers must never sense that they are at the mercy of a company or product.

3. **Simplify after-sales processes.**

Complexity, confusion, and lack of clarity equate to a lack of control. Strive to reduce the waves of automatic telephone prompts that your customers are required to navigate. There should be only one prompt required to get the customer to the appropriate customer service representative. Make returns easy and free. For example, one medical device supplier sends its customers a FedEx box to return equipment if needed. Offer online bill pay and other services, but don't use the Internet as a buffer between the company and the customers. For example, too many businesses force customers to rely on user forums or frequently asked questions (FAQs) to help them with questions about the product. Instead, give them a phone number where they can explain the problem to a live person.

* * *

CHAPTER 4

The Need for Self-Expression

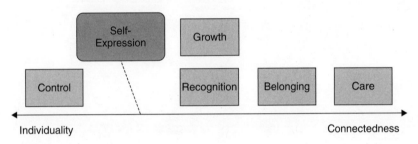

Figure 4.1   The Self-Expression Need

CHAPTER 4

The Need for Self-Expression

"Nice to see you back, Mr. Howard," the hostess says, leading the party to a table beside the window. Darryl Howard smiles as he invites his clients to take their seats, welcoming them to his home turf. It is, after all, his table, the table where deals are made, where relationships deepen.

The new restaurant on Franklin Avenue is Darryl's favorite. The floor-to-ceiling windows show off the downtown better than any other restaurant. It's quiet and comfortable. A perfect spot to win over clients.

For thirty years he's been building client relationships for a brokerage firm in the Bay area. It doesn't hurt that Darryl exudes charisma and confidence. He knows the art of first impressions. His demeanor is a billboard for his company's brand, which screams, *We get our work done, and smile while doing it.*

While his small-talk autopilot function kicks in, guiding the conversation through lighthearted laughs and industry buzz, Darryl discreetly trains his eyes on the menu.

Business aside, Darryl cherishes these client lunches for a very personal reason. Even if he knows an agreement is remote or destined to fall through, at the very least, he gets to enjoy fine dining on the company's dime. His finger traces vertically down the list of entrées, searching again for the description of the duck confit—his favorite meal in the city. Check that. His favorite meal period. *A pair of duck legs cured in salts, allspice, thyme, garlic, and ginger, preserved in its own rendered fat, served over a bed of lemon basil risotto.* The listing itself elicits a Pavlovian reaction in him.

The waiter returns for their orders. His clients mostly decide on the day's seafood specials. After nodding and complimenting their choices, Darryl grips his napkin as the last client, the female vice president of his client's company, asks the waiter, "How's the duck?" The waiter nods in affirmation. "I'll get that then," she says, turning to Darryl, the last to order.

"And for you, Mr. Howard," the waiter says. Darryl freezes. "I think I'll try the steak frites today. Thanks."

Behind his smile, Darryl's emotions are at war. His duck confit was the prize awaiting him after an exhausting round of morning presentations. Internally, he regrets not ordering it, but he fights through the dissonance and justifies his selection. Why, in the heat of the moment, would he change his mind on what's typically a no-brainer decision? Why would he delay the satisfaction of a foundational need—the need for pleasure?

To answer these questions, we have to get inside the mechanics of what this decision actually is. Seemingly a choice between competing options that can either be very simple or hopelessly complex, any decision is confounded in the context of social situations. On the playing field of group dynamics, decisions aren't just about what they will do for you. A decision can easily come to represent who you are – or at least a part of who you are. Darryl's choice becomes a symbol conveyed outwardly that gives others a picture of who he is. **In essence, all decisions are potential vehicles for self-expression.**

Already that day, beginning with choosing the right style of tie, Darryl had made countless decisions that were dictated by his need for self-expression. While it might seem silly or illogical, Darryl's gut instinct told him that echoing the vice president's order would be a mistake. The decision could convey more than a preference, but rather, a clue to his personality that might affect his clients' perception of Darryl. The decision could become a symbol of meaning. What if the client saw Darryl's copycat order as a sign of brownnosing? Or indecision? Or conformity?

True, we might think that in most cases the client wouldn't bat an eye. It'd certainly be a stretch if she showed any outward discontent at the table. But Darryl opted to play it safe regardless. And the safe decision in a culture that values individuality is a decision that errs on the side of uniqueness.

But there's more to Darryl's conundrum of choice at play here, and it speaks to the transient nature of the need for self-expression and individuality.

The prior week, Darryl had taken his family to the same restaurant to celebrate his son's college graduation. Darryl, like always, picked up the menu, found the description of the confit (reading it is somewhat of a mental appetizer!), and let his family order ahead of him. His wife ordered a steak. But then his mother ordered the confit. His son said, "That sounds great. I'm getting that."

"And for you, sir?"

"I've got to go with the confit, as well. Too good to pass up."

So in one setting, his preferred choice is "too good" not to choose it, even though half the table has already ordered the same thing. But not more than ten days later, his insatiable desire for the duck leg braised in its own juices was subverted by the need to express his individuality. The same decision, with the social situation changed, can produce distinctly different emotions in the subconscious and activate different needs.

Think back to the introductory chapter for a moment. A key reason we need to view people as complex—whether they're romantic partners or valued customers—is because emotions are fuel for the multiple roles we play in order to satisfy our needs. **We're always presenting. We're perpetually conveying something about ourselves to the self and others.** As William Shakespeare writes in *As You Like It*, "All the world's a stage." In this case, Darryl is presenting different selves to different groups. His personality is already established with his family. His role is stable. The ordering decision does not activate the need to express or the need to stand out and be different. Instead, the decision boils down to what item will be the most pleasurable.

The implications here are as complex as they are profound: there exists a multiplicity of selves. They underscore the value and complexity of one of our most important emotional needs: self-expression.

But let's first take a step back from Darryl's story and explore why self-expression is necessary to begin with. We're always expressing ourselves in different ways to different people for different reasons. But why do we need to do so? As with every need in this book, the goal of this chapter is to explore how businesses can satisfy a consumer's need for self-expression. The mechanics of this important emotional need revolve around the inner and outer meaning of brands, products, or services and the development of identity. More specifically for businesses and marketers, a brand has the potential to become both a symbol and a vehicle of expression.

Hard-Wired for Self-Expression

In 1940, four teenage boys and a dog from southwestern France happened across what would end up being a major clue to the enigmatic origins of human culture. While wandering in a series of caves near their home, the boys discovered a fantastic display of figures etched on the dark walls. The Lascaux caves are dotted with over two thousand of these images: animals, human shapes, and abstract figures. The site quickly became a tourist destination, and while it is now closed off to the public for preservation, it remains a magnet for researchers today. Scientists estimate that the images date back seventeen thousand years.[1]

No one will know for sure what function the cave paintings served. Were they used as written language? For ceremonial purposes? Or are they evidence showcasing the evolving skills of human creativity, or the codifying of the earliest culture? Whatever their purpose, they illustrate who humans were in that time period (hunters and gatherers), what they valued (animals), and how they lived (sparsely!). Had they not expressed their livelihood and cultural identity, we'd be without this window into the past. The ancient paintings might just indicate that the need for self-expression is both universal and timeless. The fact that people from various cultures around the world pierce and tattoo their bodies, and have been doing so for centuries, speaks to this too. Novelist Pearl S. Buck said that, "Self-expression must pass into communication for its fulfillment."[2] Millennia later, we're still learning how our ancestors turned thoughts and knowledge into creative, perhaps culture-defining expression.

So if we were to flash forward seventeen thousand years from now, what would be our current culture's cave drawings? What signs and symbols that we encounter everyday will clue in our planet's successors to who we were? They might discover shells of our libraries or somehow access our accumulated knowledge (and inanities) logged in the infinite expanse of the blogosphere and Web. They might discover our art galleries or trophy rooms, or stumble into a million different closets with a million different clothing styles. Our words, our thoughts, our possessions are all modes of expression, all markings on the wall illuminating the labyrinthine floor plan of our identities.

We need to express ourselves because, without the means to show off or communicate who we are, we have no way of conveying to ourselves and others that we're even relevant or alive! Without such modes of expression, we'd exist only in a prison of our own thoughts. Self-expression is self-confirmation of our individual worth. Unless we can fulfill this need, we are mere drones, ants marching. So we express ourselves through speech and writing. Through art and fashion. Through ideas. Through attitudes. Through the showcasing of possessions and purchases.

Note that for this need to be met, in most cases, our need for self-expression can be satisfied even if no one else receives the self-expressive message we are sending out. Being recognized is a different need entirely (see chapter 5). Surely, we express our personality to others in the hope that they'll take note, but we do so in part to satisfy our drive to communicate outwardly. Expression is a need to release our bottled-up self-image into the open air. It's a core process that helps us figure out who we are and who we hope to become. In a culture that values distinctiveness and defined personalities, what we choose to wear, what we choose to drive, even what we order at a restaurant are all potential opportunities to fulfill the need for self-expression. Freedom of choice is synonymous with the freedom to express.

Of course, the future observers of our material lives will wonder how the multiplicity of mass-produced logos and commercial symbols functioned for us. What did these objects and messages mean for the individuals who used and interacted with them? We still create the richest form of self-expression in our minds, through art, speech, and literature. And for many people, the most satisfying vehicle for expression is often the work of one's career. But we can't deny the leading role that symbols in the marketplace play in our persistent need to express our individuality and personality. If for no other reason, these company and brand logos are among the most recognizable and universal symbols in public spaces. From Apple stickers to Wrangler jeans, we use a near-infinite number of commercial symbols to give meaning to individual identity. We associate the meanings of brands and symbols with the owners of personalities and identities who voluntarily decide to populate their lives with these symbols. Brand identity, then, is not just about generating public recognition of a company. It's about what the symbol of the brand says about the individual who equips him or herself with it as a badge of identity.

Symbols illuminate just why marketing communication is not merely a game of pitching and selling. Again, Sydney Levy offers a definition of marketing that underscores the prominence of the self-expression need:

> Marketers do not just sell isolated items that can be interpreted as symbols; rather, they sell pieces of a larger symbol—the consumer's lifestyle. Marketing is then a process of providing customers with parts of a potential mosaic from which they, as artists of their own lifestyle, can pick and choose to develop the composition that for the time may seem the best.[3]

So we express not just an identity, but a way of life. Our psyches press us to affirm a sense of where we are and where we're going in life. Of course we are not the brands and the products we use, but sometimes they offer us a *feeling* of stability, an affirmation that we're expressing to the world who we want to be at that *particular moment in our life.*

Consider fashion's role in self-expression. People dress a certain way to help maintain a consistent identity and affirm aspects of their personality. Sometimes part of expressing oneself through fashion is a means of fitting in with a group. Sometimes it's used to stand out from the group. But in most instances, fashion as self-expression is a way to boost one's self-esteem. To a lot of people, there's little discernible difference between a department store brand polo that costs $15 and a Giorgio Armani polo that costs $220. Walking down a crowded street, it's possible that only a few people would notice the expensive shirt, but to the owner, that doesn't matter. It's the feeling that the individual wearer is expressing high self-worth that sets it apart, based on his knowledge that his shirt places him in a different, higher-class of polo wearers. Low fashion is mass produced and relatively non-unique. High fashion on the other hand, is exclusive and typically quite expensive. In other words, low fashion is functional. High fashion, which can include hard-to-find vintage relics, is exclusive, unique, and therefore, is considered by the wearer to be a superior vehicle of self-expression. Rebecca Mead, in an article in the *New Yorker*, describes how Japan's fashion industry is remarkably different from America's in that clothing options available to the masses allow Japan's shoppers to craft *truly* unique identities. Sometime it's simply easier to have something no one else has:

> In Japan, however, all the skill goes into engineering the scarcity: designers produce only limited editions of T-shirts or jackets, items of the sort that can be easily mass-produced. This means that shopping in Tokyo feels a little like a bizarre parody of grocery shopping in Soviet Russia: you might want to buy a bunch of bananas, but the only thing for sale is pickled cabbage.[4]

Whether it's the clothing label we wear or the brand of car we drive, our association with this personalized system of symbols is emotional—in other words, much of self-expression is done outside conscious awareness. The idea that possessions and material goods are extensions of our identity has long been discussed in the fields of sociology and personality psychology. But we must admit, many business leaders may only pay lip service to the notion that possessions and symbols play a major role in our lives. While self-expression can exist more purely in the realm of thought and art, our possessions still function as markers of identity, even for those of us who tend not to place a high value on tangible goods or commercial brands. Both research and common sense show that the value of important possessions becomes strikingly evident in a person's reaction to loss.

Imagine what it's like to lose everything in a natural disaster. Survivors of floods, tornadoes, or fires who have their homes and lifestyles reduced to ash or rubble are foremost thankful that their families are safe. They wipe back the tears and tell the reporter and camera crew that now it's all about trying to rebuild. But it's not just the literal process of putting back together the pieces of the ruined physical space. It's also about rebuilding the identity and memories that were tied into the fabric of that space. Losing something fragile like a family photo album destroys an intimate connection with the past and leaves us bereft. When we hear, "We lost everything," we're not listening to a dirge mourning the loss of inanimate stuff and material acquisitions. We hear a verbal symbol suggesting that aspects of the family or individuals' identities suffered the same fate as their possessions. More than one hundred years ago, in 1890, the philosopher William James challenged those who would trivialize the loss of such expressive symbols:

> Although it is true that a part of our depression at the loss of possessions is due to our feeling that we must now go without. Yet, in every case there remains a sense of the shrinkage of our personality, a partial conversion of ourselves to nothingness, which is a psychological phenomenon by itself.[5]

This discussion is valuable in that it shows that our self is made up of more than our brains and bodies. The complex web of symbols—a brand, an object, individual decisions, words and actions—tie together a collage of ourselves. This is ever so apparent in times of deprivation or loss. In research about human needs, this is called "addition through subtraction." For example, if a researcher wants to see how cell phones interplay with individuals' emotional needs, they might see how various users live without their cell phones for a week or two. In a short time, the role of cell phones in shaping and expressing an individual's identity will become apparent.

* * *

SO BY NOW we know that the psychological need for self-expression is broad and complex. Like all emotional needs, satisfying the need for self-expression requires an intimate understanding of how people seek to portray themselves and for what purpose. How can a business determine whether and how it can help its consumers satisfy this vital need? This chapter will cover three general ideas. First, there must be a general understanding that people evolve, experiment, and shift their identity, therefore changing the ways in which they express themselves. Because our self is always refining itself, making a brand, service, or product into a valuable and an accurate symbol to an individual requires a sense of how people adapt and contour their self-perceptions across time and place. Second, businesses can help the individual identify with a brand or service if the brand creates an easily definable, emotional identity over time. Third, we will see that businesses don't have to be the symbol with which consumers identify. Many products or services can facilitate or be the vehicle by which the individual fulfills the need for expression.

Malleable Selves: Self-Expression Changes as We Change

We certainly know that people act differently in different situations. We know that a 40-year-old man will want to express who he is and what he stands for differently than a 16-year-old boy. Broadly speaking, traditional demographic marketing data is successful at identifying trends between and among large groups of people. But within that mountain of data, we'll find an infinite expanse of life stages and personalities— myriad different selves toward which to market products and services. Businesses are increasingly becoming savvy and taking advantage of transitional life phases as opportunities to witness how people redefine themselves. Experiences like career change, job loss, graduating college, closing on one's first home, and confronting an "empty nest" are all pivotal "tipping points" when we are more likely to reevaluate our self-concept and find new means of self-expression.

The old way of thinking about the need for self-expression relied on the assumption that one's identity was stable over time. This is because we didn't have a nuanced understanding that took into account a person's multiple, malleable selves. One conceptual way to view and understand multiple selves is to see an individual as having a set of personality traits consistently expressed in specific situations. For example, my firm has observed in ethnography research how an extroverted opinion leader orders a premium, lesser-known microbrew at a bar to express his "finer taste." As a researcher, it is important to think about what aspects of personality are involved when the customer is thinking about using a product, and which situations (and where) they are accessed. Looking at audiences this way, we can learn how best to satisfy self-expression for different personality dimensions, including:

- Influencer—e.g., Opinion leaders and group leaders express as a means to be noticed. They are more likely to early adopt/try unique products to share with those in their social circle. They feel they have something to say. For instance, distinct groups of physicians are willing to try and recommend new treatments prior to peer acceptance.
- Creators—e.g., Creative persons are receptive to services that give them the most control over their work. My carpenter swears by his Stanley Tools, likely because they reliably facilitate his creative process.
- Introverts—e.g., Introverted personalities may be more likely to publicly express through digital media.

But with that said, a business cannot reach any individual if there is not a clear understanding of what a brand, product, or service means and represents. Some brands are iconic, define a generation, or become part of a cultural history. This rarely happens by accident. It is possible for a product or service to represent or become a part of an individual's identity. The question is: How are these symbols of expression accepted, rejected, or considered by the owner?

The Importance of Being on Emotion and on Message

"There is no force more powerful or more beautiful than self-expression," reads copy from a 2001 Super Bowl advertisement. It was the sponsor company's first national ad campaign. The annual opportunity, among the most watched events in the world, defines this primetime, high-stakes investment. In only a few seconds, the message can alienate or engage the American public. This ad underscores the danger of using emotion without any connection, and the bigger folly of not creating a stable and clear identity for a brand.

Artist Dan Keplinger was the focus of the one-minute spot. Keplinger's speech and movement are severely impeded by cerebral palsy, but as the ad begins, we see that his condition does not prevent him from creating beautiful paintings. "I speak to the world in light and color," reads a subtitle. Over angelic hymnal choir music, we see Keplinger at work, crouched atop his canvas, painting with a brush attached to a helmet. With still no indication of the ad's sponsor, the screen fades to white, with text that asks, "What do you have to say?"

The result was without question emotionally wrenching, and when juxtaposed with the rest of the standard postadolescent bathroom humor that has come to populate Super Bowl night, it stood out from the crowd. *USA Today* ranked it #1 among the ads that night. The spot was lauded by disabilities organizations nationwide. So who was the sponsor? While engrossed in Keplinger's world, the audience might imagine the sponsor being a stem-cell research fund or an arts group.

But, in fact, it was a spot for Cingular Wireless.

"We see an opportunity to separate ourselves from the pack by being the first [wireless] company to emotionally bond with our consumers," said Cingular Wireless chief marketing officer Virginia Vann upon the launch of the campaign.

The spot was never designed to promote cell-phone service. Rather, Cingular desired a relationship. They wanted to equate their brand identity with a powerful emotional need first and foremost, one that their audience could relate to and feel. They wanted to be the symbol for self-expression in a world that increasingly was communicating via cell phones. Advertisements—through both their pervasiveness and their essential role in creating a brand identity—are the most important symbols of marketing.

Like all symbols, advertisements are negotiations of meaning. The advertiser attempts to create an emotional tone, rational pleas, a visual style with the art of brevity, to strike an instant connection with the people most likely to purchase their product. But negotiation is a two-way street. The presentation of the symbol goes only as far as the meaning the individual recipient takes from it. If it hits, if the emotion and attitude facilitate the meaning of the featured product and present a match for that person's identity, the brand itself can become a symbol for that person's lifestyle or self-concept. The challenge for the advertiser is to replicate the connection again and again to expand their audience. Advertising these days is akin to a trip with a group of people through a modern art museum. One person will fall in love, even come to tears, over an abstract painting, while the others in the group see only a series of squiggly lines and opaque shapes. Likewise, show an advertisement to ten people, and you may get ten different interpretations of meaning. Thus, to become a stable symbol whereby which multiple people can discern the identity of a brand or organization, the communication must be consistent; it must own the emotional territory.

The Cingular self-expression ad took a strong, emotional first punch at associating the company's identity with creativity and self-expression. Other commercials in the campaign varied in style and tone, but all ended with the "What do you have to say?" appeal to self-expression.

But there was a problem. They removed the flag from the ground! For one reason or another, Cingular's statement on the diversity and beauty of self-expression was abandoned shortly after football's big night. The Keplinger ad didn't make too many additional appearances. Perhaps it was so jarring that it didn't lend itself to regular primetime spots. The ad may have been an attention getter. It may have made a strong case for the persistent need to give voice to our identity—no matter our life circumstances—but ultimately it fell short because it did not prove to be a good way to sell cell phones.

What began as a declaration of being a distinct, humanistic brand quickly became another voice lost in the fray of the "We have the best coverage/the best plans/the coolest phones!" campaigns that permeate the mobile market. If the goal was to equate the Cingular brand with the need for self-expression, two things had to happen. First, they had to keep the flag planted to establish the brand as a stable symbol. And second, they needed a strong connection between the brand, the service, and the symbolic meaning of their message. So here's a rule of thumb for appealing to emotional needs that can be drawn from this example:

Communicating a brand's connection to an emotional need is effective if...

- **The brand will become an effective symbol if and when the product owns the relevant emotional territory**
- **The product or service provides a connection between a core human need and the function of the product or service.**

If Cingular had kept that flag planted and owned the emotional territory, the Keplinger spot could have been seminal. In other words, if they wanted to be the wireless company that symbolized expression and diversity, it would take more than a one-time campaign to drive that emotional message home. If the brand's symbolic character shifts constantly, it becomes difficult for an individual to pin the brand down and use the product or service as a stable symbol of his or her lifestyle or self-concept.

Moreover, Cingular's corporate philosophy, as illustrated via the Keplinger spot and as noble as it might have been, also had to connect to their product and service. However, there wasn't a clear and direct link. The emotion of the ad didn't help the audience. Take this logical reaction to the ad:

> So Dan Keplinger is an amazing artist and has a moving life story. Very touching. Beautiful, even. So this ad is telling me what? I should express myself by using a Cingular Wireless cell phone?

The problem was that Cingular phone service was never truly connected to the need for self-expression. While it might very well have been designed purely as a bold corporate public-relations statement (it did after all get a significant amount of post–Super Bowl buzz), the highly emotional Keplinger spot wasn't the most efficient road to high sales over the long haul. Cingular may have connected to the consumer in that very moment—but the need for self-expression was not clearly linked to the service being offered over time.

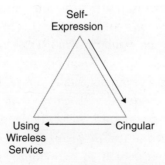

Figure 4.2 Needs/Company Connection Triangle—Cingular

We can treat this common problem in marketing and advertising like a triangle missing one side. At the top sits the human need, in this case, self-expression. At the points of the base we have the brand, Cingular, and the product/service, cell phones.

There's a side connecting self-expression to the brand. And a side connecting the brand to the product (until it was merged into AT&T, everyone knew Cingular Wireless had something to do with cell phones.) But where's the side linking self-expression to the product via the right tone and message? It's nowhere to be found in the Keplinger ad. We see the value of the need and how Keplinger expresses himself, but all we're left with is a tenuous connection (at best) between the three points.

So what does a complete triangle look like? One of the most consistent advertising campaigns in the past ten years helps illustrate what owning emotional terrain is all about. A product we've worked with, Corona, a pale lager made by Mexican brewer Cerveceria Modelo, is one of the best-selling beers in Mexico, one of the top imported beers in the United States, and is consistently among the best-selling beers internationally. It doesn't hurt that when many people see or hear "Corona," vivid images of white sand, blue skies, and rolling waves flood the senses. Each installment of the famed advertising campaign (most noted for its television spots) varies only in backdrop and action. Everything else—from the setting, to the sound, to the colors—was etched in audiences' minds for years.

Note how Corona steps around the complicated task of homing in on a marginal portion of the general public. The ads don't appear to be targeted at a subgroup or a specific audience. In fact, the actors in the ads underscore this most of all. The panoramas of the beach, in most spots, are shown from a first-person perspective. The audience

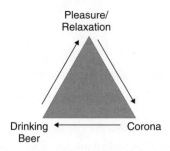

Figure 4.3 Needs/Company Connection Triangle—Corona

isn't watching other people relax in peace while enjoying a drink. We're transported into the experience; we're the ones invited to skip our cell phones into the water, use a parrot as a bottle opener, swing on a hammock. We're the actors invited to "relax responsibly."

Corona built their brand around an emotional need and was unrelenting in how the product and marketing aligned with it. At the top of the Corona triangle we have the need for pleasure, and in this case pleasure takes the form of relaxation/escape. At the other points we have the brand, Corona, and the product/function drinking beer. All sides connect.

- I need to strive to relax and just enjoy life while I can.
- Corona makes beer.
- Corona's marketing communications impress upon me how beer can facilitate emotional pleasure—an everyday vacation from life's stresses—escape and relaxation while we kick back and listen to the breeze.

* * *

OWNING EMOTIONAL TERRITORY is a necessary objective on the path to a product becoming an iconic symbol. If each of our decisions is a potential act of self-expression, it's important that shoppers know what a brand represents and how that might fit with who they are and also who they want to be. But that's not the only way to satisfy the self-expression need in the marketplace. Many businesses can partner with their audience's yearning to self-express.

The More We Change, the More Vital Needs Stay the Same

A peek inside people's diaries from the eighteenth and the nineteenth centuries teaches us in the twenty-first century another key lesson about self-expression:

April 27, 1770: Made Mead. At the assembly.
May 14, 1770: Mrs. Mascarene here and Mrs. Cownshield. Taken very ill. The Doctor bled me. Took an anodyne.

Sept. 7, 1792: Fidelia Mirick here a visiting to-day.

Jan. 26, 1873: Cold disagreeable day. Felt very badly all day long and lay on the sofa all day. Nothing took place worth noting.[6]

Do these remarks look a bit familiar? Do they sound, perhaps, like a noise a bird might make...like a Tweet?

Diaries during this era were not personal journals in the sense we think of them now. They were among the earliest forms of social media. The small notebooks were semipublic in nature, chronicling the news of family and day-to-day events and mailed to relatives who lived far away. For all that changes in a society, it's easy to forget that emotional needs continue to drive human behavior in similar ways. Centuries-old "Tweets" are further evidence that the ways we choose to express sometimes differ only via the platforms available to us.

This list of historical "tweets" was made by Lee Humphreys, Assistant Professor of Communications at Cornell University. "We tend to think of new media as entirely new and different," said Humphreys in an interview with Cornell's newspaper. "But often we see people using new media for old problems that people have always had to think about and engage with."[7]

At the same time as Humphreys presented her findings, the Library of Congress announced its plan to archive all "Tweets," preserving these billions of snippets of self-expression for current and future study. It's quite possible that two hundred years from now researchers will look to these ancient Tweets to understand who we were as a society and, like Humphreys, will be surprised by how closely these ancient Tweets resemble a similar method of self-expression popular in their time. We tend to think of the immense growth of the social media giants—Facebook, MySpace, Twitter—as an example of how people are ceaselessly attempting to stay connected with friends in a faster-moving world. It is "social" media, after all. But psychologists are discovering how these platforms are more about the "me" than the "we" than we generally acknowledge. Expression is perhaps more important than connection. Websites provide avenues for communication with friends and family. But the most frequent users—mainly younger people, adolescents to college-aged—literally become addicted because the sites provide a quick and simple vehicle for their need for expression: a workshop for identity.

Tweets and profiles are digital advertisements for the individual. Self-documentation of every daily mundane activity is nothing more than a quest to show the world, "Hey, I'm here. Look at me." It's almost as if they were to stop self-expressing, they'd disappear in a cloud of dark matter.

New Atlantis writer Christine Rosen compares the way we express via social media to the way people once acquired self-portraits:

> "By showing the artist both as he sees his true self and as he wishes to be seen, self-portraits can at once expose and obscure, clarify and distort. They offer opportunities for both self-expression and self-seeking. They can display egotism and modesty, self-aggrandizement and self-mockery. Today, our self-portraits are democratic and digital; they are crafted from pixels rather than paints."[8]

We've come a long way from the caves of Lascaux. The Internet increases the ease with which we experiment with identity. The ease of communication that blogging and social media provide clearly allows us to take expressive risks that we wouldn't venture in face-to-face communication.

Online games and Web-based chat rooms increasingly allow users to alter their digital self-representations dramatically and easily. The game "Second Life" offers players more than 150 sliders that allow them to change everything from T-shirt color to gender and species. On these online interactive social forums, what social cues do players use? The gap between one's virtual representation and one's real self can be worlds away (a grim reality for online dating sites, too). Generally in social situations, we read into the way people carry themselves, their tone, eye contact, body language, the context in which we find ourselves, and yes, what they look like. With many of these cues stripped away in the virtual world, we rely heavily on visual information—the presentation of the avatar—to determine the user's personality and how we should respond in kind. Amazingly, researchers have found that, as in real life, more attractive avatars are treated with a bit more courtesy than average or less attractive avatars.

Digital identities are malleable. It's psychologically a lot less risky to vocalize a brazen opinion on Facebook than it is in the conference room; it's less risky to the ego to post one's own artwork on a blog than display it in one's work office. The Internet, according to technology sociologist and Massachusetts Institute of Technology (MIT) professor Sherry Turkle, allows us to pull and push the boundaries of our identity.

Researchers are finding that people with narcissistic personality disorder (NPD) often use social media as a vessel of expression and self-promotion. Moreover, San Diego State University psychologist Jean Twenge surveyed more than one thousand college students nationwide, asking "How much do you agree or disagree with the statement, 'People in my generation use social networking sites for self-promotion, narcissism, and attention-seeking?'" Two-thirds agreed.[9]

But that statistic misses the point. Of course people use social media for self-promotion. If anything, social media represents the increasing importance of individual expression in a world that is more and more disconnected in a physical sense. Social media provides a forum for sharing ideas. It is a digital laboratory for identity, a vehicle for expression that reaches the masses at a low emotional and economic cost to the user. Think of how artists and musicians use blogs to give life to their work. Everyone has a billboard—and for a relatively minor emotional and financial investment.

The social-media phenomenon is often seen by marketers as important in other ways. Every company seems to have a Facebook and a Twitter account to assemble a template of their most active supporters (or critics.) It's also a solid public relations tool and has proven to be a creative way for business-to-business firms to market themselves.

But as far as marketing relates to vital human needs, the real lesson of social media is that if a brand or service provides individuals a platform for expression that fits their lifestyles and self-concept, it can be mutually beneficial for the expresser and the provider. In other words, businesses should create services that help people express their individuality. Social-media entrepreneurs know the value of appealing to this need. Shawn Gold, a former senior vice president of MySpace. com, an online community of more than eighty million registrants, said, "We created a platform to facilitate the core human needs of individual expression and identifying with others, and then we listened to our members—their opinions and actions drive the development of the site."[10] Note how the whole concept of the platform began with the need. Future iterations of the website were microalterations to better facilitate users' ability to express and communicate.

The lesson here extends well beyond the boundaries of digital experience.

Some companies deliver products and services that will never be sexy badges of identity. Big-ticket items, like a laptop or a car, or other highly visible, public goods, like clothes or jewelry, readily lend themselves to being meaningful symbols of expression. But the type of pens we write with, the cleaning supplies we buy, or the nails we use to hang pictures are all purchasing decisions that may or may not necessarily activate the need for expression.

This leads back to Darryl's parallel ordering decisions. Just because every decision is a potential act of expression does not mean we associate—consciously or unconsciously—every decision with an effort to affirm our identity.

Sharpie markers may not be as "cool" as a touchscreen phone is "cool." For most people, it's not a brand that can seriously become integral to how they view themselves. A grade school teacher isn't going to embroider the Sharpie brand on his school sweaters because he uses the markers for a number of his lessons. Popular kids at the school won't be showing off their new Sharpies. But the markers are easily integrated into art lessons, and they facilitate classwork. Their function is to be a vehicle of expression. Thus, much of the Sharpie marketing budget is used to encourage creativity and expression. A recent tagline for Sharpie: "Uncap what's inside." This isn't much different from what Cingular tried to do, but it's clear that the brand is the vehicle for untapped expression and not just an errant cheerleader for it like the Keplinger spot.

So if a brand can't be an Apple-esque symbol of culture, meeting the need for self-expression can be approached from a different angle. If your brand can't become the symbol of a generation, try directly facilitating self-expression.

Integrated marketers are reaping the rewards of encouraging their audience to express themselves. Brand "interactivity" has morphed into a recognition that people will seek out opportunities or competitions to express themselves in the right forum. In many instances, companies are embracing coproduction to the point that the consumer is essentially becoming the marketer. It's ostensibly direct democracy at the branding level.

In other words, companies are inviting audiences to express their creativity—often with the incentive of cash and prizes—in order to enhance the visibility and relevance of the brand. The attitude of the company becomes: "Express yourself to us and we'll listen."

One significant trend in recent years: promote new products by involving the audience in creating products. When Dunkin' Donuts invited people to create the next flavor of doughnut, it combined creativity with marketing. This initiative resulted in more than 130,000 entries and 3 million Facebook wall posts, showing that the appeal to creativity appeared to be an inexpensive and easy way to virally enhance buzz around the brand. Similarly, Vitamin Water asked consumers to help decide what its next flavor should be via a Facebook application called Flavor Creator Lab. After the promotion began, Vitamin Water's Facebook page grew by over 11 percent in just one week. Since March 2010, when the page launched, it has grown to more than 400,000 fans. Additionally, Mountain Dew tapped into the nation's political fervor at the advent of the 2008 presidential elections by running a flavor campaign dubbed DewMocracy. The website mirrored election-night campaign maps, breaking down votes by county.

Similarly, for the past several years Doritos has aired user submitted advertisements for their Super Bowl ads. In 2008, Twix invited aspiring comedians to submit sketches and routines loosely tied to their branding. Freecreditreport.com held a competition for alternative rock groups to play a jingle in an advertising campaign. Whatever the vehicle, the sheer number of people participating makes the facilitation a fun, harmless, participatory forum of creativity, spurs word-of-mouth marketing, and gives new sustained life to brands.

And what about traditional forums that promote expression? Today, magazines are finding ways to drive profit by showcasing user-generated talent. *ReadyMade* magazine, owned by Meredith Corporation, publisher of age-old giants *Better Homes & Gardens, Ladies Home Journal, Fitness,* and several other consumer magazine brands, was founded by a small staff of artists and do-it-yourself (DIY) lovers. Each issue includes a dialogue between editors and the readers who submit ideas. Targeted toward young, ecologically minded readers, the monthly publication features dozens of artistic DIY furniture and art projects pieced together from salvaged household and rummage-sale fare. Each article provides a step-by-step guide and a materials list and cost estimate. The issues are pieced together from the suggestions of the readers, professional artists, and designers, but the projects can be replicated by anyone with a tool kit and a few spare bucks.

By fostering creativity and expression, brands can easily become communities of like-minded creative types. What's true at *ReadyMade* is true for the traditional media companies that rely on user-generated features and stories to stay viable and connect to an audience that wants a platform to present their equally valuable opinions. This format has always existed in the form of talk radio shows, where callers have been known to script their rants of ahead of time. One such mutually beneficial talk-radio program is the British Broadcasting Company's (BBC's) "Mark Kermode and Simon Mayo's Film Reviews," where the hosts depend on the listeners to call in with "a pithy" film analysis to give fresh perspectives on blockbusters as well as champion independent films. Given the sheer volume of movies produced, the hosts realize that unless listeners submit their opinions, some deserving films will be overlooked. Or some nondeserving films will overshadow their competition. We've come a long way from Siskel & Ebert's thumbs up or down evaluation.

The old media—radio, broadcast news, newspapers, and magazines—are surviving only as well as they're adapting to the two-way nature of modern journalism. Cable news, which is often bereft of substantial news coverage, is forced to address the growing influence of professional bloggers. Grassroots websites like the liberal Daily Kos or the conservative Town Hall are communities that have deeply affected the landscape of government and politics. Now that we can express and be heard en masse, via YouTube, a blog, or Twitter, traditional media must be less constrained by established methods to maintain their audience and keep advertisers advertising. Journalists have to engage in a reciprocal conversation with their audience or face increasing irrelevancy. A tell-tale sign of twenty-first-century news media: turn on one of the 24/7 cable channels and you might just find a reporter keeping tabs on Twitter feeds, Facebook pages, and professional blogs rather than doing his or her own reporting.

We're a country with three hundred million people and three hundred trillion opinions. We have and will continue to thrive on self-expression.

Fieldwork

Projecting a Light on Self-Expression

When Numbers Lie

As we have discussed, turning a brand into a true symbol of a person's identity can be an elusive process. And owning emotional territory takes consistency, connection, and confidence. Providing a vehicle for expression, à la Vitamin Water, works for some brand categories in the short term. But clearly no brand can or should turn over the creative direction to its audience 24/7.

It's easy to say, "Self-expression is important for everyone. Let's make that the focus of a new campaign." It's simple for the company to hire an agency to draft storyboards showing how creative their audience is, layering it over a bed of the latest indie music hit, maybe adding some stop-motion animation and high-tech digital effects. Find a compelling tagline that ties the brand into the importance of individuality. And then, of course, conduct research to find out if people like it. Send out surveys to five hundred people in the demographic target. Ask questions like, "How does it make you feel?" Tabulate the answers. Did 65 percent of respondents check both happy and curious? A great result! Develop the idea and run the ad.

But surveys can be limiting. Asking a person whether he or she has bought X product in a certain time frame is valuable when cross-analyzed with 15 other data points. But asking a person how message X makes him or her feel leads generally to more questions than answers. A survey may suggest that a key subgroup thinks the joke at the end of the commercial is rip-roaring hilarious. But is that number a reflection of how the key audiences actually responded, or how they *say* they've responded? Moreover, data can be like a prisoner—interrogate the numbers long enough, and they will tell you what you want to hear.

Our firm did some work with an advertising agency representing a major brand of women's hosiery. It's a product area where the emotional accessibility of the message matters. With 15 different options available to the consumer, all offered at similar prices, sizes, and styles, the only basis for choice is emotional: which brand matches the type of person the shopper wants to be? How the marketing (advertising campaign) makes the person feel is as important as how the product itself makes them feel, sometimes more so. Advertisers know this. The agency I worked with knew this, as well.

The agency put together a reel of four prospective ads. Each featured a woman in a different scenario. Each focused on the importance of being confident with one's femininity and sexual expression. The message relayed: if you've got it, flaunt it! Women showing off their legs conveyed a sense of youth and vitality that women feel, and that men definitely notice.

The agency identified their favorite of the four.

The imagery of the ad featured a confident, talented woman at work and at play, illustrating that the product was not only desirable but also versatile enough to match a professional woman's lifestyle. The woman was a veterinarian, and she loved her work. Ads with puppies and adorable children are commonly sure-fire winners. Another set of images in the ad showed the same woman's legs being checked out by a man. She's still all smiles. Her legs are looking great.

A quantitative survey was used to support the client's opinions of the four prospective ads. It supported the hunch that the vet ad was the way to go. People generally thought it was satisfying. The ad met all the standards of an appealing and effective 30-second spot. It was simple, told a good story, and was visually engaging. The numbers confirmed this. Across the board, it was rated well enough to get the green light, but the agency was not sold on it quite yet.

Our role was to see if the underlying emotion elicited by the ad supported the hard data. When one asks people to explain honestly how they feel about a video, they put on their critical hat. But people don't react to ads critically. We react viscerally. What we needed to know was whether the story optimally connected with the audience's emotional reality.

Beyond the Numbers: Using Projective Insights

After running through a number of questions, we asked women individually to take part in a projective imagination exercise. Psychologists use projective techniques to get beyond participants' thoughtful, rational responses, beyond what their rational brain is telling them. Through fantasy scenarios and by activating participants' imaginations, projective techniques reveal underlying emotions about an object, idea, or image that would have previously gone unnoticed. These techniques produce the rawest of data. Projective exercises run the gamut, from word association, to picture analysis, to stream-of-consciousness verbal exercises.

The most famous example is the Rorschach test, more commonly known as "ink blots." These tools make some executives (and some scientists) nervous, because how can anything so subjective be reliable? A fine question. Especially when a million-dollar national television campaign rides on it. Skeptics fear the projective, but at the same time, many agree that the unconscious drives behavior. Quantitative methods have their place. But typically they don't provide insight into the thoughts and feelings that consumers may not even be aware of.

Projective techniques were first developed in 1935 by psychologists Henry Murray and Christina Morgan. In the thematic apperception test (TAT), subjects are asked to make up stories for black-and-white pictures in which it is unclear what's happening and why. The exercise unearths insights into the respondent's personality, life challenges, and conflicts. The subjects are asked to spend three to five minutes talking at length about each picture. Murray and Morgan matched their interpretations of the stories with a list of 35 separate personality needs. The stories, according to Murray and Morgan, illustrate the need for projective techniques:

> "The test is based upon the well-recognized fact that when a person interprets an ambiguous social situation he is apt to expose his own personality as much as the phenomenon to which he is attending... He becomes naively unconscious of himself and of the scrutiny of others and, therefore, defensively less vigilant... The subject reveals some of his innermost feelings without being aware he is doing so."[11]

Murray and Morgan ran the test in 1952 with 57 recent Harvard graduates, and again fifteen years later with the same 57 participants. The data generated from their experiments in 1952 turned out to be highly predictive. Men who revealed a deeply held desire for intimacy as postgraduates had the healthiest marriages and were most successful in their careers. Without the projective testing, these behavior-driving traits would have easily gone unnoticed. Similar projective techniques were used in the groundbreaking 72-year longitudinal study run by Harvard's George Vaillant, a developmental psychiatrist. The massive study tracked 268 men (who, incredibly, included the future President John F. Kennedy) through college, war, marriage, family life, and old age to uncover the traits resulting in a satisfying life.

So what value do such projective techniques have for the hosiery commercial mentioned above? Our goal was to reveal the uninhibited feelings behind the ambiguous "satisfactory" rating. We wanted participants to tell the conclusion of the story. We wanted them to be the veterinarian in the ad. To do this, we went through a fantasy exercise that required each participant to imagine what happened to the woman after the ad concluded. Would the imagery of the hosiery become a successful symbol of their sexuality? Listening to the women, we were able to glean a sense of their personalities, their unrestricted feelings about lingerie and women's clothing, and what significance they assigned to their feelings about their body.

Across the board, the women I spoke with began revealing pronounced discomfort as they imagined the rest of the ad's story. The symbols used throughout the ad triggered a conflict between separate needs competing for priority. There was something off about the veterinarian's overtly showing her sexuality while at work. In the minds of our participants, they felt she (and perhaps more importantly, they) had worked hard for their acceptance and success, and didn't want to appear frivolous or feel sexually objectified in the workplace. But this revelation didn't show up in the other ads. The women's need to be seen as a competent, influential professional, independent of socially agreed-upon ideas of beauty transcended their need to feel sensual. The juxtaposition of professionalism and sexuality, initially so subtle and ordinary that it went unnoticed, struck a different chord with their emotional unconscious and their previously unexpressed reactions.

The sexually charged professional alienated viewers on an emotional level. This response contradicted the quantitative data, which indicated the female viewers initially "liked" the ad. The insights caused the agency to select a spot that avoided these deeper, conflicting emotions.

Earlier we discussed how, when it comes to self-expression, certain key personality traits transcend how individuals act at particular points in their life. Personality traits are a platform for self-expressive tendencies. The research lens that helps businesses identify the traits is nontraditional. But when key insights are found well beneath the surface of consciousness, beyond the quantitative survey data, it pays dividends.

Chapter 4 Summary: How Business Can Empathize with the Core Need of Self-Expression

People are always looking for ways to express themselves—their personalities, their values, even their uniqueness. Self-expression gives people a sense of self-worth and identity. The need for self-expression offers a variety of opportunities for business. Positioned and marketed correctly, a brand can be either a symbol of or a means of expression.

Below are a few key steps businesses can take to effectively respond to consumers' need for self-expression:

Suggested Follow-Up Steps

1. **Find the emotional identity that best fits your product or service, and build your marketing around it.** Your brand can become a symbol of who people are or what they want to be—an identity badge—but only if it clearly represents a specific emotional need. What does your brand stand for? What emotional territory does it own? Corona owns leisure, relaxation, and escape. Sports car brands want to own success and "cool." Minivans want to own family safety and comfort. Big-box hardware chains own independent do-it-yourself. What need does your brand own? What will your

customers express about themselves through your brand? When building the self-expression symbol of your product:

a. **Focus on one emotional identity and be consistent.** Connecting your brand to an emotional identity takes time—in many product areas, at least 18 months. Don't frequently switch marketing campaigns or switch the emotional need on which campaigns are based. The result will be a brand that doesn't symbolize anything. Once you've identified the emotional identity you want to own, stick to it.

b. **Look for opportunities in life transitions.** People are constantly redefining themselves, especially when transitioning to new life phases. They are looking for ways to express their new selves. Launch products and services that address these transitions. What, for example, do you have to offer new college graduates or the newly retired?

2. **Products don't have to be symbols. Turn them into *tools* of expression.** People don't express themselves through the Sharpie markers they buy. No one says, "Wow, that's a cool Sharpie, it's so you!" But Sharpies can be a tool for self-expression that enables or facilitates self-expression. Can your products be the paintbrush rather than the painting? If new college graduates want to show their independence, how can your products facilitate their expression of independence? Perhaps your kitchen products can help them cook gourmet meals. Perhaps your financial services offerings can help set up their financial independence, which will help them buy the cars, the apartment, the clothes that express the independence they've achieved.

3. **Use coproduction to build your company through consumer self-expression.** Let customers name a new product, build their homes, boats, or cars, choose a new flavor, or pick the next color of the product. You're giving them an opportunity for self-expression by letting them coproduce the product. At the same time, the coproduction campaign generates significant buzz for its new product or flavor.

CHAPTER 5

The Need for Growth

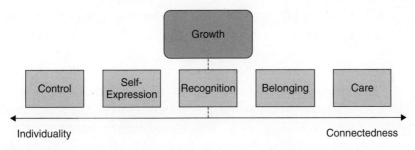

Figure 5.1 The Growth Need

CHAPTER 5

The Need for Growth

Adriana hit the wall, that invisible but physically and psychically crippling barrier they say affects marathon runners around the twentieth mile. It happened at the dinner table three nights after their last child moved out of the house for college. Tearing up, she pushed her plate aside, put her head to the table, hands over her eyes.

Eric, her husband, panicked for a moment. He'd rarely seen his wife break down. She was a mental fortress. Implacably confident. Immune from vulnerability. He stood for a moment, hands on her shoulders, waiting for her to come back to life before they talked. He flipped off the music and cleared the table while she gathered herself.

"I was wrong," she said after several minutes, raising her head with a slight smile. "I told you I didn't believe in any existential crisis."

Adriana had always been a thrill-seeker. Not in the "sky-diving" sense, however. Spontaneity was more her guiding philosophy. She was addicted to change. Outside of her marriage, she was never the type to settle down in a single place for too long. She shopped at different stores. Never read the same book twice. Forbade herself from becoming a constant viewer of any television show, regardless of how much her husband tried to convince her. She was afraid of any and all habits—no weekly routines, no long-term extracurricular commitments, no behavior that could even resemble stagnation. She switched the companies she worked for every five years for no other reason than to start anew. She took the opposite track of Eric, a structural engineer going on thirty years at the same firm. In a haphazard sort of way, she felt she could actually live each day to its fullest.

But none of it added up to anything of great significance. "I'm empty," she said. "This house is empty. I've done next to nothing with my career.""Have you ever wanted anything from it?" Eric asked. "You've mostly made lateral job moves. You've been so busy outside of work, it never seemed to bother you."

"I know, but with the kids being gone, isn't there an alarm in your head saying life is well past halfway over? How does one go about shutting the thing off?"

"Here's the problem," he said, sitting back down next to her. "You are a Bhaskara Wheel."

"I'm a what?"

He explained. The Bhaskara Wheel is the first known attempt by an engineer or a physicist to create a perpetual motion machine: constant movement generated from the object's self-sustaining force. Bhaskara, a twelfth-century Indian mathematician, designed the device so that it would theoretically produce more energy than it would exhaust. As the wheel turned, containers of mercury would shift in such a way that one side of the wheel was always heavier than the other, creating a never-ending cycle. But despite his design, no such device was ever built. In fact, no such device can be built. For centuries onward, countless engineers attempted to build their own perpetual motion machines, one after the other failing to trump the laws of physics. And even though modern thermodynamics have proven that such machines are impossible to construct, curious basement scientists around the globe still want to see for themselves.

"You think you can always be in motion," he said. "You're driven frantically by the idea that if you keep changing, keep rotating through life, you'll never hit a low point. But that's impossible. It's a physical anomaly."

Adrianna was obsessed with change, but lost to the concept of personal growth. By maintaining a false sense of perpetual motion, she masked over significant self-exploration. Growth is change. But not all change is growth. There are times and stages in life when we call into question who we are, evaluate where we've been, and forecast where we'd like to go. This process of self-insight can be remarkably difficult. Midlife crises, such as Adrianna's, are necessary for our evolution as individuals. But sometimes, we pretend we can avoid such barriers by plowing through them. We change without considering the implications, and when the implications do make their presence felt, we're already changing again. But this cycle—the perpetual motion wheel—is an invention of fantasy. Change that satisfies the need for growth is gradual and buoyed by both stability and decline.

So when is change alright, and when does one really need growth? Adrianna hinted that work might be a future source of meaning. But it hadn't been before. She had other priorities. When she got bored with work, she switched jobs to keep life fresh. That's change, but not necessarily growth. Growth entails seeking out permanent new skills for a career. Growth involves making a concerted effort to derive deeper personal meaning from one's work. It is forward movement, the gradual acquisition of enlightenment.

The Need for Growth

The lesson of Adrianna's story, at first glance, may make businesses in the consumer marketplace quiver a little. If consumers aren't constantly changing to the "new" and to "more," how will businesses that don't deal in essentials stay afloat? It's actually not that difficult. Growth plays an important role in the marketplace. Many times, consumers need change, and there's no shame in that if it doesn't override the more important needs (more on this later). But do businesses that cater to personal growth really understand what growth is and what it isn't?

We can approach that question with a relatable marketplace example. Satisfying the need for growth in a marketplace context is most easily seen in the mega-"self-help" industry. Self-help is a staple of American identity in many circles. Autonomy, control, and meaningful personal expression are by no means bad sentiments for an industry to encourage. They're essential to the individual. However, the emphasis on "self" poses a problem semantically. It implies that there is no "other" in self-improvement.

To clarify this idea, let's pick on an easy target of the self-help industry: weight loss. For every useful, scientifically valid diet or workout plan patented and sold to the masses, there are in all likelihood hundreds of borderline scams. *Get six-pack abs in three weeks. Drop 3 dress sizes in a month. Lose 100 pounds without cutting your diet of pizza, burgers, and fries.* Most people are sharp enough to know these claims are puffed up and unrealistic. Even if the dramatic before-and-after pictures are authentic, we know that the subject in question was an outlier, or relied on much more than the product in question.

But some of us (despite our hunch that it is in fact snake oil we're staring at) are persuaded to buy the product anyway. It's an impulsive fantasy that a quick and easy road to the ideal body exists. However, the mettle of the 1-in-100 diet and exercise plans that are actually honest and valuable is measured by honesty. Simply put, these plans state plainly:

1. You'll likely need the support and consultation of others to achieve your goals.
2. It might take a long time.
3. Success will require both diet and exercise.

Those "truth-telling" products and services are hard to market because, in all honesty, a lot of times we'd rather believe in the five-minutes-a-day, three-days-a-week route to perfect health than tackle the difficult prospect of an intense, but effective, diet or workout regimen.

Because growth in many ways relies upon both personal strength and social support, it is arguably the most difficult need to satisfy. It is the product of successfully balancing the needs along the continuum. Growth is our need to positively evolve our abilities, competencies, and attitudes in an attempt to better realize our best self. The need is satisfied through intrinsic motivation, meaning, to grow toward our ideal selves, we have to first imagine who that ideal self is, and take the necessary steps toward achieving that self.

And as Adriana teaches us, growth is not change for change's sake. It is an effort that results not in a scattering of identity, but in solidification. We don't need to maintain a rampant pace of growth. Growth is gradual, up and down, marked by life events and epiphanies that spark us to refine and reconsider who we are and where we'd like to go.

In chapter 1, I discussed Carl Jung's concepts of the persona and the shadow. A persona is our social mask, the detachable identity we assume in different settings that can often serve as a placeholder or a disguise for our true selves. The shadow is the unconscious's collection of disowned character traits that, while forgotten by us, emerge subtly in our behavior until we recognize them. To satisfy the need for growth, we chip away at our life-hardened exterior, looking for our ideal selves. When we expand our minds and the idea of who we are, we shed the persona, getting to the core of our shadow. It is a process of self-discovery, but it isn't necessarily a conscious, existentialist game of "figuring it all out."

Growth, in other words, is the idea that, within each of us, a better, authentic self awaits release. Throughout life, we take steps, chip away the excess, to liberate the finished figure. Rarely do we ever complete the process, though, and at many times, our lives may not resemble a masterpiece, but that's really beside the point. It's the moving toward meaning that matters. It's not the pursuit of perfection, but the unlocking of and movement toward potential that reflects our psychological evolution.

Many people live comfortably with who they are throughout life, and don't quite realize or consciously try to contemplate their evolution. But when a major life transition occurs—the death of a loved one, illness, a career transition, graduation, the birth of a child, or a personal achievement or setback—we are more likely to directly survey our personal landscape and call into question who we are and who we want to be. We become motivated to actively pursue our notion of the ideal self, as manifested in an ideal job, an ideal home, ideal relationships, and so forth. There is no escaping this process. The slow plod of growth is essential to healthy maturation and development. But there are two sides to every coin. Part of this effort requires that we also experience temporary decline. We're not always growing psychologically. We have setbacks and failures, and without our acknowledging these vulnerable moments, growing stronger would be impossible.

A recent study found that the three human qualities identified most often in people who've achieved stable personal growth are sociability, openness to change, and goal directedness.[1] Why are all three of these qualities necessary? We need to be ready, we need to know where we're going, and most importantly, we need people in our lives to affirm our ideal self—they help further the sculpting process.

In other words, there are few shortcuts to true personal growth. Positive thinking can't do it. Mega-best sellers like *The Secret*, although they are likely to inspire a long line of people, are sure to disappoint most of their readers. They sell personal growth like undervalued stock. Everyone can have it—for a low price and with little effort. We rarely evolve toward our ideal self alone. It takes a combination of conscious willingness and control of our aspirations and achievements, along with relationships and social connections, to affirm the effort.

The themes mentioned above are just a few to keep in mind as we discuss the need for growth. So what are businesses to make of these themes? How can businesses meet this need? And where can they potentially slip up or harm their customer or their bottom line?

We'll discuss these questions as they relate to four areas. First, we explore how businesses can leverage the *affirmation* role in growth. If growth is about movement toward a positive self-ideal, the marketplace has a role in playing the third party that affirms an individual's roles and identities. Second, businesses must investigate the role of growth in major life transitions—crises, milestones, and rites of passage. Opportune moments to facilitate growth arise at these monumental life stages. Third, we investigate a core component of personal growth: competency. Expanding the mind is a timeless anecdote to a stagnant existence. Some businesses cater to this need perfectly; others miss opportunities to affirm this desire for intellectual growth. Finally, we return to the question posed at the beginning of this section: what is growth and what is it not? Companies are notorious for instilling in people false hopes of personal growth, but there's a less explored misstep involved here, as well. Too often, marketers assume or project the ideal self onto an audience. They narrowly predict the type of person their product is said to represent, thereby potentially alienating large segments of people who do not see or do not wish to see themselves painted in such a light.

E.R.A.: Empathize, Reconcile, Affirm

To successfully sell any brand, product, or service, businesses know they have to ask the most important question of the consumer: *Why?* Why do people need a product? What job does it perform? Why do people choose one brand over the other when both brands do virtually the same thing? We know, after exploring the needs along the continuum, that the answer to why is often associated with the needs buried in the unconscious. In a mass market, the products that fulfill deeper human needs will likely have the edge over the brand that performs well, but that cannot draw the third line connecting the consumer, the product, and the underlying emotional need.

However, the need for growth is trickier to identify. It is not easily associated with the why behind the consumer's decision. The discovery and satisfaction of the need must provide a promise to the ideal or best self. Let's consider one important why of the marketplace: *why do people begin looking for new cars?*

Surveys that ask this question reveal that car shoppers consider purchasing a new vehicle for a litany of rational responses—their current car has high mileage, a spouse needs a new car for work, they need a safer vehicle for the family, and so on. But according to one survey, 22 percent of car shoppers are looking for a less precise reason: "tired of the old car, wanted something new." This is psychological code for: *the respondent can't articulate the emotions coloring his or her desire for a new car.* So the question is: what needs might the new car fulfill?

Imagine that two different young professionals are in the market for a new car. The first has long deliberated a major career change. He achieves this and decides to complement this transition by buying a hybrid for his new commute. He is more likely to fulfill the need for growth than a person unhappy with his life and career who purchases a $30,000 vehicle out of impulse. It may certainly be the ideal short-term fix, and may satisfy his need for self-expression, but it is unlikely that the car itself will heal or transform the other negative aspects of his life. For the first buyer, the car became a symbol of his psychological evolution rather than a trigger to make something happen. So if a marketer wants to satisfy the customer's need for growth, the message should not be, "You are imperfect without this vehicle. This vehicle will make you your best self," but rather, "This vehicle could come to represent or serve as a symbol for who you want to be or who you've become"—a metaphor for individual growth.

Three Steps to Affirmation

Affirming a customer's need for growth is not an easy or obvious task for salespersons or marketers. Facilitating the need for growth requires a deliberate three-step process: salespersons or marketers have to, first, **empathize** with the customer to identify his or her sincere motivations, then **reconcile** their old sales tactics with the newly discovered information gained from seeing through the customer's eyes, and, finally, positively **affirm** the customer's idea of his or her *ideal self* to help the customer achieve it.

Empathize

By now, we know what empathy means. But it is, again, an essential tool in the sculpting process of growth. Marketers and salespeople must be able to see from the perspective of individual customers if they are to assist customers in the attainment of the ideal identity. The car salesperson must step into the young professional's world and learn about his milestone and transition into a new career. He must sense what a new car symbolizes and how it registers with the buyer's ideals.

Reconcile

Before companies or individual sales representatives can assist the client or audience in the growth process, they have to acknowledge that their previous approach to the process of making the sell will have to change. If they empathize with the customer's sense of ideal self and with their hopes, dreams, and aspirations, the standard pitch will no longer suffice. The marketing and pitching must be reconciled in a manner congruent to the direction the person wants to grow.

The car shopper is using the vehicle as a reward, marker, or metaphor for his growth toward a stable career and future, for example. He's not directly using the purchase to self-express an eco-friendly consciousness. He's not using car ownership as an opportunity to practice fiscal responsibility. For his or her message to resonate effectively, the salesperson has to switch gears and not make any claims that distract from the reason the young professional is making the purchase.

Affirm

The third step in the process of facilitating an audience's growth is the most important. After business or salespersons understand the customer's motivations or ideal-self and reconcile that knowledge with their existing strategy, they must affirm the customer's motivation. Affirmation is confirming what is already said.

The car salesperson, once he or she is clear that the new car represents the young man's growth toward a meaningful career track, can affirm his self-ideal by discussing how the car is perfect for commutes, is a durable and sustainable option (just like the young man wants a durable career), and is an excellent choice that will communicate great potential to friends and colleagues. Hearing these affirmations will reassure the young man that he deserves the car as a metaphor for his personal growth and as a reflection of his achievements and of who he is and who he wants to be.

Milestones, Developmental Stages, and Rites of Passage

The need for personal growth is one of the most pervasive and fundamental human needs, but it reveals itself differently throughout life. In early life, we work towards becoming the person we will be as an adult. This means experimenting, changing, and trying new things. Later in life, we become focused on finding meaning and reprioritizing our values in life. Marketers need to recognize the importance of personal growth and the meaning it has to different segments of the population.

People go through different stages of personal growth throughout their lives. The ways in which people express such growth are different in childhood and youth compared to midlife and retirement, for example. In childhood, adolescence, and early adulthood, growth is marked by gaining independence, establishing an identity, and discovering oneself. Young people seek variety and innovation in the products they buy and the behaviors they exhibit. They are constantly working to redefine and prove themselves to others, gain access to new groups, and cultivate an image that they are proud of. They may convey their growth through the products they buy, or buy products that cultivate growth.

One of the most successful advertising campaigns for the U.S. Army was built around the slogan "Be all you can be." Instead of focusing on traditional military themes such as patriotism, history, or adventure, the army promised the young men and women who enlisted personal growth and achievement. "Be all you can be" could be the motto of a university; it's use as a calling card for the armed forces dramatically widened the definition of military service.

Turning to another example, on behalf of a leading electric shaving company, we interviewed a number of men who used wet shavers (those who use razors and cream to shave) to discover insights that might help the company increase the market share of its dry shavers. For many participants, shaving was just a chore. But younger participants viewed shaving in a completely different light: as an exciting way to affirm one's growth from boyhood to manhood. More than just a new habit, the first shave was seen by many as an important rite of passage. "I like to shave," said one participant. "It's a part of growing up...I have the option of being a slob and being unkempt, but it's really important to me—for them to see me as doing what's acceptable." Young shavers comprised a segment who were most inclined to consider alternative shaving systems. This group maintained that they were willing to take the time and effort to get a good shave.

Another facet of the experience of young shavers revealed in our interviews was the bond between father and son. The son had seen the father shave (usually using wet shavers), and the father guided the son on how to do the same, providing, according to the participants, encouragement and support in the son's entrance to the "male club."

One advertising strategy that we proposed was to use this theme of adolescents' "rite of passage" into manhood via the electric shaver. The advertising campaign would focus on the positive aspects of the emotionally important relationship between the father and son and the first shaving experience: acceptance of the boy as a man and recognition of his physical development. Highlighting the increased bond between father and son, we believed, could counteract the traditional image of "men" as blade users, and electric shavers as more appropriate for "younger" beards. We wanted to show that the electric shaver was the way for boys to redefine themselves proudly as budding young men.

Personal growth in the young is manifested through identity and emerging independence. In midlife and adulthood, by contrast, individuals seek to establish a more complex understanding of themselves and the world around them. They work to establish their material lives within certain limits and become more interested in finding meaning, reprioritizing personal values, developing meaningful relationships, and beginning to contribute to society. Young men may cease to make changes and try new products simply for the sake of change and experimentation. They are more interested in maintaining independence and defining meaning in their lives.

One of the life-changing opportunities for personal growth for adults is becoming a parent. Suddenly, the priorities change as the focus of attention shifts from themselves to children and family. Their own personal growth is manifested in the growth and success of their children: part of growing and evolving as parents is feeling good about sacrificing for one's children, seeing the world through their children's eyes, and providing the best experiences for them.

Insight Consulting Group's (ICG's) research with Disney/Universal and Six Flags showed how these brands could appeal to this need. For young adults, vacation and theme parks are vehicles for their own enjoyment. For parents, theme parks become opportunities to provide their children with new experiences and a sense of growth and achievement through conquering challenging new rides. Children are proud when they no longer go on what they dismiss as the "kiddie rides" and start trying out the more "grown-up" rides. But there is a parallel sense of growth in the parents as well. They are no longer the children being taken to the theme parks by their parents. Now, *they* are the mentors providing guidance.

Retirement and later life is a major period for finding meaning and purpose in life. Seniors are now living long, healthy lives that give them the opportunity, with the time and freedom that comes with retirement, to seek out opportunities for growth. Once again, however, growth does not necessarily mean change.

In a study of the French perfume market, perfume lines launched before 1962 had a 37 percent marketshare for 80-year-old consumers compared to 11 percent for 29-year-old consumers. Similarly, 74 percent of new car buyers age 75 and older purchased one of the three well-established national brands compared to 49 percent of consumers ages 18–39, and radio stations established before 1981 have a 58 percent share of the 60-and-older market, compared to 30 percent of the 30-and-younger market.[2] These findings suggest that older adults establish preferences for products that last throughout their lives and tend to remain loyal to those products.

When we understand life stages, we see how many marketers and business strategists pervert the idea of growth. *Appeal to people's needs to evolve and grow through purchasing products that act as quick esteem fixes.* An impulsive buy can certainly make the consumer feel good, but its effects are like a drug. *This $200 shopping spree at the mall will make it all better,* we might tell ourselves. True, the clothes may have helped us feel better about our social or professional image. That's self-expression, a vocalization of identity. But it's not growth. Weeks later, we might come down from the high we experienced during and after the impulsive splurge. The panging that prompted us to shop still lurks. The dopamine-fueled temptation to satisfy short-term pleasure is hard to resist. We are faced with a choice. Find a new fix: *Shoes, entertainment system, phone upgrade? Anything to distract from underlying issues.* Or are there other underlying needs troubling us that we can't see? Perhaps we're looking for a more significant step forward.

This is the difference, again, between growth (evolution) and aimless change (faddism). Growth and consumption only align properly when a purchase is a product of the individual's growth rather than its source.

Intellectual Expansion: Growth and Competency

In 1988, the *Economist* launched its now iconic "white out of red" advertising campaign, which became the foundation of their highly successful advertising efforts for almost 20 years. The highly recognizable print ads featured simple white text on a bold red background, with witty messages positioning the *Economist* as essential reading for the smart and successful, providing a competitive edge and a sense of "membership in an exclusive club" for those in the know.

While this campaign included countless different ads, the underlying message was always: *"Read us, or you will go nowhere in your career." "You're not that interesting of a person are you? Read us." "We will make you smarter. Read us."*

Since its origin in 1843, this British magazine/newspaper has aggressively marketed to an audience who thinks they're smart, thinks they need to be smarter, and values the ceaseless acquisition of knowledge. And they build their readership by making their audience self-conscious.

The *Economist* borderline insults and goads nonsubscribers. After all, the ads described here are just clever challenges to one's vanity. And it works. Most people naturally grow defensive when someone challenges their competence. But the challenge, even if we think highly of our knowledge base, lingers in our minds. We know that we could always learn more. And we know how good it feels to feel smart. After seeing the ads, we're reminded that the *Economist* is a reputable source for political and market news, and we consider accepting their challenge to obtain that pleasant feeling.

This approach is essentially selling lingerie for the mind. The *Economist*, for so long, has successfully appealed to our need for growth. And few journalism brands do it that well. Knowledge is one of the Western world's greatest commodities. We need to grow our minds to grow ourselves. Imagine if you had learned all the things you now know by the time you had reached the age of 30. No more knowledge to be gained; you've hit the cap. Live out the rest of your years comfortable with what's stored inside your intellect, because that's all you're going to get. One needs no imagery to speculate about what a terrible existence this would be. A stagnant mind is a dead one, in the view of many philosophers. "The unexamined life is not worth living," proclaimed Aristotle.

One of the surest ways to achieve personal growth is to ceaselessly and relentlessly pursue new knowledge. Those who seek out knowledge, who act as an intellectual sponge, absorbing information as if their very livelihood depends on it, hold an advantage over those "unexaminers" roaming the planet.

It's important to note that we grow most fully when our enlightenment leads to competency, which is extraordinary knowledge in a given area or subject. In one's career, those who learn more about their niche will get ahead of those who do not. The mind is not built to plateau until a person reaches a very late age in life. But like our waistlines, if we don't work out our mind, it won't grow the way we'd like it to.

Marketers can also play a role while affirming those who believe they've achieved significant growth in their lives. The hair coloring product Just For Men recognized that many middle-aged men find slightly graying sideburns and facial hair to be a symbol of accomplishment or wisdom. But unless the look came about naturally for an individual, there was no way of expressing that. So the brand launched Touch of Gray, a product that on the surface seems to subvert every reason a man would want to color his hair in the first place. Isn't it supposed to be about hiding the gray? For some consumers, yes. But when the company empathized with men who feel they've done a lot with their life and connected that to a specific look and reconciled their product lineup to affirm this niche group, a new market emerged.

However, the advertising for Touch of Gray took a negative turn with a campaign at the height of the 2008 economic crisis. The ad is set in a job interview, an apparent attempt to stoke the fears many older job seekers have in the tough market. The female interviewer evaluates two versions of the same man based purely on his looks. One version has dark brown hair, which to him represents "energy." The other's is solid silver, which represents "experience." The ad represents ageism through and through: neither look is good enough. The job seeker needs a combination of both colors to win over the attractive interviewer.

Although the insinuation of employment discrimination was carried out in a sardonic manner, the ad was a gross misfire in my estimation. Rather than focus on affirming the positive attributes of the "touch of gray" look, it instead played on the fear of not having the right look to get the job. The distinction is slight but critical when affirming the need for growth. Affirmation is about positively showing an existing ideal to be within one's reach or true already—not scaring someone into using a product.

False Appeals—The Danger of Disaffirming and Misaffirming

If there's one demographic shift over the past 30 years worth noting, it's the arrival of a new developmental phase called "emerging adulthood." Because fewer people are getting married in their early- and mid-twenties, in part due to a focus on school or career, the ranks of single households are skyrocketing. Marketers, however, have been generally slow to portray single people in their advertising, despite their dominant purchasing power.

Some facts about singles:

*For the first time, there are more single households than married households in America.

*Before the 2010 Census, there were more than ninety million single adults in the United States.

*Never-married single people ages 25–34 outnumber married people by 46 percent to 45 percent.

*More than 30 percent of new homes were bought by singles in 2009, with two-thirds of the purchasers being single women.

*Ten percent of singles are gay or lesbian.

*Twenty-five percent of singles are baby boomers.

The point is: no group comprising more than a third of America's adult population should be considered homogenous. There are single men and women of every class, race, ethnicity, career, and lifestyle. Yet oftentimes in advertising and marketing, singles are either invisible or carry with them a stigma of a life incomplete. There are plenty of policies and services tailored for couples. But rarely do singles get acknowledged. When they are represented, singles are too often shown as lonely, insecure, and irresponsible. Singles expert Bella DePaulo notes that marketers depict singles as wanderers in search of one thing only: the perfect mate. This is most notably the case with single women.

In her book *Singled Out: How Singles Are Stereotyped, Stigmatized, and Ignored, and Still Live Happily Ever After*, DePaulo recounts a recent ad for Coldwell Banker, a San Francisco-based real estate franchise. The ad starts positively enough, telling the story of a single woman buying her first home. At least the company recognizes that singles are capable and ambitious people. It also conveys the fact that single women buy new homes at a rate double that of single men. However, the ad ends with the woman falling in love and marrying the bachelor next door. "For almost a century, Coldwell Banker has known that real estate is only part of the story," the copy reads. DePaulo's response: "I, a single woman, might go to a Coldwell Banker agent in search of a home. The agent, though, will just know that what I really want is a husband."[3]

Coldwell Banker uses an appeal to growth—buy a home as your first step on the path toward happiness—with a vague suggestion that happiness as a single is impossible unless you find love. They clearly see the importance of their single-woman segment, but by attaching the buying power and self-reliance of these women to their more important aim of getting hitched, they're potentially alienating single women who are buying a home to celebrate their independence. Nowhere in research that investigates home-buying motives will one find data listing "for future husband and children." In fact, one recent study discovered that more than half of single female homeowners purely wanted independence, to own their own property. That sounds like the opposite of "the part of the story" Coldwell refers to in the ad.

Successful advertising featuring singles cannot affirm ideals that only exist for a portion of the single population. But aren't people suckers for those happenstance romance stories, some may counter. True, but when a brand makes an affirmation about a target audience, it had better be sure the audience wants that type of affirmation. The Coldwell ad merely reflects a long line of singles marketing that defines this group as people just waiting around for "the one." Adrian Fogel, a planning director at the ad agency Leo Burnett, wisely instructed in *Advertising Age* that successful ads are "not about making them being single a negative. I think it's about trying to connect them with what they do or love."[4]

I don't mean to pick on Coldwell as being any sort of an egregious actor in the marketing world. They merely illustrate a trend in marketing that needs to be broken.

One of the most interesting questions and points of contention in the branding world asks whether marketing/advertising culture shapes people or whether people shape the contents of the marketing. It's sort of the chicken-and-the-egg question. What came first, the brand personality or the person? But critics of marketing and advertising have a good point here. So much of the advertising we see conditions its audience to accept preconceived notions of how certain people should act. The singles ad illustrates this clearly. By reinforcing cultural stereotypes, personality types, sexuality tropes, and gender roles, marketers and advertising are doing more than reflecting the existing culture. They are propagating it. For better or worse.

This is the opposite of the E.R.A process discussed earlier. Rather than empathize and affirm, some marketers start with their own idea of who people want to be, based on trends and myths that are often decades old, and craft their message in hopes that people will latch onto that culturally crafted ego ideal.

Marketing that appeals to our need for growth makes these mistakes most readily. Rather than affirming the ideal self, these advertisers disaffirm diversity by imposing on the audience their own ideas of the ideal self. Young Americans are supposed to get married and own a home and have two children, so let's reflect this as the endgame in our advertising. That is where people should go, they think. But it's not necessarily an accurate reflection of where people are in their lives, nor is it an accurate depiction of the ideal path of growth many people choose for themselves.

Fieldwork

To Help Customers Grow, Understand Them Fully

The Ecstatic and Anxious World of Moms

Abbott Nutrition, the manufacturers of such nutrition products as Similac and Pedialyte for children, and Ensure for older adults, hired ICG to help them develop a better understanding of the needs, desires, pressures, and responsibilities of mothers. Specifically, Abbott wanted to obtain insights into mothers' attitudes and behaviors relating to wellness, health, and nutrition; to better understand how mothers chose what to feed their families and what role health and nutrition brands played in those decisions; and to develop insights into how Abbott Nutrition and its products could better connect with mothers today.

Our methodology was diverse and comprehensive. We conducted in-home discussion groups in the home of a "host mom," and six or seven of her mom friends. We also asked all mom group-discussion participants to complete a number of homework assignments. One was a creative expression assignment on motherhood in which participants could create a current versus ideal life collage or a mom's advice letter.

We asked them to keep a written or video diary. The third was a grocery-shopping activity in which they would purchase two to three nutrition products that they normally bought and two to three products they didn't, but would if cost wasn't a barrier and then fill out a purchase-decision questionnaire.

An ICG ethnographer spent a "day in the life" with one mom in each of the four markets covered by the study. He or she also conducted "shop-along" grocery-shopping activities with each mom. The study was conducted in four markets: Milwaukee, Boston, Atlanta, and Seattle, and included new or pregnant mothers, older or multichild mothers, and empty-nester mothers.

Emotional Turbulence

From these studies, we drew some significant insights into the emotional lives of mothers. First, no surprise here, we learned that being a mom is the central identity of mothers. Any other element of one's identity—being a wife, daughter, employee, friend, or anything else—becomes secondary. Every aspect of life is about the child. But we also learned that this near-total subjugation to the needs of the child could be emotionally and physically draining. Mothers complained of the total lack of "me-time." Being a mother was also an emotional rollercoaster, with periods of being overwhelmed and exhausted alternating with periods of deep contentment and fulfillment. At times, moms would feel in command and competent, convinced that they were "hardwired" to be moms. At other times, they would be filled with self-doubt and uncertainty. Being a mom, said one participant, "is having your greatest joys, sorrow, hopes, fears, frustrations, and successes all rolled into one." At the same time, moms could not predict from moment to moment what the future had in store for them, and were living somewhat of a crazy existence.

One consistent sentiment, however, was the feeling among mothers that there was a deep disconnect between the reality of their lives and what they would like their lives to be. Real life was stressful, chaotic, and often overwhelming. The mothers did not have enough time to get everything done, and not enough sleep to maintain the energy they required to keep going. There was little opportunity to focus on one's health or on the couple's relationship. Keeping the house clean and the laundry done was a constant struggle. Preparing perfect, balanced daily meals for the family was a constant challenge. Financial worries were common. And, finally, mothers also suffered from a strong lack of identity outside of their children. Not an uplifting commentary on the state of young motherhood.

The ideal life that mothers aspired to was a life of calm, tranquility, and contentment, a life in which they were confident about what they could accomplish and had accomplished, were well rested, had time for romance and intimacy, and had time to work out and take care of themselves. The house was always clean and organized, the family always ate home-cooked, fresh, nutritious meals, and there were few financial worries. Finally, the mothers had the time to maintain a social life and a secure, satisfying identity outside of the children.

As far as knowing what to do for their children, mothers saw parenthood as intuitive and experimental. Overwhelmed with the amount of parenting information thrown at them from myriad sources, they often become distrustful of "experts," and resent unsolicited advice and information. As one mother explained: "No one knows your child better than you. There are definitely times when I think I have no idea what I am doing or wonder if I made the right decision—but no one else can tell you the right thing to do. You just have to trust yourself and listen to your instincts." The only people, outside of pediatricians (and mothers even sometimes listened to them with a degree of skepticism), to whom mothers will listen are the people who are walking in their shoes: other mothers.

However, while new moms used to depend almost entirely on family, the pediatrician, and close friends for advice and support, they are increasingly using the Internet as a major source of advice and support. In matters relating to diet and nutrition, many moms turn to the Web for information with a greater degree of confidence than to their pediatrician. The Internet offers new opportunities for moms to connect through online communities, blogs, and forums. Many moms are going online to find or start groups with moms in their area that evolve into real-life play groups and other support systems. Mom-to-mom support is no longer just about "stitch and bitch"—it's about connecting, bonding, getting sustenance and support from a peer group, and helping each other to blaze through this new life passage.

Our research highlighted the deep need and desire of moms to grow as a mother, to strive to fit the idealized role of the perfect mother. We also learned that all moms struggle, have uncertainties, look for help to grow and be the best mom, and provide the best for their kids.

We saw a key opportunity here for nutrition, which has a strong symbolic value, equated with love. Providing good nutrition for kids is seen as a key to being affirmed as a good mom, helping their kids to grow and reach their potential. Providing the best nutrition helps parents feel that they are growing into being successful parents.

Opportunities for Abbott

Brands that can recognize their customer's need for growth and realistically help people attain the growth they aspire to will have an edge up on the marketplace, because they can become a respected authority that creates trust. But it's not just a matter of telling people they can do it better, quicker, or faster, or of overpromising what they can achieve. Brands have to make sure that they are truly practicing *empathetic* marketing—that they truly understand the challenges of the consumers and can offer solutions to those challenges.

With moms, if a brand can position itself as a trusted adviser that can help them navigate this new area in their lives and empower them to *achieve* the growth they want for themselves (and not just try to sell them a product that overpromises this growth), then it can create an important emotional connection between the brand and its customers that will drive brand loyalty and sales.

In our view, recognizing that moms are looking for ways to grow, and helping them to become the mom they aspire to be gave Abbott a better vantage point for selling its whole portfolio of products. From the very beginning, with its baby formula, Abbott could position itself at the side of new moms, helping them to grow and feel confident as a mom by helping the infant to grow and thrive. As a result, moms would connect with and trust the Abbott brand, giving Abbott the permission to sell Pediasure and the other subsequent products in their portfolio.

Empathetic marketing starts with dialogue and conversation, talking with moms, not at them. Abbott also recognized that there are different segments of mothers, with different needs in terms of growth. The company could provide financial help (coupons, Women, Infants, and Children [WIC] reimbursements) to moms struggling with limited resources. It could help moms concerned about issues with breast-feeding and what is best for their children. It could help moms overwhelmed with the demands placed on them to feel confident and good about their decisions, to grow into someone who they want to be, to effectively navigate this challenging new area in their lives.

Past ICG studies with pediatricians showed that a significant number of office visits were focused on quelling moms' fears and concerns. Growth isn't just about achieving an ideal but also learning to accept fears, conflicts, and anxieties, which help a person navigate growth.

Recognizing this need and understanding moms' experiences and challenges helped Abbott to better tailor its products and services to connect with moms. Abbott placed special emphasis on connecting with new moms, helping them to learn, develop, and grow. They launched a new website, www.strongmoms.com, that effectively appealed to this need—incorporating community support, tips, advice, and more from other moms.

In moving forward with new ideas and products, a company must always be mindful of its customers' underlying need for growth, which will help it develop more effective ways of communicating with them. Like all companies focusing on personal growth, Abbott has to address two masters: reality and aspiration. It has to be aligned with a mom's underlying aspirations to grow and become an idealized mom, but it also has to realistically fit into her lifestyle and be attainable.

The need for personal growth is a powerful reason for customers to purchase product or services. But fulfilling that need requires careful positioning and marketing. Emphasis on the product and the standard product benefits won't truly resonate with customers who desire personal growth. They are not looking for a solution to get a stain out or for a pretty dress, but rather they are looking for proof that the brand will help them grow internally and succeed in their eyes. Successful brands will do their homework to connect with the internal needs and motivations of their customers, and will be very deliberate in what they can actually provide. The fastest way to lose a customer's trust is to overpromise and underdeliver.

Chapter 5 Summary: How Business Can Empathize with the Core Need of Growth

As with other core needs, such as self-expression and belonging, people fulfill their need for growth in different ways throughout the various stages of their lives. The goal is always the same, however: to release the better self that resides within all people. Business must recognize the difference between growth and change for the sake of change, and match growth-related offerings to the life stages of their consumers.

Below are a few key steps businesses can take to effectively respond to consumers' need for growth:

Suggested Follow-Up Steps

1. **Develop a plan to identify your customers' core set of growth ambitions.** "Growth" means different things to different people. What does it mean to your customers? What is their "ideal self"? Only by knowing where they want to go can you help your customers get there through your products and services. Demographic statistics and marketing surveys aren't good enough for this task—you need one-on-one marketing techniques. The end result: a short list of customer "self-ideals," expressed in a short phrase. Here are two areas on which to focus as you identify this list:

   a. **Identify the major life transitions—crises, milestones, and rites of passage—that have an impact on your customers.** Self-ideals are not static. Different life stages leads to different expressions of growth. Businesses have opportunities to facilitate these expressions of growth. If the first shave is a rite of passage for teenage boys, a razor company may consider creating a marketing and product strategy that celebrates that rite of passage. Identify the changing self-ideals of your customers.

b. **Help consumers become more competent.** Competency is a core component of personal growth. Investigate innovative ways for your company, through its products or related services, to help customers become more knowledgeable and capable. You might have an affluent customer base that wants to manage its money. Do you have the supporting processes in place to help them do that? Supermoms want to access medical information so that they don't have to count on doctors' appointments every time the baby is sick. Is there an opportunity for your business to help them get that information?

2. **Put your products and your marketing on your best customers' path to the self-ideal.** Do your customers want to be the "best moms in the world"? Do they want to be "highly successful career climbers"? Or perhaps they want to be "serene seniors, healthy, wealthy and content." Once you've specified a limited number of self-ideals, identify the self-ideal(s) with the optimal brand fit and greatest potential for revenue and align product development, product delivery and service, and marketing to those self-ideals. Seniors represent a growing market. What do they want to achieve, and how can you help? Seniors might want to have more active lifestyles, for example. They don't want to be the grandfatherly/grandmotherly types in a rocking chair on the porch. If you're in the optical industry, that could translate into more fashionable or stylish eyewear for seniors.

CHAPTER 6

The Need for Recognition

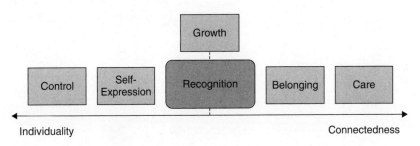

Figure 6.1   The Recognition Need

CHAPTER 6

The Need for Recognition

Her job title suggests she's simply a middle school language arts teacher, one of hundreds in her city. But Janet Norris considers herself more. A manager. A strategist. A creative director. She's tasked with cultivating the reading and writing skills of 120 diverse 12- to 13-year-olds. It's not so much the challenge of getting through a grammar lesson on independent and dependent clauses that keeps her up at night. Rather, it's the daunting mental chess match of motivating dozens of hormonal adolescents to succeed in a subject most of them could not care less about. Her students are sometimes insolent, sometimes kind-hearted, sometimes hardworking, sometimes downright cruel to each other, but at this age, without doubt, they are all smart and cunning individuals who will try most anything to have it their way.

This is why Janet, after 30 years in the classroom, let's the seventh graders have it their way. Sort of.

On the first day of school every August, Janet announces to her classes that their opening moments together will not be spent going over coursework or terrifying them with upcoming standardized test dates. Janet says, "Today, I give you the floor. By consensus, you tell me how you want this class to be run. You pick the daily routines. You write the classroom rules. This is your very own Mrs. Norris Language Arts Bill of Rights." The students murmur breathlessly to one another, eyeing their new teacher with skepticism. They wait for the fine print, which Janet gives them when the room grows silent. "This is my gift to you. So take it seriously," she says, pulling out a marker. "I reserve the right to use my veto pen when one of you inevitably tries to ban homework." A mixture of laughter and groaning erupts from desks, giving way moments later to a spirited discussion.

At one point early in the debate, a girl in the front raises her hand and proposes a rule, "I don't mind when people talk during class when nothing's going on, but I hate it when I try to answer a question and people are whispering and chatting. I can't focus on what I'm trying to say."

After the class discusses, Mrs. Norris asks the girl to write the rule on the white board: *No side chatting when the teacher or another student has the floor.*

Other students follow with their own provisions, such as: *Bullying will not be tolerated; Students may choose their own seats if they follow all other rules; Ten minutes of book report silent reading time will conclude each class period; Students have a right to discuss why they get a bad grade with Mrs. Norris; Students get one due-date extension with prior notice to Mrs. Norris.*

The class votes on each measure and signs a typed final list. A poster of the document is hung for each class before the period begins each day. When a rule is grossly broken, most of the time Janet needs only to point to the poster and their signatures, invoking the rules crafted at the beginning of the year. Confronted with a disobedient, unruly class, she says, "I was so proud of you all when you came up with this excellent set of rules. It showed a level of maturity years ahead of most students your age. But apparently I'm wrong...." The class goes silent, and the students who continue to disrupt are written up—a reminder that they didn't rebel against the teacher's rules, but their own.

But of course, the rules aren't really their own. Janet's policies would be nearly identical to what her students come up with. By creating the impression that the students are self-governing, she rightly comes across as a teacher standing for fairness, a teacher who respects the individuality of her students at an age when kids begins to reject authority more than respect it.

Janet knows that it's impossible to motivate or effectively communicate unless there is a foundation of trust. Her tactic won't by itself create the perfect learning environment. But it is a tangible gesture that shouts, "Hey, I'm on your side. I see where you're coming from—I see you."

This is but one way Janet and other teachers like her successfully recognize their students. **The need for recognition is the universal human drive to be seen, understood, and validated as an individual.** As we'll see in the pages to come, there are many ways we can recognize others and feel recognized ourselves, but Janet utilizes one of the most powerful ways for her students. She bestows on them rights and liberties that they do not receive (or, more likely, do not think they receive) in other classrooms. She *recognizes* that they are not lab rats to be conditioned into memorizing answers on a test, but instead, are people who need to learn and to love reading and writing if they are to succeed in higher education and throughout life.

And Janet provides this recognition by empowering them in a way similar to how marginalized groups have been recognized throughout history. Giving a man or woman the right to vote, erasing racial barriers or inequalities, and establishing laws that apply to all people rather than some people are all expressions of mass recognition that engineer the foundation of liberty and equality.

Surely, allowing students to make modest revisions to their classroom experience does not compare in substance to any of the above. But the principle of recognition resonates. It's easier to foster participation and trust when a group feels they are not locked in a box. For Janet, recognition opens the door to trust and more deeply inspired connections with her students. Even in the mind of thirteen-year-old students, it's harder to rebel, slack off, or take advantage of a teacher who obviously values them and recognizes their potential.

Recognition is paramount anytime the need to motivate groups, and individuals within groups, is central to accomplishing organizational goals. This notion, naturally, extends well beyond adolescence and education. We need look no further than the workplace.

In 1973, Harvard professor Harry Levinson published an important series of essays in the *Harvard Business Review* regarding organizational and management psychology. Called "The Great Jackass Fallacy," Levinson's essays argued that a crisis of motivation in the modern workplace derived from an antiquated view of human psychology. Dominant theories of motivation centered on the classic "carrot-and-stick" (reward and punishment) approach to productivity. The idiom is simple. The driver dangles a carrot in front of the donkey, knowing the jackass will pull the cart in a vain attempt to reach its prize. The problem? Workers aren't jackasses, don't like being led around like foolish jackasses, and retaliate by becoming less productive or resistant to the demands of their employers. Thus, the objectifying of employees in the bureaucracy of business kills productivity and ingenuity. Employees unhappy with their work will do anything to protect their esteem and ideal self-image—steal, slack off, stretch the rules as they see fit, and so forth. Managers who view their workers as anything less than complex emotional beings will miss this idea and not be able to connect with them productively.[1]

Extrinsic rewards like bonuses, holiday parties, or even more flexible rules can be incredibly effective when used at the right time. But they are in no way more powerful than an employee feeling truly appreciated for the impact of his or her work beyond material compensation. An acknowledgement or a thank you and positive encouragement can work wonders for employee morale, trust, and loyalty.

Without recognition, the carrot-and-stick doesn't work with employees. It doesn't work in romantic relationships. It doesn't work with consumers. And it certainly doesn't work with young adults.

Janet Norris frequently hears from her friends and family that the job she does is undervalued and underappreciated. It's a profession not enough people aspire to do, and a job that many who do undertake it don't do well enough. Teaching is more art than science, more interpersonal intuition than managerial logic. For primary school educators, the product of their work—how that student fares in his or her academic and professional life a decade later—is very rarely witnessed. So why is it worth it? Are the teachers themselves recognized adequately?

For Janet, the best recognition is not from her principal, superintendent, or student teachers; it's not sewed into the paycheck or pension— though it certainly helps she was recognized with a $20,000 bonus as a highly effective teacher under the ImpactPlus system. For Janet, the most meaningful recognition is when a familiar-looking college student or young adult knocks on her classroom door or stops her in the grocery store, thanking her for the experience many years earlier when she gave them creative license over their classroom. She may not always remember their names off the top of her head, but she always recognizes faces, and always appreciates the reciprocity of recognition.

Recognition: The Pivotal Need

Leave it to *Seinfeld*, the self-avowed "show about nothing," to portray relatable, excruciatingly awkward daily experience with a level of clarity perhaps sharper than any program in television history. Life is governed by social mores and unwritten rules that the infamous *Seinfeld* characters negotiated hilariously for nine years. Here's one of the main characters, the neurotic, slightly paranoid George Costanza seeking advice from his best friend, Jerry, regarding a problem that captures the essence of our need for recognition:

> **George:** *So let me ask you a question about the tip jar. I had a little thing with the calzone guy this week. I go to drop a buck in the tip jar and just as I am about to drop it in he looks the other way. And then when I am leaving he gives me this look, "Thanks for nothing." I mean, if they don't notice it, what's the point?*
> **Jerry:** *So you don't make it a habit of giving to the blind.*[2]

Tipping for George is symbolic social communication. A tip is a customary act of recognition for a skilled and valued service. But if the recognition (dropping a dollar in the jar) goes unseen, it's as if the deed itself never happened. George wants to be recognized for displaying recognition!

He consciously sought to be recognized for an act he thought didn't have any value beyond the reward for his ego. He, like most people, positions himself so that he can be seen in a certain light, be recognized as an admirable individual. When recognized, we are satisfied that people see us, see what we do and who we aspire to be. It is proof not only that we exist, but that our words and actions have meaning, for better or worse. Consider the literal meaning of "recognition." Ethicist Charles Taylor breaks it down etymologically: re-cognition. Cognition is the process of knowing or perceiving. Recognition, then, is to *know again*. We recognize a familiar face because we may have met that person or know someone who knows or likes that person.

We recognize a logo on a new billboard, because we are familiar with the symbol from previous exposure to it. We know when it's going to rain, because we see the familiar pattern: the clouds roll in, the birds sing loudly, the temperature may dip. We know the difference between an exceptional work presentation and a poor one, because we've seen enough of each to recognize the difference. Our navigation of day-to-day events depends on a system of recognizing.

The verb "recognize" means to identify something or someone previously seen or known, to identify from knowledge of appearance or characteristics. Recognition can be as simple as, "I remember this guy from somewhere...," or as esoteric as, "I see the best of the human spirit in this woman...." The first is literal. When someone looks familiar, we recognize a quality in that person, usually the facial characteristics that mirror distinct memories of past encounters with the recognized person or someone similar. The second is a dive into the deep end. It suggests that we can know a lot about a stranger by observing his or her personality, values, or behavior. We recognize qualities and traits, both ideal and aversive, in other people that reflect our diverse and complex experiences.

In the Fieldwork section, we'll talk more about the psychological process of how people recognize and connect to familiar images. It's impossible to show recognition to a customer or client if the company cannot see what it takes to get the customer to recognize the company's brand.

With Taylor's definition in mind, imagine what it would feel like if everything in the world felt foreign or alien. Worse yet, what if no one recognized us? Feeling invisible is among the psychologically most desperate predicaments in which a person can find him- or herself. There's a reason why moving to a new city is as anxiety-inducing as it is exciting—unfamiliar territory is a step into the unknown. There's also a reason why it's hard for dog owners not to smile when they return home from work. All the tail-wagging, barking, and jumping is unbridled recognition of the master's return—its provider, walker, playmate, and protector. If parents figure out how to get that type of welcome from teenage children (or a spouse), then we'll truly have a societal breakthrough!

Arguably, the need for recognition is the most important of The Needs. It rests smack in the middle of our continuum because its fulfillment requires in equal parts "individuality" and "connectedness." It is pivotal. Organizations that undervalue the role recognition plays internally and externally risk skirting one of the most psychologically influential needs. We cannot see or realize ourselves as an individual without recognition, which requires the presence of the other. This characterization explains how recognition relates to the previous needs for self-expression and belonging. Recognition is not a requirement of satisfying the need for self-expression (for example, the creative process of an artist is often fulfillment in and of itself). However, much of what we express is designed to catch the eye of an individual or a group that we hope sees us in a certain way thereafter. When we are recognized, our life is reaffirmed, our meaning validated, and often our role or status within a group to which we belong is confirmed—we matter.

Contemporary German scholar and philosopher Axel Honneth writes about the paradox of individualization and the role of recognition. To know oneself, to be an individual, one must be connected. Honneth observes a common trait in highly individualistic societies: the more independent, autonomous, and unique we feel we must be, the more existentially empty inside and cut-off from the world we are. For Honneth, this is one theory that explains the skyrocketing rise of depression cases and other mental health issues. In our quest for self-discovery, we've theoretically thrown out the role of community and connectedness in the process.

Recognition, therefore, becomes the axis, the turning point by which we come to see how we operate as individuals in an interconnected social universe. It's an idea long shared by philosophers and psychologists. G. W. F. Hegel, the nineteenth-century German philosopher, used the analogy of the master and his slave. If one party did not recognize his role, the other could not have his confirmed. So in other words, if George's calzone guy did not recognize his customer's tip, his impression and future recognition of George would be altered.

Honneth proposed three types of expressing recognition that we'll use to navigate the need in the marketplace:

1) **Recognition in the form of care, respect, or love**
2) **Recognition through validating achievements within a community**
3) **Recognition by extending rights to a person or group**[3]

The first expression, care, is so important in relationships and in the marketplace that it is a need of its own on the connectedness side of the continuum. Care is the most intimate act of recognition, and is a critical factor in growing self-esteem.

These concepts are undoubtedly not lost on most businesses. But the larger a company becomes and the greater the size of its audience and potential market, the more difficult it is for the company to show recognition to individual customers meaningfully. Recognition is a need that must be instilled as a core organizational value.

And why is that?

Our need to be recognized does not disappear when we take our wallets and purses into the marketplace. The first two needs discussed—self-expression and belonging—help us evaluate whether a product or service will enhance our individuality or help us feel like we are part of something larger than ourselves. If an organization can successfully and truly recognize their audience, then loyalty and market growth are but one step closer.

The Psychology of "Thank You"

When sorting through mail, we employ an instantaneous filter of what's important and what's junk. In the important pile, we place bills and personal correspondences. Outside of party and wedding invitations, personal correspondence via the ordinary postal system is so rare that when we see an envelope with our handwritten address on it, a mental exclamation point fires in our synapses. Our heart rate increases in expectation and surprise. It's the first thing we open.

Oftentimes, we find that what captures our curiosity is the timeless tradition of a hand-written thank-you card. Perhaps we recently let a friend crash on our couch for a weekend as they passed through town. Or loaned a tool to a neighbor. Or returned a lost item to an acquaintance. In any case, there's a palpably strong feeling of satisfaction when we see that our good deed is recognized in the form of a tangible symbol of validation.

The words "thank you" are the most culturally pervasive form of recognition. The basic expression of gratitude is among the first words taught to a toddler. It is a nicety uttered at the end of a transaction. It is often the first idea associated with politeness. But why? How does the presence or absence of a thank you affect behavior, if it does at all?

New research suggests that saying "thank you" is more than a perfunctory reply. It affects the way we consciously and unconsciously perceive others. In 2010, Adam M. Grant and Francesca Gino reported the results of four experiments related to the psychological effects of "thank you."[4]

In one experiment, Grant and Gino tracked how the inclusion of a "thanks" factored into a person's decision to help another person in the future. About 70 volunteers were asked to give feedback on a cover letter for "Eric," a fictional student. After they sent their response, "Eric" asked for additional help with a different cover letter. In half of these replies, "Eric" inconspicuously left out a statement of gratitude. The other half received a simple "thank you" for their critique. Those thanked by "Eric" helped him 66 percent of the time. Only a third of the participants who didn't receive any gratitude helped him again.

These results shouldn't be too surprising. But this experiment alone doesn't tell us why a thank you prompted more people to continue their mentorship. Subsequent studies by the researchers led to the intriguing finding that the idea that we're capable of successfully performing a task, had little to do with the decision to help. Thus, the "thank you" did not confer the idea that a participants' cover letter critique was enlightening in its advice to "Eric." Instead, the "thank you" conveyed self-worth, in other words, "I'll help you again because you told me that I'm valued as a person." In another study, Grant and Gino found that those thanked will even pay the kindness forward to others. More than half of a different set of participants thanked by "Eric" were willing to help "Steven," another job seeker in need, days later.

So what are the implications of this for business? Does this mean that all a business has to do is simply convey "thanks" to a customer at the check-out line? As with all emotional needs, it's not that simple. In short, an organization should never *not* say "thank you," but in order to deeply satisfy the customer's need for recognition, how the "appreciation" is delivered is essential to the organization's standing out and fostering loyalty.

Corporate-speak is skillfully, and sometimes ostentatiously, polite—so much so that we've come to expect and dismiss the superfluous niceties. We inoculate ourselves from what we see as faux gratitude. We see the words "thank you" on shopping bags, marquees, receipts, spam emails, and coupons, and tune them out along with the rest of the commercial clutter in our mental lives. A large business telling us "thank you" may be sincere on their part, but it certainly feels perfunctory—an expectation that doesn't move or surprise us. If recognition is the optimal path to self-realization, as Honneth claims, it's hard for me or anyone to feel recognized when we are but one of millions "thanked" for purchasing a product or service.

This doesn't change the fact that companies sincerely want you to know how important you are to them, because without you, they can't exist. They genuinely do value your business. But the reason why their thank you's fall flat is because you know that in most cases they don't appreciate you as an individual; rather, they appreciate your financial transaction. Certainly there's nothing wrong with that, but as a vehicle of recognition, it doesn't quite get the returns businesses desire. So what's the difference between a thank you that can legitimately build customer loyalty and a thank you that is not even heard? In short, to truly value an alert, skeptical audience, businesses have to travel an extra mile or two to break the patterns of recognition.

The following sections illustrate both potential for recognition opportunities and pitfalls.

Personalize to Recognize

A work colleague's home is wrecked due to a water main break. You (along with two dozen of his other friends, colleagues, and family members) volunteer your weekend to rebuild and clean up. Later that week, he sends out a terse but gracious email thanking the group for helping him through the crisis. The sentiment is nice, but you don't really pay much heed to it. You're not going to make a big deal about it, but the email didn't make you feel appreciated individually. On a different level, this is how you likely react when a company sends you a junk letter gushing with thanks. You know that whoever wrote the copy for that letter doesn't really know you at all. Like a Hallmark card that does not contain a personal letter from the sender, it makes it that much easier to pitch it straight into the recycling bin.

Companies that invest in one-on-one personal communication reap the rewards of increased loyalty. Throw out the form letters. Send personally addressed messages rather than LISTSERV emails. Cut out automated menus. Empower retail employees to address consumer issues without requiring them to cut through 18 miles of corporate red tape. If possible, try sending handwritten letters (because who doesn't read a handwritten letter?).

These strategies require time, effort, funding and commitment. But depending on the industry, loyal customers on one end can generate new leads and lower costs on the other.

It's been said that personalization is a form of recognition, and validation is among the oldest sales tricks in the book. But I hesitate even to call it a "trick" if it's done tactfully, which is not always the case. For example, most direct mail today is addressed to the potential customer by first name—all it takes is a list of prospects and the print-merge function of the printer. In some cases, the first name is printed onto a fake Post-it note so that it seems as if someone at the company wrote a personal message to the prospect.

This kind of fake personalized marketing is hardly inspiring and can easily backfire—who wants to buy a product from a company that is trying to fool you? However, there are many ways to create authentic personalized interactions with customers.

For example, a representative's taking notes on clients' personal lives, important dates, or milestones for future recall allows the customer to feel recognized even though the representative may have hundreds of contacts in his or her book. When your broker can easily reflect on your current transactions and balance as soon as you call and compare them to key indices (and ask you about your family and your recent vacation), it can even cushion and diffuse some of the upset from significant losses in the stock market. Naturally, the need for recognition is tailor-made for customer service and public relations departments. Database companies abound that specialize in recording information about past transactions, customer behaviors, and feelings or service snafus for call-center employees. If an event is significant enough that a customer will remember it, it is flagged for the representative to recall so that the consumer is reminded about the service resolution, reminded that the company knows exactly who he or she is, and what his or her needs are past, present, and potentially in the future.

Twitter and other forms of social media offer opportunities for one-on-one personal communication that was literally impossible just a few years ago. Imagine that we are in the year 2000, and you complain to a friend about the bad service at the local bank. Within a few hours, the phone rings: the caller is an executive in that bank's public relations department apologizing for the bad experience. Such a scenario would, of course, have been pure fantasy in 2000. But not today. Through the use of Twitter, companies today can in essence "listen in" on what customers are saying about them and respond immediately, if necessary. C. C. Chapman, who runs a digital marketing agency in Boston, was watching a National Basketball Association (NBA) playoff game when he noticed a problem with the high-definition reception from his cable company, Comcast Cable. The unhappy Chapman blasted a quick Tweet about the problem to his followers. As reported in the *Boston Globe*, "Minutes later, a Twitter user named ComcastCares responded, and within 24 hours, a technician was at Chapman's house in Milford to fix the problem."[5] Technology doesn't have to be impersonal.

Best Buy has been particularly innovative in using social media to connect one-on-one with customers. For example, the retail giant has a new Twitter service called "twelpforce," through which customers can ask questions about electronics, and any Best Buy employee can respond through Twitter. Social media consultant and author Charlene Li relates in her book that, in response to her question to Best Buy, an employee of the company contacted her and offered to meet her at a nearby store. I can personally attest that Best Buy sent a representative to my home at no charge when my amplifier blew, and then he returned and replaced it with an upgrade.

Unfortunately, as companies slash costs during tough times, resources devoted to person-to-person outreach is often reduced to nil. But these interactions, few as they may be, are critical to fostering loyalty. Advertising can set the spark; it importantly allows the individual to recognize a brand over time. But the glue is connecting to customers by letting them know that you recognize them, thus making them want to relate to you. A positive personal interaction can do wonders for satisfying this need that a $1 million television spot never could.

In fact, all other components can be right for the company when a breakdown of recognition occurs. A 30-second television spot can emphasize how much the business cares about us, good public relations on the product can convince us to adopt it, and the product itself might work fairly well. But when you call customer service and wait 30 minutes listening to ear-rattling generic pop music and a looped "We value your time, and will be with you shortly," it can very well trample all the good will you have built up for the company. It is faux recognition. And it is off-putting.

But not all companies make this mistake. Apple gets much love in the marketing world. Yet Apple's extra investment in customer service "geniuses" reinforces their successful branding and product design.

For instance, after accidentally deleting some music I had originally purchased from the iTunes Store, I sent an email asking if I could retrieve the music that my technological ineptitude had caused me to lose. Within hours I received a friendly, nonformulaic set of instructions from a representative. The problem was resolved. Assuming it was a simple form letter, I discarded the email without response. A couple of days later, I got another email from Apple:

Mandy here again from the iTunes Store, I hope you are having a fantastic day.

This is just a quick follow-up to your previous request regarding the items I posted back into your account. I haven't heard back and just wanted to touch base and ensure everything has been resolved to your satisfaction. As a valued member of the iTunes Store family [*sic*] didn't want to leave you without any type of resolution.

If I don't hear from you by today or tomorrow, I wanted to let you know that at that point I will be closing this case out. However, if you do require assistance agai [*sic*] in the future, another agent will be more than happy to help out. It's been my pleasure working with you and I hope that you will continue to enjoy the iTunes Store.

Sincerely,
Mandy
iTunes Store Customer Support

Compare that to the all too familiar "We value your call" nonsense. Consumers are sensitized to this alienating, insincere language. They know that when a company says something like this, it's a sign that it won't devote the resources to addressing their needs. These pronouncements of "recognizing every consumer" reek of insincerity to the consumer unless proven otherwise. Even though the Apple email says I'm a "valued member" of their "family," I know the customer support representative might very well value me. And I know that, given the typos (unless Apple is really going to the max to trick me by purposefully making an error in the email), Mandy is actually a person typing at a keyboard and not a machine shooting off form letters. Those little touches don't undo the necessity for mass marketing and advertising, but they sure create glue. This type of recognition elevates Apple beyond the 99 percent of large corporations that profess personal attention and the validation of each customer, but do so in name only.

Creating the types of processes and systems that allow direct and personalized communication with customers requires a company's dedication of significant financial and personnel training and development resources, but these are essential if the company is to stand out and satisfy the recognition need in the Internet era of email, social media, and other instant connectivity tools. As Chip Conley, founder of the highly successful Joie de Vivre boutique hotel, points out in his book, PEAK, satisfying this need is especially important in a recession!

Right this Way, Madam: Recognition and Bestowing Rights and Privileges

Working with United Airlines, we learned that the negative effect of fee increases can be offset and cushioned if paired with new privileges and rewards for maintaining loyalty to the airline. Specific segments of travelers are willing to pay more to feel special. They are recognized when they're able to move through an expedited security line or have a separate boarding area roped off, in clear view of the coach class. People are motivated by different forms of status, and importantly, by the recognition they expect to receive once that status is achieved.

Incidentally, showing is better than telling. A "thank you" in conjunction with a tangible symbol of that recognition is often unexpected, and thus, a sure way to encode the validation into a lasting memory. Many retailers recognize loyal customers by giving them store credit or big discounts, but that token isn't appreciation as much as it is a tactic (and by no means a bad one) to get people back into the store as quickly as possible. But even those perks are delivered so often to the extent that they are expected and they do not hit the "I'm recognized" button in your brain. I received discount offers every day from the shuttered retailer Borders. The discounts were nice and all, but how could the company be sending them under the guise that I am a valued customer when I hadn't shopped there in a year?

Companies can diversify their thank you's by allowing you to send a $5 gift card to a friend (a small cost for the potential of getting a new customer and solidifying the loyalty of another). A store can give a complimentary gift or candy during holiday seasons. If it's an online order, a company can ship a thank-you card or a small gift the customer didn't expect.

Note how these strategies simultaneously engage with our need for belonging. When our favorite bartender every now and then pours us a fresh drink on the house, the acknowledgment of loyalty in turn breeds devotion and solidifies attachment to that establishment. Having a place where "everybody knows your name" is a commodity in our digital era, and it is one that more services and retail businesses, large and small, should strive for in their business model. We'll learn about this type of service in the care chapter.

Fieldwork

To Recognize and to Be Recognized

Familiar Territory: The Psychology of Brand Recognition
When the words "business" and "recognition" are used together, the concept that comes to mind will often be brand recognition, or the process of identifying, recalling, or associating with one brand over another. Brand recognition is quite different from the individual's need for recognition, as discussed previously. The need requires individual validation for the purposes of self-esteem, self-worth, and self-awareness.

We need to be recognized.

But we navigate the world, including the marketplace, via a perceptual system of recognizing familiar patterns and sensory information.

The former is the need of the individual, while the latter reflects the business's need to ensure that their brand is easily recalled by their audience.

However, for the business strategist, the two concepts are very much interrelated. If a person cannot recognize a particular brand, it is impossible for the company in question to satisfy the person's need for recognition in any way—or any other of his or her needs, for that matter.

Let's briefly walk through a few concepts related to how we recognize.

Linguistics

Linguists have long been interested in the role of language in recognition. That is, how we define the world around us and the words we use change our perspective. The most famous anecdote is the arctic-dwelling Sami population who, as myth would have it, have over three hundred words for snow.[6] Given their environment, one isn't surprised by this. Snow of different weight, consistencies, intensity, ice, and so on shapes how they see the world. Yet if a native of Phoenix, Arizona, were dropped onto the Sami's frozen tundras, the landscape to their eyes would be consistent and unvaried: white snow. To the Sami, their location is a sea of diversity, from powdered flaky snow, to rough dense patches, to pervious ice trails, to thin and dangerous ice. How we define our surroundings enhances our recognition of important stimuli; words give solidity and borders to our world. But by defining and recognizing a brand or an object for what it is, we simultaneously define it by what it is not.

Mirrors

Of the many discoveries worth noting in the neuropsychology field over the last few years, none has garnered more attention than the concept of mirror neurons. These neurons are found in the motor cortexes of our brains, and they fire when we observe the actions of other people or animals. The neurons mimic an observed action, allowing us to see how the actor feels during the action. Although the research is hardly complete, it appears we're literally hardwired to mimic and feel emotion when watching others. This phenomenon has moral psychologists chomping at the bit. Are mirror neurons responsible for empathy? We recognize when someone else is experiencing pain or sorrow because we experience a neurological response in our own brains, which causes us to feel and identify with the same emotions just by observing the state of the afflicted individual.

Patterns

Mirror neurons are another factor in the long stream of research on how we learn and recognize. The brain's ability to store information in the unconscious is incalculable. Why can we drive home from work, exit our vehicle, and not remember the trip at all? The brain's autopilot function allowed us to spend our attention elsewhere, while the unconscious brain performed the recognizable and patterned steering, route planning, and reactions. Even when we're mentally distracted on the road, our eyes scan for irregularities in the pattern, for example, a pedestrian in the road, a car door opening—that allow us to react quickly enough to adjust course.

If we were not capable of recognizing patterns and sorting familiar stimuli, imagine what inefficient, helpless beings we would be in the modern world. Nothing would get done! We would spend entire weekends wandering the grocery store aisles, overwhelmed with the unfamiliarity of the products and the confusing layout of the aisles. We'd never be able to learn the most basic tasks.

How we recognize encapsulates this aphorism: all brands are not created equal. Some brands—by their nature, history, pervasiveness—will always be more easily recognized than others. Brand recognition is a pretty straightforward concept. How do we distinguish Brand A from Brand B, given that both products are practically identical? Brand A's initial success in the marketplace attracts many imitators. Unfortunately, Brand A's mechanics are pretty simple to replicate, and Brands B through G are now battling for space on the aisle. Similar prices, more or less equal efficiency, the same quality. Yet, customers prefer Brand B again and again. Why? Brand recognition. Through engaging ad campaigns supported by marketing, Brand B developed its message to appeal to the appropriate population segment. Its catchy slogans, showy veneer, and ideal positioning enhance one's ability to recognize the brand and differentiate it from the competition.

In most consumer categories, we can point to a "pioneer" brand, the creator or first widely successful entry into an emerging market. They are the brands we weigh all others against, and that usually, but not always, dominate market share. Marketing scholars Gregory Carpenter and Kent Nakamoto note that pioneer brands have a distinct edge over competitors:

> "A pioneer brand is novel. We devote cognitive effort to understanding the product and what it does.... By the time we observe the sixth or tenth brand, redundancy increases, novelty decreases, and we devote much less to understanding new brands and what they do. The pioneer, having received the most attention early on, is most easily and most positively recalled."[7]

For the lucky few brands rewarded with the status of being easily recognized, there's a great risk in adjusting the pattern or messing with the systems of recognition. Remember New Coke? In 1985, Coca Cola famously threw out its highly successful formula in the face of an intense market-share challenge from Pepsi. What resulted was a disastrous flop that led to the return to the old formula, and the rerebranding, "Coca-Cola Classic." The company changed the brand recognition that was the source of its market dominance. It was a betrayal of loyalty, an unwarranted step into the unknown. In his book, *The Real Coke, The Real Story*, Thomas Oliver said that the company hired a psychiatrist to listen in on customer calls to Coke's hotline. The psychiatrist likened the emotional trauma some customers expressed to the death of a family member. Recent headline examples hearken back to Coke's dramatic marketing decision. National Broadcasting Company (NBC) pulled the plug on Conan O'Brien's short tenure on the *Tonight Show* to much fanfare and discussion. While they suffered a lot of public relations blowback, they didn't want to prolong a ratings decline in the competitive 11 o'clock hour. So they went back to their old formula, Jay Leno, the entertainer whom their older audience recognized and preferred over the off-beat, quirky Conan. The Gap exchanged its age-old, tall, serif typography logo in 2010 for a jarringly poor logo that subverted any and all recognition to the classic, casual image it had built for itself. They, too, reverted instantly to the original before the new look was fully implemented.

Thus, the process of recognizing is biased toward the tried and true, the classic feel, the comfortable, generation-defining appeal, giving it the competitive advantage.

However, stellar research and product innovation combined with carefully conceived marketing, advertising, and public relations efforts can catapult a brand to the forefront of a person's recall list.

A Familiar Face and a Clean Face: Nivea For Men's Dual Challenge of Recognition

The constructs of masculinity have dramatically changed in the past two decades. Even the term "metrosexual" is too broad to define the changing consumption patterns and image ideals of the American man. Western men are finally coming around to the idea that skin care is more than a quick shave in the morning. Yes, less and less, men of all ages are not using the same bar of soap their fathers used for their face, torso, feet, and every nook in between, thanks to highly informed girl-friends and wives and a culture's growing acceptance of male fashion and personal-care products, some of which were once stereotypes of a gay community.

The notion that women take too long in front of the mirror is trumped by new data that suggests a surprising cultural reversal. A 2006 survey found that 73 percent of European and US men stated that spending time in front of the mirror was "important" or "very important." Women who said the same thing? Seventy-two percent. More and more men are taking the time to pamper themselves and take care of their face, making the market for skin and facial care products among the fastest-growing sectors in the industry. In fact, between 2000 and 2005, the men's segment in the skin-care market grew 42 percent. The market for both men's and women's skin-care products only grew 23 percent as a whole during the same period.

The emerging audience for these luxury products provided new opportunities for personal-care companies, but a new set of challenges, as well.

At the height of this market growth, my firm was commissioned to conduct qualitative research on behalf of Nivea For Men's advertising agency. As with any new market looking for a pioneer, there was no established brand authority in the men's face-care category. Our initial goal was simply to identify what factors would make Nivea products recognizable to men of distinct age groups.

What stimuli: messages, information, settings, and tones would foster the quickest connection and recall?

Using a research design our firm entitled "Ad Lab," we showed about five dozen males of three different age groups dozens of television and print ads in the skin-care category, including drafts of Nivea For Men ads. The findings revealed several distinct trends. Among them, we found that in all age ranges, men were intimidated or turned off to some degree when exceptionally attractive models were used. This finding opens the door to a legitimate criticism of traditional focus-group qualitative studies. Respondents might articulate in a group that they're put off by attractive women who come across as discerning and dignified, but we already know from earlier chapters and other psychology work that people don't always say what they think or mean what they say. One might think the potentially sexually arousing ads is an effective psychological strategy. *Make men feel inadequate by showing perfect-ten models. This feeling will in turn prompt them to take skin care seriously.* This seems like sound logic, but after empathizing with these men and learning about their backgrounds, we found that their lack of connection to this ad set came from a place of sincerity. Many of them were in relationships and took their face-care advice from their wives and girlfriends. The suggestion that grooming would get a man into the good graces of unrealistically attractive women caused them dissonance with their perfectly healthy, existing relationships. Many men were older, and thus explicitly thought they were being shown an ad that didn't apply to them.

In all, the ads were most effective when they suggested: "Scrub, moisturize and exfoliate for YOU—your health, your esteem, your confidence."

This finding was all well and good, so long as the participants connected to the service. Yet in the television ads, Nivea For Men ran into a problem that ran up against everything we know about how we recognize.

The men in this study felt disconnected from the Nivea ads, and stated that they did not see themselves in the actors. Nivea, owned by the German company Beiersdorf, used European-looking models to exhibit their products. It's a fine distinction, yes, but because skin care was an emerging market in the United States at the time, the ads signaled to the viewer's unconscious: "For some reason I can't relate to these people, there's something foreign or different, it doesn't feel like I could be standing in his place, it doesn't apply to me."

They could not connect because the ad, from the actor to the sterile, minimalist background, did not activate the participants' systems of recognition. Our filters are strong. What we can't recognize, we won't relate to. This was a huge problem for a brand trying to be a pioneer in a new market. By having the ad agency create a diverse set of more "American looking" models that spanned ages and perceived lifestyles, we drew the attention of a wider swath of men to the ads.

However, investigating "how will they recognize us?" led us to another critical insight that directly links to the individual's need to be recognized.

The men were rampantly confused about how, when, and why they should use these products. This finding mirrored sales data on the subject, as Karen Grant, a beauty industry analyst commented[8]: "The products that we see in the prestige market that are doing well are those that are simple and multi-purposed, products that are part of a basic regimen, like cleansers, moisturizers, and shave treatment products. Any product that requires extra steps is a much harder sell for men."

Meaning, before you can sell a box of exfoliating cream, you'd better take steps to make sure men know what exfoliating is!

By recognizing this predicament in product design, ad copy, and packaging instructions, Nivea For Men had the opportunity to show their prospective customers that they recognized more than their interest in a new product area. The company learned that many of these men had no clue what to do with the product. And, yes, recognizing this need for education is surely one form of showing recognition.

Unlike females, who had decades of accumulated knowledge about skin and face products that were marketed to them, men were an interested but naïve entrant into the category. Some men who had the support of their wives or girlfriends but were interested in conquering new territory on their own, sought a new face-care regimen without the help of their partner.

Chapter 6 Summary: How Business Can Address the Core Need for Recognition

Positioned in the middle of the needs continuum, equidistant from the poles of individuality and connectedness, is the core need of recognition—that is, the individual's core desire to be appreciated and valued. Businesses that fail to offer recognition in specific ways will lose their customers. The challenge is providing authentic recognition; however, it is not simply rote messages of recognition that have no emotional value.

Key Business Success Factors

Below are a few key steps businesses can take to effectively respond to consumers' need for Recognition:

Suggested Follow-Up Steps

1. **Personalize to Recognize.** Strive to make every effort to recognize customers as individuals, not as customer segments or anonymous statistics behind the daily sales revenues. Here are some ways to personalize transactions:
   a. Send one-on-one personal letters, signed by a real person, complete with their contact information.
   b. Ensure that representatives of your company, from customer service representatives to sales clerks to other customer interface employees, refer to customers by name and show they know them without being intrusive.
   c. Create a dedicated social-media staff to maintain contact with customers through Twitter, Facebook, and so forth. If someone tweets about your company, do you have someone who will see that Tweet and respond?

2. **Bestow exceptional rights and privileges.** Push the boundaries of standard marketing and customer service practices, and deliver meaningful and even surprising privileges; leave no doubt that you personally recognize the customer for his or her loyalty like the Ritz Carlton, who places a bottle of wine or candy in the room and says, "Welcome Back". Granting an outward symbol of status is especially effective, as exemplified most explicitly by first-class seating on a plane. While there is no first-class service available in a grocery store, consider dedicating a cash register for selected customers (who are high value customers).

3. **Recognize specific needs.** Identify and accommodate specific needs of customers or segments. Do you accommodate mothers with small children? IKEA and McDonald's do.

4. **Show that you care.** The most intimate act of recognition is proving to customers that the company cares about them. This will be covered in more detail in chapter eight.

CHAPTER 7

The Need for Belonging

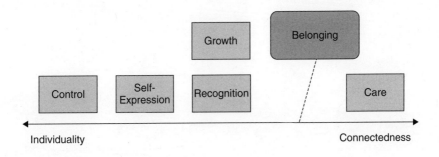

Figure 7.1   The Belonging Need

CHAPTER 7

The Need for Belonging

It didn't take Frannie very long to decide her new job wasn't working out. The cleanup effort seemed insurmountable, and even more irksome, her volunteers appeared to be enjoying themselves.

Sweat weighed down her T-shirt like a backpack. She rolled down her sleeves, covering the strawberry-red burns up and down her arms. Frannie set down her box of plastic bags and metal prongs and wiped her brow. It was a 90-degree, near 100 percent humid, suburban Chicago summer afternoon. It was only ten a.m., and Frannie, a shift manager for the cleanup, would clock out and collect her $120 honorarium for the week at two p.m. that afternoon.

The wooded area along the river was the site of a massive, summer-long community cleanup effort sponsored by the township's council. The city was expanding its bike path along the river. An unsightly mass of garbage and debris had to be cleared from an abandoned industrial complex located a hundred yards off the water. Frannie had signed on to supervise groups of volunteers, a two-month commitment to spend every Saturday roasting.

She tried hard to convince herself that the good cause with the added cash incentive was worth it all. But at the end of the day, she was stiff and exhausted, and the area still looked like a postapocalyptic wasteland. The cleanup coordinator handed her the check and said, "See you back next week?"

Frannie avoided eye contact. "Actually, I just found out my son has a baseball tournament scheduled. I'm so sorry. I won't be able to come back," she said. It was a lie. The city official knew it too. Frannie's family had just moved to the area. Her son couldn't join a team until the following spring.

This tedious part-time job was not worth the low pay. And that warm glow from doing good works? A sunburn.

She quit.

Several weeks later, she returned to the job for no pay, with a markedly better attitude. Why?

Frannie had lost her job in Portland, Oregon, earlier that year. She had been a middle school art teacher for four years before getting pink-slipped in the wake of drastic budget cuts. Soon after, her husband, an information technology (IT) technician, was given the "choice" of resigning or transferring to Illinois. They had little choice. With college tuition right around the corner, two out-of-work parents was an unmanageable scenario.

They packed their belongings, but left behind everything they *belonged to*.

Frannie had to say goodbye to her life-long friends. The summer book clubs, Saturday arts groups, church, the moms from her son's team, teacher friends. She even cringed at the thought of finding a new grocery store and coffee shop.

Adding to her anxiety, finding an open job in an Illinois school district, like most places in the country at the time, was as likely as taking up a successful career in basket weaving. She called about the riverside cleanup project minutes after seeing the listing. Work was work.

Later that summer, after quitting the cleanup gig, Frannie and her husband joined the local church. She didn't consider herself particularly religious, but cherished the strong sense of community they had with their church back home and figured it was a way to rub elbows with the neighbors. Frannie signed up for a summer activity group.

"What exactly do you do?" she asked Jill, the group's organizer and a new neighbor.

"Lots, actually," Jill said. "You'll learn the town in no time. We help with projects at the school, organize some of the city festivals over the Fourth. Oh, and this week, we're doing some volunteer work, helping to take care of that eyesore blocking the bike path expansion."

The thoughts of sore muscles, dirt clinging to her face, and the smell of the polluted water at the site wove together a tapestry of aversive memories.

Was this the only way in? she thought.

But she showed up. And to her surprise, she worked with new energy. Frannie decided not to tell the group she used to supervise the effort. Yet, her experience helped her become a competent motivator and guide. She zipped around the woods, striking up conversations and working up a relaxed sweat like it was her old yoga class. By day's end, the area only looked marginally better, and physically, she was just as exhausted as the month prior. The task itself was just as tedious, but she enjoyed every last second of it.

She wasn't working as a manager collecting cash at the end of the day. She was working as part of the group.

Frannie's 180-degree turn is confounding when we think of her actions in terms of rational economic behavior. How could anyone turn down the money, only to turn around and do the same thing for free? But ask this same question from the perspective of Frannie's social psychology. Frannie's attitude reversal isn't abnormal at all. The money, frankly, in some way poisoned her enjoyment of working toward the cause. The initial Saturday was a job and only a job in Frannie's mind. Attach a dollar value to the tedious work and no amount of money could make the job "a good job." Attach a sense of purpose and a potential group of friends, and suddenly the hard labor becomes desirable even when the miserable physical conditions persist.

Frannie's need to belong overrode her need for extra spending money. The task itself didn't change, but she was able to justify the unpleasant work in return for creating a new life and social group. **The need to belong and connect with others deeply motivates us to create and maintain strong social attachments.** Thinking in terms of the Needs Continuum, we can see that belonging is connectedness plus community—our drive to be affiliated with ideas and other people.

Research in the social sciences tells us that, when in the right situation, most people will behave like Frannie. This observation (a product of cognitive dissonance theory developed by Leon Festinger) is backed by numerous social psychology experiments, all demonstrating the powerful sway of the group. An explanation for Frannie's rationalization is best explained in Morton Hunt's *The Story of Psychology*:

> The harder it is to gain membership in a group (as, for instance, when there is grueling screening or hazing), the more highly the group is valued by a person who is accepted. We convince ourselves we love what has caused us pain in order to feel that pain was worthwhile.[1]

While there is a dark side to the implications surrounding Hunt's observation, there remains a positive opportunity built into this essential element of our roles as social beings. What if we only acted independently, driven purely by these extrinsic rewards? The answer is, a lot wouldn't get done. The need to belong moves people in directions that seemingly run counter to self-interest—sometimes even economic interests. However, when we look closer, we see that belonging has everything to do with self-interest.

At the end of the afternoon, the city coordinator approached Frannie. "Hi there... You know I can't pay you this time?"

"No worries," Frannie said. She was paid in a different way, with a heftier payoff.

The Pull of Belonging in a "Self"-Driven Culture

Famed psychologist Soloman Asch discovered the powerful influence of the need to belong. In a small group, Asch showed research subjects

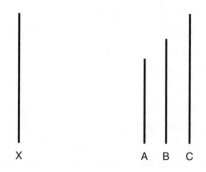

Figure 7.2   Asch Conformity Study Example Comparison Lines

two cards with vertical lines, asking them simply to pick the two with the same length.

It was a visual logic game clear and simple enough for a toddler to grasp. But for some of the cards, embedded actors sat around the table chose and agreed upon obvious wrong answers. Seventy-five percent of the research subjects agreed with the actors at least once. One in four of the subjects conformed to the group consensus at least 50 percent of the time.

The phenomenon of conformity is a product of our need to belong. This need for connectedness to the group is essential to our well-being—so much so that it can override what we initially consider as a fact.

However, one question remained unanswered in the decades that followed. Did the conformists actually know they were giving the wrong answer? More recent research, powered by the latest brain-scan technology (yes, there is a place for it), indicates that the group can influence what the individual's brain perceives. If we are faced with the possibility of being the dissident, areas of the brain responsible for perception actually reinterpret our surroundings, redrawing the truth before our own eyes . . . or brains, rather. The implications are profound. They suggest that our emotional needs affect perception, distorting our world and consequently our behavior.

Thus, Frannie is not alone in her behavior. Those misled by Asch's actors are not alone, either. We all, from time to time, follow the crowd. We're wired to belong, even if it betrays reality. This carries with it many scary implications—entire nations duped by totalitarian propaganda, brinksmanship, and potentially catastrophic group decision-making.

But these risks do not eradicate the necessity to feel connected, to be part of the crowd. Despite living in a society that values individual accomplishments, we need communities, peers, and families to help us achieve the infinite number of tasks that individuals cannot do alone.

Even if self-interest is outwardly one's prime motivator, the push to belong is strong under the surface. Voluntarily or involuntarily, we belong to groups, organizations, ideas, movements, and cultures. Our memberships in or affiliations with these social constructs give us a sense of place and identity. Belonging helps us see our individual self against the backdrop of our relationships. We equally define ourselves by our chosen social circles, as well as by whom we choose not to associate. Groups may provide trust and comfort, and act as a vehicle for self-expression. Abraham Maslow placed belonging third in his hierarchy of needs, right after physiological needs (health) and safety needs (shelter, security of resources).

Satisfying the need to belong is simple on the surface. However, its fulfillment seems to run against the grain of our need for individuality. We both need others to help us achieve our individual goals, while at the same time reciprocating with a stable, enduring framework of "affective concern for each other's welfare."[2]

Belonging is important, but because we are a culture that largely values the individual over the larger group, how do we prioritize this need? For one, the need is all too often latent. We don't realize the extent to which social yearnings drive us through our day. Like many other needs within Maslow's hierarchy, the needs become apparent and are most salient in their absence. In Portland, Frannie naturally moved through her day in well-established social groups. It never was a priority for her to seek acquaintances because that need was already "met" according to Maslow's hierarchy. It was only after her move to Chicago when the impact of her loss was most heavily felt.

Social psychologist Eda Gurel-Atay tracked the evolution of social values held by American adults over the past few decades. Note the backwards movement of belonging:[3]

Table 7.1 Evolution of American Social Values

Value	1976	1986	2007
Self-Respect	21.1	23.0	28.8
Security	20.6	16.5	12.4
Warm Relationships with Others	16.2	19.9	20.9
Sense of Accomplishment	11.4	15.9	10.3
Self-Fulfillment	9.6	6.5	8.1
Being Well Respected	8.8	5.9	8.3
Sense of Belonging	**7.9**	**5.1**	**3.3**
Fun/Enjoyment/Excitement	4.5	7.2	9.3

As we head into the second decade of the new millennium, a sense of belonging is the least important value, inverting itself with the "fun-enjoyment-excitement" value and the "warm relationships with others" value. This is significant. Our need for connectedness and interpersonal relationships grows, but it comes at the expense of a core vehicle for connecting: groups and communities. Given the pace of American life in the twenty-first century, it's understandable many tend to forgo belonging to groups and organizations and focus on a few close interactions with others. (Either that, or we belong to so many groups that the meaning of these affiliations becomes diluted.)

Despite belonging's decline in the chart above, we cannot devalue the continued importance of the need. What we think we want may be different from what we unconsciously need. Society may place less emphasis on belonging, but for individual psychological health, the need remains paramount.

Companies must account for the effects of these human needs in product and service design, beginning with research strategy. People tend to see themselves as highly independent individuals, and rationalize their behavior based on personal views. They often overlook how the group affects their behavior. But much of behavior is actually determined by the social and emotional context. It's a fact that businesses cannot undervalue.

Organizations that research an audience as a data set of autonomous individuals—unaffected by the unseen pull of social needs—will have an incomplete and inaccurate view of how and why their audience acts. It's acceptable to study the individual; it's important to recognize that American culture often places the development of individual needs and priorities above any group-related needs such as belonging. But let's not throw the baby out with the bath water. The emotional truth is that we all still yearn for a sense of belonging. Our behavior is constantly altered by our connections. Businesses that cater to and help us meet the need to belong will uncover previously unexplored opportunities.

The opportunities, if capitalized on, can help consumers avert the distress of feeling alienated.

Psychologists Roy F. Baumeister and Mark R. Leary spent much of their careers studying the effects of belonging. "A lack of belongingness should constitute severe deprivation and cause a variety of ill effects,"[4] they write. Ill effects include depression, low self-esteem, anti-social behavior, suicide, and poor health habits.

We can imagine that if a culture fails to satisfy one's yearning to belong and be accepted by a coveted group, commerce no doubt suffers as well.

We'll discuss the need for belonging in a marketplace context in several different ways, focusing on how people are driven by this need and how companies can analyze and satisfy it.

Belonging and the Book-Clubber: Bringing Groups Together

> "What's great about this country is that America started the tradition where the richest consumers buy essentially the same things as the poorest. You can be watching TV and see Coca-Cola, and you know that the President drinks Coke, Liz Taylor drinks Coke, and just think, you can drink Coke, too. A Coke is a Coke and no amount of money can get you a better Coke than the one the bum on the corner is drinking. All the Cokes are the same and all the Cokes are good. Liz Taylor knows it, the President knows it, the bum knows it, and you know it."
>
> —Andy Warhol[5]

Most brands no longer have this luxury. Warhol understood that when a brand becomes a cultural symbol, it transcends commoditization. Again, this is the man who made a fortune with paintings of Campbell soup cans. Suddenly it's no longer just a soda, but a signifier of something more: Santa's Coca-Cola red suit, capitalism, and even America. Of course, this idea runs counter to pure free-market philosophy: the more options the better. There are hundreds of alternative soda options, and Pepsi, Sprite, and Mountain Dew are close seconds, but they fail to reach the saturation and cultural dominance to emerge as #1. Coke as an American ambassador crosses national boundaries, unifying everyone under the label the "Coke generation."

Coca-Cola has inundated our lives, from childhood birthday parties to our first legal Jack-and-Coke. The brand not only connects us to a global brethren, but it reestablishes connections to past experiences.

When we purchase Coca-Cola, we aren't consciously associating Coca-Cola with America or capitalism per se, and yet for many, somehow, we feel it's part of our American upbringing—and our American future. Memories of Coca-Cola span our lifetimes, and our purchase ensures more memories.

But, as Warhol would agree, few companies are able to achieve this level of emotional impact. How do other products and services satisfy this deep need to belong? We'll explore several ways in the following pages, but first, a general rule of thumb: it takes creativity and a strong understanding of how and why an audience connects to their social world.

*   *   *

JOHN SHORS SPENT FIVE YEARS laboring over his first novel, *Beneath a Marble Sky*. It's a story of a forbidden romance behind the creation of the Taj Mahal, told from the perspective of an Indian princess. It was published to good reviews but very low sales numbers. Shors, a former public relations professional and journalist, took a highly unorthodox step to drive readership. He went clubbing—book clubbing.

Writers who are fortunate enough to be published have it tough. About 1 percent of books account for 80 percent of sales. In other words, you probably have better odds landing a role on a reality television series about surviving in Bora Bora than hitting a best-seller list. Publishers naturally focus their resources on what's selling, perhaps leaving many "great American novels" collecting dust, read only by their creators' closest circles and supporters. Shors's novel was given a chance, but the window was closing on that coveted 1 percent benchmark.

After accepting friends' requests to discuss his novel for their book clubs, Shors saw his opening. He started calling on and visiting book clubs. Word spread, and the novel was eventually picked up by Penguin books for a paperback edition. On the inside flap, Shors encouraged his readers to invite him to any and all book clubs. True to his word, through a combination of in-person and teleconferences, he was soon meeting with about three book clubs a week. It may not seem like the trajectory of a best seller, but it ended up creating a groundswell in the crowded publishing world.

He knew that literature, like movies, television, and sports, is best enjoyed when you have someone to *share it* with. Book clubs weren't new, but the idea of a first-time novelist traveling the country and attending any book club that requested him was certainly unprecedented.

"I'm just trying to do my tiny small part to make reading fun again, on a group level. And this is what I can do to do that, so I'm trying," Shors told Columbia Broadcasting System (CBS) news during his tour, which was mostly self-funded.

And by the way, it also landed him a lucrative multi-novel deal.

Reading is by definition a solitary activity. But sharing, critiquing, and discussing literature is very much a social endeavor. The featured book at a book club often takes a back seat to the social gathering. People join book clubs not just to share an opinion, but even more important, to share some time together. The club is merely a means to facilitate connection. But there still has to be a book in order for there to be a book club. The picks usually come from Oprah Winfrey or the *New York Times* best-seller list, which speaks to the cleverness of Shor's strategy. He reversed the game by recognizing the power of belonging. His success was fueled not by elite reviews and aggressive mass marketing, but by a recognition that many Americans read to connect, as well as to entertain.

During his tour, one thousand copies of *Beneath a Marble Sky* were sold a week! Shors understood the power of groups on commerce. The novel reached thousands of readers who otherwise never would have laid eyes on it.

Today, there's a marketing obsession with using social media as a platform for understanding consumers and generating brand awareness. For instance, the Facebook page for Skittles candy generated hundreds of thousands of hits by burying a man in Skittles live on web cam for every new person who "liked" their page. That's great free publicity. But don't be fooled; there's a difference between generating "likes" on Facebook and turning those people who "like" you into a meaningful community.

To satisfy belonging, if that's a company's goal, audiences must be moved beyond the "like" button. The product or service must facilitate our yearning to feel a part of a valued group. Further, they must utilize those emotion-based insights to craft strategies that truly strengthen those groups by bringing people together in the flesh or through real dialog.

WWMRGD? (What would my reference group do?)

In the late 1960s, Californians Doris Fisher and her husband, Don, were preparing to open a store with "a simple idea: to make it easier to find a pair of jeans."[6] Mass retailers at the time typically sold jeans that took a one-size, one-style-fits-all approach. However, a nice-fitting, casual pair of blue jeans was hard to come by if the shopper couldn't afford a boutique label. What if a retail store allowed customers to actually try on different styles and sizes until they were satisfied? It was an idea that hit home with a distinct segment of the nation's young adults and adolescents, who were looking to distinguish themselves from older generations.

Doris named the store "The Gap," a direct play on the growing recognition of the generation gap emerging between the baby boomers and their parents at the time. The brand became a symbol proclaiming that people with divergent lifestyles and self-concepts needed different market experiences.

In order to belong to a "cool" group, members inherently reference cool according to what they deem not cool. *I belong with this group— not those people.*"

When we satisfy the need to belong, our perspectives and individual decisions change according to the group with which we affiliate. This phenomenon is connected to human developmental stages. The groups we belong to change as we evolve through life. "Being cool" among one's peers is far more important to a teenager than to seniors. Connecting and maintaining influence among work colleagues is important for any worker to achieve their career goals. The middle-aged and elderly commonly focus on making family, faith, or their larger community their bedrock of belonging while they pursue other personal interests. New parents or households with lots of children may put all other groups aside for their children.

We unconsciously make a mental map of which groups are important to us and for what reasons. In different purchasing situations, one group's consensus or opinion can affect what we buy, whereas a different group has little effect on the decision at hand.

For decades, consumer psychologists have labeled these "reference" groups.

We have primary and secondary reference groups. *Primary reference groups* are our closest connections: family, best friends, close business colleagues. Even the demarcation lines between primary groups breed conflict. A teenager considering a tattoo on her upper arm may be torn between the disapproval of her father and her need to express herself to her social circle. *Secondary reference* groups have a narrower influence. Friends in one's golf league might be an anchor for which brand of putter the golfer switches to next, but may not be relied upon to guide decisions on matters away from the clubhouse.

Reference groups are used for two reasons: informational and identification functions. First, reference groups establish standards that the individual follows or aspires to. There probably aren't too many upper-middle-class corporate employees without smartphones these days. When an individual is deciding on a new phone, the group standard gravitates toward the high-tech, application-rich options, and that collective norm influences the individual's decision. We also rely on reference groups for their specific expertise in product areas as well. A hunter, for example, will reference his purchasing decisions on clothing and gear or tattoo based on the group's consensus.

Second, as we touched on in chapter 2, the groups to which we belong often become a meaningful part of our individual identity. A Christian may proudly wear her crucifix necklace wherever she goes as a symbol of her faith. A Harley Davidson fanatic wears her brand's gear to signify that she belongs to an exclusive group.

Similarly, we all have reference groups that help us decide *who we don't want to be*. We're competitive beings, and frequently make decisions that are more about distancing ourselves from unfavorable groups than affirming ourselves wholeheartedly to a favorable group.

All in the Family: Belonging and Facilitating Close Emotional Ties

The most poignant centers of belonging lie with our closest social circles and families. To really feel you belong somewhere, you need near unconditional love or intimate bonds with a core group of friends.

One salient lesson for businesses on the topic of belonging come not from a social scientist or research data, but in a comment from a high school student responding to an entry on the class blog. The student said:

> "For the people who can be in a hundred clubs and feel that they belong to each, more power to you! But...it just doesn't seem possible to spread yourself that thin and still feel that you belong."[7]

If we belong to too many groups, do we really belong to anything at all? We have limited mental capacity and limited time. So if we're emotionally economical, we focus on belonging to the groups that are most important to us and provide the most meaning.

The lesson for business strategists: don't expect to satisfy your audience's need to belong by trying to be the center of a community itself. Only a few brands can do this (e.g., John Deere, Harley-Davidson, Apple, Starbucks, etc.). Businesses can facilitate an individual's need for close connections, but they cannot supplant them. Like Shors, focus instead on how a brand, product, or service can serve to strengthen and create connections between members. At every level of business strategy, there's potential for this facilitation to exist. Here are a few examples of how this can be accomplished.

Be the Right Place

This smacks of being obvious, but remarkably, many businesses undervalue the role that atmosphere plays in a group's satisfaction. Movie theaters started buying rights to classic children's movies, showing them without charge in the late morning hours, and watched as mothers and caretakers bussed in toddlers.

Independent coffee shops in New York City understandably started bucking customers who crowded tables and cozy chairs with laptops and headphones all day, deciding to make their shops less intimidating to patrons who wanted to meet and relax with friends by banning laptops in their stores. Shopping malls began selling space to furniture retailers alongside women's clothing boutiques so their boyfriends and husbands would be more inclined to shop. *Go ahead honey, I'll just sit here in the leather massage chair.*

People want to be together. Retailers that live and die on customers attending a physical space must ask: does my space cater not just to the primary customer, but to the people they'll be there with?

Cater Services to the Group

Cell phones may be the twenty-first century's most important vehicle for connection. Their mass adoption has caused academics and consumer psychologists to scramble to examine how in the present and in the future people integrate cell phones into their daily lives. High-tech networks and the advent of smartphones have expanded the functions of the device as a tool of social networking—the ability to ceaselessly stay in touch with every tedious movement of family and friends. Sociologist Kenneth Gergen coined the term "absent presence" to describe relationships in the cell-phone era.[8] Absent presence means that even though we may not be physically near our closest friends and family, their presence is usually less than two presses of a button away. T-Mobile cleverly applied this dynamic in the pre-smartphone days with their My Five campaign. By signing a contract with T-Mobile, the customer could choose five contacts for which no minutes or fees would be charged. Our firm pioneered similar work for AT&T's Friends and Family plan. These simple services harness our need to be virtually tethered to our loved ones, which is perhaps why "family plans" dominated cell-phone marketing before the smartphone era besieged the airwaves.

Similarly, businesses targeting young children and adolescents must cater to their media gatekeepers—parents. One of our clients, Radio Disney, a traditional-format radio station targeting tweens, thrives because they successfully built a community of young listeners (who call into the station, participate in contests, interact with each other, and are "cool"). But Radio Disney works because the listeners' moms and dads are concretely assured that the radio platform was inoculated from the violent, sexualized content of the bulk of "teen" radio shows, with lyrics "sanitized" and altered for the ears of their younger audience.

Observe the Group

How can a commonplace grocery store item strengthen the bonds of a family? An example from the excellent book *Made to Stick*,[9] by Chip and Dan Heath, illustrates how product positioning can unintentionally interfere with the fulfillment of the need. They tell the story of Hamburger Helper's brand manager at General Mills. "When she started she was given three huge binders full of sales and volume data, ad briefs, and marketing surveys," said Dan Heath. "The data was too abstract to provide much intuition." Instead, she launched an ambitious ethnographic research project that followed working mothers through their evening routines. Family dinners were important to these women. But time was also a valuable commodity. Cooking fresh meals was not always an option. The researchers quickly realized that these women were so busy that Hamburger Helper's 28 flavor options were overwhelming. The moms needed something efficient, something that was consistent, good tasting, recognizable to the kids, and available everywhere. There's truth to Danish philosopher Søren Kierkegaard's famous pronouncement: "Anxiety is the dizziness of freedom." Too many flavors actually compromised family time.

The observational research led Hamburger Helper to cut back the options. It made shopping easier. It was simpler for moms to find flavors kids would like. Production costs went down. And it provided a key ingredient to strong families: dinner time.

The success of grocery stores like Trader Joe's capitalizes on similar psychology. Some people don't want to wade through a 200,000-square-foot megamart with three dozen brands of frozen pizza. They want quality products that are easy to prepare and allow more time for the real reason families eat together: growing closer together or connecting as a family.

Belonging to Causes and Movements

Belonging to a community or larger group is different from our bonds with family and friends. The most powerful forms of community are sometimes comprised of strangers unified by a shared thread of ideas and purpose.

Nonprofit or advocacy communities rally people to a cause and high-minded goals in ways that corporations are rarely able to (although some do especially well via cause marketing). They capitalize on the power of inclusion.

We stand for a cause, but don't have the funds to effectively lobby. Please, be a part of our community. Please, lend your dollars to keep our lights running and the fight continuing.

If audiences don't donate, the nonprofit ceases to exist.

These appeals to our need for community by charity groups can be highly effective. We like to feel that our money is going to a positive cause that we believe in and support. Additionally, the extrinsic benefits (tax deductions), the giveaways—gifts and auction prizes—further enhance our feeling of reward. We give and receive equally. But mostly, charity helps us feel like we're being benevolent, generous, going beyond self-interest to be part of something larger than ourselves. We feel connected to the community and the world. We belong to something that in our hearts and minds stands for good.

For nonprofits, harnessing this ideal of belonging can make or break their balance sheets. And sometimes the idea they stand for and the objectives they work for die with it. After the recent financial collapse, hundreds of 501c nonprofits shut their doors. Major donors that had propped up personal charities of choice could no longer fit such generosity into their budgets. As people saved more during this period of extreme uncertainty, charities suffered.

National Public Radio (NPR) craftily develops campaigns casting listeners who donate as members of their *community* ("member-supported" is the near-constant phrase), inducing guilt in avid listeners who don't donate. "Stop freeloading" is their not-so-subtle message. For two weeks every six months, programming is dedicated to driving home this message. Individual donors sign up to have celebrity hosts like *This American Life*'s Ira Glass call their nondonating friends to playfully shame them into paying up. Local stations talk about the value of their community presence, their partnerships with other community groups. People donate to support the idea of public radio itself. No matter the size of their donation, they belong to a greater community of like-minded individuals. Local stations subscribe to nationally produced shows, and must raise their own funds to pay for the fees to air them. Some stations put a face to the otherwise faceless medium by organizing events and station meet-and-greets, where fellow donors can meet and discuss the station programming with its employees.

This sentiment can just as easily fuel for-profit success, as well. Greenheart Chicago, a gift shop that sells only sustainably produced, fair-trade international products, hosts weekly events, bringing residents of Chicago's upper-middle-class neighborhood Wicker Park together to discuss sustainability and third-world development.

For the consumer, not-for-profit marketing is really all about belonging and self-expression. It's self-expression in that the decision for the consumer often becomes a question: "What does it say about me if I don't choose to buy the product that donates 5 cents to breast cancer research?" Consumers are more and more interested in being socially responsible, and understandably they seek to reward companies with similar values.

The idea of cause marketing is a classic win-win-win. A win for the consumer who believes his or her purchase can help benefit the world in some cases. A win for the nonprofits that benefit from corporate partnerships. And a win for the business's bottom line. A compilation of statistics from Changing Our World, Inc., a philanthropy organization, shows that the public relations benefits of "doing good" pay off handsomly:[10]

*Coca-Cola: "In 1997, Coca-Cola donated 15 cents to Mothers Against Drunk Driving for every case of Coca-Cola bought during a 6-week promotion in more than four hundred Wal-Mart stores. Coke sales in these stores increased 490% during the promotion."

*Bayer Aspirin: "Bayer Aspirin partnered with the American Stroke Association (ASA) to create the American Stroke Challenge, an effort designed to raise money for the ASA and educate the public about strokes. During the May 2000 Challenge, Bayer sales increased 9% over the same month the previous year."

*American Express: "In 1983, after American Express pledged to donate a penny to the restoration of the Statue of Liberty for every transaction made by its cardholders, use of American Express cards increased by 28% and new users increased by 17%."

What's more, the report found that given the choice, consumers are highly inclined to vote with their pocketbooks:

*"76% of American consumers surveyed have contributed money or volunteered in at least one cause-related marketing campaign."

*"60% of consumers surveyed planned to buy a product during the 2004 holiday season of which a portion of the purchase price would be donated to a relevant cause."

*"77% of women and 64% of men considered a company's reputation for supporting causes when purchasing gifts during the 2003 holiday season."

*"48% of American and British consumers surveyed reported that, in the past, they had been motivated by a cause-related marketing campaign to change brands, use a product more, try new products, or get information about new products."

*"In a survey of twelve thousand European consumers, 20 percent said they would pay more for a product if it were affiliated with a good cause."

Strength in Numbers: Belonging and Tribalism

Q. Where's the site of America's largest family reunion?

A. Ann Arbor, Michigan. The Big House. Football stadium of the University of Michigan Wolverines.

On a handful of Saturday afternoons every fall, 112,000 people pack "The Big House," America's largest stadium (not including National Association for Stock Car Auto Racing [NASCAR] racetracks), singing the fight song in unison after every point scored. Professional and collegiate sports represent America's most financially profitable form of belonging. Humans can be viciously competitive, and will pay—via tickets, cable subscriptions, and retail merchandise—to align themselves with their chosen team. Athletes train and practice because they know the other teams will handily defeat them otherwise. Politicians consistently leverage the dangers of their opponents to foster affiliation to their own platform.

Belonging is about defining *who you are not*, just as much as it is defining who you are. *Bob is liberal, and proudly not a conservative. Christine is a Texas Longhorn and proudly not an Oklahoma Sooner. Kathy works for Oracle, and seems to find many things wrong with how IBM does business. Todd finds his school's drama department stuck-up and cultish, while the debate team, which he is captain of, is welcoming to all. Becca rides a Harley, and can't understand why anyone would ride a Yamaha crotch rocket.*

These divisions exist anytime and anywhere there is an "us" and a "them." Competition brings out the best and the worst in us. It can lead us to stronger motivation and clearer thinking, great accomplishments and innovations, and can help us develop leadership skills. On the other hand, competition can also result in foolish disputes, degradation of the competitor, xenophobia, or arbitrary irrational refutations of fact. Men are more susceptible to outright volatile competition, but women are equally susceptible to biases that divide groups.

A classic social psychology experiment conducted in the 1950s explored the phenomenon of "in- versus out-group" dynamics. Muzafer Sherif, widely considered one of the fathers of social psychology, took two groups of 11- to 12-year-old boys on a three-week summer-camp experience at Robber's Cave State Park in Oklahoma.

The participants in both groups—11 boys per group—were white, middle class, and Protestant, and had comparable athletic and camping abilities. The participants were as homogenous as middle-school kids get. Each group had a different cabin on the two-hundred-acre Boy Scout campground. Their respective cabins were on opposite sides of the camp. Each group did not know of the other's existence, and for the first week of the experiment lived without adult supervision. As predicted, the boys in each group developed a group structure, complete with roles, hierarchies, and even group names: the Eagles and the Rattlers. The boys accepted each other and cooperated to achieve their goals.

It was inevitable that the two groups would soon notice the existence of one another. Immediately, they began working toward reinforcing the superiority of their own group internally. They became insistent that the other group was treating the campgrounds with disrespect. Both groups asked the researchers to set up competitive activities with the other group. Keep in mind, they hadn't even met each other yet!

During the second week, the researchers organized a team competition, with the winning group receiving medals and pocketknives for their accomplishments. The losing team would get nothing. The battle lines were drawn, and when the two sides met for the first time in the camp mess hall, things got a bit ugly.

"There was considerable name-calling, razzing back and forth, and singing of derogatory songs by each group in turn. Before supper that evening, some Eagles expressed a desire not to eat with the Rattlers."[11]

The second week featured many open hostilities: cabin raids, threats to burn the opposition's team flag. In order to prevent the scenario from eroding into a replay of the Lord of the Flies, Sherif and the researchers constructed situations in the third week that would unite the two groups. Only by intervening so that both groups had to work together to achieve the common goal (e.g., collaborating to fix the camp's water supply, raising money to see a movie) did the researchers break down the divisions. Given the option, the boys agreed they should all take one bus home, and on the road, one group pooled their resources to buy milkshakes for the boys in the other group.

In three weeks, Sherif created among the boys: a) the natural need to form alliances and bonds when more than two people are assembled, b) a resulting tribalism when a group was introduced to a competing group, and c) a simple erasure of the divisions once one group got to know the other through shared experience.[12]

We're tribalistic by nature, but when distinctions between groups begin to blur, the nastiness can swiftly be eradicated.

But it's a mistake to discount the benefits of friendly group competition. For one, it's a core vehicle for satisfying the human need to belong. It's often difficult to develop skills if there's no one pushing an individual to be better. Without competition, complacency becomes the norm, and progress is stifled. It's true in sports. It's true in industry. Companies accentuate the in-group, out-group dynamic, because it enhances a sense of consumers belonging.

Harley-Davidson is a club for a particular type of person. It's a close-knit community rallying around a single brand that offers deep meaning to the individuals making up this exclusive group. They know who they are, and against the dark contrast of who they are not (Honda, Ural, Yamaha bike riders), they confirm their identity. Belonging-based branding and marketing can be seen across a wide variety of products and target consumers. For example, marketing for the hugely successful film adaptation of the *Twilight Saga* generated an immense amount of buzz by asking its teenage-girl fan base to choose which male suitor they supported for Bella, the heroine. Were they on Team Edward (the laconic vampire) or Team Jacob (the buff werewolf.)

Our competitive nature drives the logic surrounding a lot of beer and car advertising dominating the airwaves. Drive a Ford, because we *are the American Company.* Meanwhile, Chevy is simultaneously laying claim to the patriotic territory. While Bud Light attempts to prove its coolness to domestic beer drinkers, Miller Lite responds with a campaign casting non-Miller beer drinkers as non-manly.

Through it all, we see the familiar incantation: Join US because we're not THEM.

Fieldwork

Reaching the Out-Group through Empathy

In society, there are always groups of people who don't belong. These are the outcasts, the pariahs, the people on the fringe. In psychological terms, they are known as "out-groups." As entrepreneurs in the United States and around the world have discovered, great products and businesses can be developed when business asks itself: how can we help those who don't belong to belong?

In India, for example, cars were once owned exclusively by the affluent. Most people did not have the kind of income that could make a car affordable to them. As a result, the poor and less privileged in India traveled on bicycles and motor scooters. They did not belong to the class of Indian society that could afford a car.

All that changed when Ratan Tata, the chairman of India's leading car manufacturer, the Tata Group, had a moment of empathy. During a downpour, he observed an entire Indian family hanging soaking wet onto a motor scooter, the only mode of transportation for the family. As Clayton Christensen et al. write in *The Innovator's DNA*, Tata knew that the family would never be able to own a car, at least, not the traditional car as manufactured by his company. So Tata, the memory of that family lingering in his mind, decided to create a revolutionary new car. It would be affordable—the Tata Nano was eventually sold for just $2,200—but it would also be a complete car. Tata didn't intend to put a chassis on a moped and call it a car. By empathizing with a group that was outside the margins of the car industry, Tata created an immensely successful product. Targeting the disenfranchised can make for effective business practices.

The banking industry was also revolutionized by an entrepreneur who reached out to a group previously ostracized by the banking community. The story of Muhammad Yunus, founder of the Grameen Bank, and creator of an entire new industry, micro-lending, is well known. In the mid-1970s, Yunus was a professor in southern Bangladesh teaching students the theories of economics. However, as famine took over the country and starving men, women, and children from the countryside began to pour into the cities, the economic theories Yunus taught seemed to him woefully inadequate. He went to the villagers and started talking to the poor, looking for an economic solution to their problems. He discovered that lending small sums of money to poor craftspeople, with nothing but trust as collateral, could have a huge economic impact on their lives.

Reaching out through empathy to the groups who don't belong to the mainstream is not just a story reserved for developing countries. In the United States, designers used to create fashions for large-sized women that were more matronly than fashionable. All it took was for a little empathy from Italian clothes manufacturer Max Mara to recognize (what should have been obvious) that plus-sized women were just as interested in being fashionable as slenderer women. Max Mara launched Marina Rinaldi, a plus-sized division that offered fashionable clothes made from cashmere, silk, and leather in sophisticated colors, such as gray and black. "Some of its new customers remember when large-size clothing meant pastel polyester pants suits and tent-like dresses with flounces," the *New York Times* wrote in a feature on the company. "Marina Rinaldi was in the vanguard of companies that brought fashion to the category."[13]

Society reinforces, via mass-media messages, organizational culture, and community values, who belongs in society and who doesn't. Commercial communication can play a very real role in shaping the cultural climate of tolerance. Acceptance of out-groups in the media and on the Web can remove stigmas and create a climate of acceptance. Businesses too often underestimate and cut themselves off from the humanness—the thoughts, needs, and feelings—of a potential audience. Empathy can easily be the first victim of a faceless, individualistic, digital world. Businesses, by making simple changes to the way they communicate and conduct research, can lift the veil and discover new ways of reaching distant groups.

This fieldwork section discusses how in-depth psychological interviews and psychoethnographic research can uncover the dynamics of belonging and not belonging. It deals with an issue facing one of the most marginalized groups in society in recent times: gay men living with human immunodeficiency virus/acquired immune deficiency syndrome (HIV/AIDS).

Erasing the Stigma

In 2005, our firm conducted research on the primary audience for a ground breaking HIV treatment: Altripla. Using Altripla, developed by Gilead Science and Bristol Meyers Squibb, people living with HIV (PLWHIV) could now take one pill a day for a complete treatment regimen. This was a huge scientific advancement over other treatments that required a cocktail approach, a mishmash of multiple pills and other medications taken at varied intervals. Multimedication treatments with heavy side effects only added to the stigma of living with HIV. One particular earlier treatment for PLWHIV had patients swallow a pill almost larger than a new iPod Nano. At the time, there was no way to make the pill smaller.

The functional benefits of the treatment were clear. The simpler the treatment, the easier it is to go on living. It reflects the amazing developments in HIV treatment over the past two decades. No longer is HIV the specter of the disease it was in the '80s and '90s. It's now treatable. Advanced medicine allows patients experiencing symptoms to live normal lifestyles for decades after infection. An HIV diagnosis is no longer a death sentence.

The emotional benefits go hand in hand with the treatment's simplicity. Among them was the overriding sense that because the treatment was easier, the condition itself could become less stigmatized, less threatening, less a reminder of the struggles so many PLWHIV felt as they grappled with fear and shame.

The primary market for Altripla was gay men. Gay men living with HIV were an especially marginalized out-group within the larger culture, and to a significant degree, remain so today despite less and less media attention paid to HIV/AIDS. In the '80s and early '90s HIV was generalized as a "gay man's" condition, the fault of irresponsible behavior : unsafe sex, sex with multiple partners, and/or drug use. Already a part of a fringe community, gay PLWHIV faced a solid wall to larger cultural acceptance. Their ostracization could further add to negative health decisions. Cut off by fear and shame, some gay men living with HIV coped by further neglecting their health.

Altripla was positioned to cut through the psychological barriers standing between this diverse out-group and a healthier, thriving life, but only if the maker of the drug knew how to connect with the target.

A Pyschoethnographic Approach

A common trait is found in all "us" and "them," in-group and out-group dynamics: the societal in-group (the wider population) broadly stereotypes the out-group. Diversity disappears in the wake of stereotypes. There are many smaller communities within the category of gay men living with HIV. If Altripla were to succeed, its developers and marketers had to first understand the psychodynamics of fear and shame associated with confronting treatment in each of these subgroups:

- men with high self-esteem, less fearful of disease
- men who quietly, yet confidently dealt with HIV

- men who felt excluded from society, and thus were hesitant to confront disease head-on

My colleagues and I conducted two dozen in-depth psychological and ethnographic interviews in the homes of gay men living with HIV on both coasts. Each segment was represented. The men were at different stages of living with HIV. About half had not gone through any treatment. The others were treatment experienced.

A "clinical analysis" is a natural fit for this type of market. Focus groups or quantitative surveys may reveal little of the personal, emotional issues that help companies empathize with their audience's behavior. A vulnerable, oftentimes skeptical population, like PLWHIV, will understandably simply not be as open in a group setting. Nor can much be gleaned from how emotions affect behavior through Likert-scale responses. What's more, we didn't want participants there purely for a check; those respondents usually aren't the type that would help us understand the psychology of a marginalized group. By working with local Gay, Lesbian, Bisexual, Transgender (GLBT) groups, we found men willing to let us into their lives and homes. Authenticity sums up the value of ethnography, a research strategy used in the social sciences that centers on close observation and evaluation of people's behavior in everyday settings as they experience life. By interviewing our participants in their homes, barriers quickly broke down.

Most readers are familiar with the main critique of this type of qualitative approach: the sample is too small. How can insights be generalized when only a few personal stories are taken into account? This is an understandable concern. However, to some extent it is more a managerial fear of not seeing hard data than it is an understanding of how the clinical lens works:

- A clinical psychologist may not uncover insights in the quantitative realm, but his or her methodologies are rooted in scientific theories that stand the test of clinical research. If there were a simple, affordable, accurate way to quantify the unconscious, psychological underpinnings of behavior, there'd be no need for focus groups or interviews at all. The expertise of the clinical psychologist is no different from the reasoning behind seeking any expert advice. Faced with a persistent, painful cough, we don't diagnose ourselves, but rather, we go to our physician.

- The goal of the Altripla study was to identify emotional attitudes representative of a large and diverse group.
- Clinical insights are extrapolated to develop messages and strategies for wider audiences. Once crafted, the study becomes valuable in determining whether the message holds water by showing it to a wider sample.

Our interviews mostly took place in participants' homes. When openness and honesty are paramount, it is critical that participants feel comfortable in the environment in which they're speaking and that they trust those to whom they are speaking. This is crucial when researching out-groups. PLWHIV are understandably skeptical of anything that remotely signals manipulation or exploitation, especially in this case, where they didn't know how the research would be used. However, our participants didn't want to feel like curiosities studied under a clinical microscope. They wanted to be heard and understood, and to contribute to research that they hoped would help their community. And who can blame them?

One man was frustrated with society's persistent misrepresentation of PLWHIV. "When people think of HIV, they think of Tom Hanks with lesions all over his body—taking pills, getting pneumonia, and dropping dead," he said, referencing the Oscar-winning '90s film *Philadelphia*. "I wish this old-school thinking would be replaced by a new school of thinking."

This "old-school thinking" demoralized many of the men. "HIV is worse than cancer. If you have cancer, people sympathize with you, but HIV is a stigma," said a participant. Several men expressed the sentiment that educating friends, family, and acquaintances, and overcoming the stigma was like "coming out all over again." Another said that feeling ostracized was "more overwhelming than the disease itself."

Their statements cannot be underscored enough. The reason HIV is perceived as dangerous relative to other treatable diseases may have more to do with the psychological effects of despair and stigmatization than the effects of HIV itself.

Faced with this intense emotional duress, gay men living with HIV are confronted with the choice to either retreat or fight. The interviews revealed that if a treatment approach along with education helped them overcome the psychological impediments, living with HIV would be a lot less stressful.

Many of the men said they hoped to thrive in the face of their diagnosis, and were mentally at ease with treatment or someday going on treatment. They were a prime audience for Gilead and Bristol-Myers Squibb for obvious reasons: this segment was a prime focus. They were more confident and vocal; they were potential ambassadors for the new drug within their community. Our analysis of each interview revealed that this classification was somewhat inaccurate. For both those men who were already in treatment or had yet to go on medication (some doctors recommend that their patients hold off going on medication until symptoms reached certain levels), these confident, thriving PLWHIV displayed the same traumatic feelings of fear and shame as their emotionally distraught and alienated peers. In some, their conscious, positive attitudes were a mask for harmful repressed feelings. Through projective exercises—card sorts, imagery analysis, sensory exercises, and story telling—we saw variations of the traits listed in the table below in almost all of the men with whom we spoke. The strong emotions of fear and shame are critical barriers to feeling like one belongs to the wider culture—a culture that lives healthy lifestyles, a normalized life. When weighed down by these thoughts and feelings, self-worth and positive health decisions can easily fall victim to paralysis and depression.

Psychodynamics of Shame

Table 7.2 Psychodynamics of Shame

Conscious Feelings	Subconscious Feelings
• Hide Emotions	• Self-blame
• Have strong desire to be accepted	• Self-hatred
• Assume they are being judged/scorned	• Inferiority
• Feel like a social outcast	• Defective
	• Experience of a diminished world

Psychodynamics of Fear

When we asked our interviewees to respond to customized imagery we had developed, they continually chose two pictures to represent their experience of diagnosis and the painful ordeal of treatment. Those afraid of treatment and the stigma associated with treatment felt trapped, imprisoned, isolated. Going on treatment was seen not as liberation from their cells, but rather it viscerally reinforced their confinement. It became apparent that medication was not a weapon against freedom. Instead, it symbolized impending fatality and vulnerability.

So how did the makers of Altripla confront these issues? How did they ensure that their treatment was antithetical to feelings of pain and marginalization?

For starters, BMS and Gilead had to target education campaigns toward doctors and patients. The fears of hospitals and waiting rooms were metaphors for their bodily demise. The relationship with their doctor could make or break their ability to cope and overcome the stigma. If Altripla is to be successful, doctors must be aware of the psychodynamics of fear and shame. The functional benefits of Altripla's simplified treatment had to be merged with the far more resonant emotional benefits—living without shame, joining the greater community, making treatment less traumatic, less a metaphor for their marginalization.

To optimize all marketing and advertising, Altripla had to avoid any tone, message, or image that might symbolize ostracization. Any missteps in communicating with this psychologically vulnerable group would not only hurt Gilead and BMS's bottom line, but further alienate

Table 7.3 Psychodynamics of Fear

Conscious Feelings	*Subconscious Feelings*
• Impending Death	• Anger, rage
• Lack of trust in relationships	• Damnation
• Isolation	• Abandonment
	• Persecution
	• Paranoia

their audience. The messaging and imagery for the resulting campaigns reflected the liberation the treatment could bring rather than the qualities of the disease.

Approved in 2006, Altripla is now the preferred medication option for treatment-naïve patients in U.S. Department of Health and Human Services guidelines. The functional ease of the once-daily treatment and the lower number of insurance copays due to the low number of medications needed are two reasons for its success.

But the related psychological and emotional benefits further help patients overcome decades-long stigma. This could not be done without the company's empathizing with the out-group.

Chapter 7 Summary: How Business Can Empathize with Customers' Need to <u>Belong</u>

Affiliation to groups of all kinds, from families to cultures, gives people a sense of place and identity, a source of comfort, and a venue for self-expression. At the same time, belonging clashes with the core needs on the individuality side of the continuum, such as self-expression. This conflict presents a challenge for companies seeking to empathize with customers: their customers all too often will explain their behaviors in terms of personal reasons without taking into account the impact of groups on their decisions. Yet there are still many opportunities for business to cater to the need to belong.

Key Business Success Factors

Below are a few key steps businesses can take to effectively respond to consumers' need to belong:

Suggested Follow-Up Steps

1. **Help your customers make or enhance their connections with their reference groups.** Companies might help teenagers to fit in with groups of their peers, career workers to connect with colleagues, and senior customers to interact with groups related to

their personal interests. To successfully help your customers with their reference groups:

a. **Observe the reference group.** Don't take market-research shortcuts or make assumptions about the needs and wants of the reference group. Depend more on individualized and personalized qualitative research than demographics or statistics. Hamburger Helper discovered that when cooking for the family, working mothers didn't need or want 28 different flavors from which to choose. Being able to cook quick, good meals that gave these busy mothers more time for their families—the most important group to which they belonged—was their primary goal.

b. **Become the group's standards. In other words, WWMRGD (What would my reference group do?)** If high-powered career people use iPads and other sophisticated communication tools, customers who want to emulate them will also buy these sophisticated communication tools. Use marketing to frame your product as the "preferred choice" of the targeted reference group.

c. **Cater services to the group.** Design products that connect individuals. Before the smartphone, cell phone companies created "family and friends" programs of unlimited minutes that facilitated the connection among the most important reference groups of their customers.

d. **Use social media to its full potential.** Company Facebook pages and Twitter accounts keep customers connected to the company and to each other.

e. **Create opportunities for consumers to belong to your sponsored causes.** People are often brought together by a common cause. Customers recognize and appreciate the efforts of a company that enables this facet of belonging through its philanthropic programs. Extensive research over time has proven that companies can "do well by doing good."

f. **Be the right place.** Create opportunities for groups to connect by creating a gathering place. Some coffee shops ban laptops to welcome friends looking for a place to meet. Cater your space to anyone who might have a reason to gather there.

2. **Don't try to be the group to which consumers belong. Facilitate their membership in already existing groups.** A few brands— Harley-Davidson, for example, or home-based sales businesses such as Tupperware or Silpada—can actually represent the center of the community. In most cases, however, the goal is to facilitate and strengthen the connections to other members of the customers' reference groups. Don't start a Widget Club. No one will join.

CHAPTER 8

The Need for Care

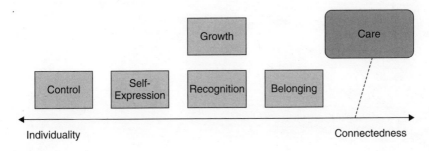

Figure 8.1   The Care Need

CHAPTER 8

The Need for Care

Marcus was never fatalistic before his injury. The T-bone collision at the stoplight was out of his control. He was fortunate that neither he nor anyone else was killed. In the weeks after the car accident, his stalwart motivation to resume life as normal didn't wane. He believed in the virtue of perseverance, the notion that despite life's randomness, there was always a way out of turmoil. The surgeries for his injuries were trouble free, and the early stages of rehab were a breeze.

But his outlook changed when the doctor flatly said his right shoulder and leg were shot, that he'd never again be able to take on the demands of his welding job at the aluminum plant. When the insurance compensation hit bottom and returning to his job was no longer an option, Marcus's career, his life as he knew it, was over. The only skilled work he knew—work that had helped him secure a solid middle-class footing—was now unobtainable.

The "way out" was now at the other end of a labyrinth.

Marcus was approaching his fortieth birthday. He had never married or had any children, and shortly before the injury had broken off a long-term relationship. His father, whom he considered his best friend, had died several years earlier. His mother lived in a retirement home several hours outside of town. Since the start of his career, their relationship had consisted purely of holiday visits and the perfunctory monthly phone call. His friends were there for him as best they could be, but while they worked and carried on their lives, Marcus grew angry, resentful, and eventually, depressed. Shortly after the accident, a friend recommended he look into a management position at the plant. "You know the place better than any one of those MBA-toting office guys," he said. "Go for it."

"That's the problem," Marcus replied. "I'd still need the degree."

"So what's holding you back?"

Marcus dismissed the idea. Any education past high school and vocational training had always been an exotic, and undesirable, concept. He applied for less-demanding warehouse jobs, as well as some minimum-wage service positions. But every time he shook a hiring manager's hand, his depleted attitude sent out warning flares: *this guy will quit or will have to be fired.* He sank further into despairing resignation. As is the difficult case with so many long-term unemployed Americans, for every month they spend not working, that's more time not developing new skills, more reason for employers to hire people with fresh experience. It's an economic sinkhole for workers in this position. Some of the most inspiring, optimistic out-of-work Americans in the current economic crisis take their free-time to volunteer and give back, but for Marcus, lingering depression suffocated his motivation to do much of anything.

Eight months after his accident, Marcus received a phone call from his elderly mother. It wasn't like her to call him. She usually waited patiently for *her* phone to ring. "Is everything OK?" he implored. "Oh, everything's fine with me," she said, "but I'm worried about you. We need to talk...I want you to come out here as soon as you can." She spoke in a tone that Marcus hadn't heard since he was a little boy, caring but stern, leaving no room for refusal. He didn't question her directive. He fueled up his truck and left town that afternoon.

Marcus opened the door to her apartment. Wordless, his mother looked at him with an unflinching, earnest expression. She kissed him on the cheek, and for a very long minute, left her hand resting on his right shoulder, still stiff from the surgery.

"Hi, Mom," he said. They sat on her couch over tea, and remained there well into the evening as his mother listened to him, reassured him, comforted and cared for him, conveying that he was capable of moving forward.

The next day, without a second thought, Marcus joined a support group and dipped into his savings for a series of private counseling sessions.

And within two months, he was accepted to his community college, received a student loan, and set his eyes back on the plant.

It may seem specious (or reminiscent of a Hallmark made-for-television special) to suggest that his mother's touch was the turning point for Marcus. It's not news that emotional support during crisis is a requisite of successful coping. But we take for granted just how important the need for care and affection is throughout life, and how subtly something like a loving touch can affect an individual's future behavior.

New experiments conducted by Jonathan Levav and Jennifer Argo suggest that the secure feelings associated with a caring touch induce adults to take perceived risks more than they otherwise would. This is especially true when the person doing the touching is a woman. According to the researchers, this is not traced to sexual arousal, but to our maternal attachments learned at infancy. Marcus could have easily remained paralyzed by his circumstance and continued to apply for low-paying, low-skill jobs. After all, taking a leap back into academia after being out of a classroom for two decades was a huge emotional and financial gamble.

For the vast majority of circumstances and people, empowerment of the self only comes with a little a love and encouragement. Self-empowerment is somewhat of an oxymoron for this reason. Even the staunchest individualist had to learn how to be independent from a caring, guiding voice at some point in her or his life. The trust and esteem that grow from the love of another can empower us to do seemingly impossible tasks or achieve lofty aspirations.

And as one classic experiment shows, care and trust encourage young humans to do literally what their developing minds deem impossible. It's called the "visual cliff test." Researchers put 6- to 12-month-old infants atop a raised platform. With their mothers standing above them, the anxious and newly mobile babies began crawling to the opposite end of the platform. Awaiting them in the middle, however, was a transparent, sturdy segment of Plexiglas. The babies, who had not yet developed a semblance of depth perception, would reach the apparent cliff, hesitate, and grip the solid surface nervously. Their first instinct was to turn back toward their mothers, with a look begging, "What should I do?" When their mothers smiled encouragingly, the infants would almost always turn again toward the cliff, and with a little trepidation, begin bravely crawling out along the glass surface, over the perceptual gorge. When the experimenters instructed the mothers to give a flat or worried expression, the infants assumed the mothers' emotional state, and would not take the risk.

Unconditional trust, bred by the experience of love and affection, allows us to step out into the void of life at all stages of personal development. Many people grow to become self-sustaining, confident individuals, but such growth does not occur without a foundation of love weighed in past experience, and walls of support propping us up throughout life.

Care can't heal all wounds, financial woes, or mental illnesses, but undoubtedly, it's difficult to progress through life and satisfy other needs without attending to this core emotional pillar.

The Science of Care

In 1876, John Wanamaker converted an abandoned railway depot in Philadelphia into one of the world's first department stores, proclaiming "When a customer enters my store, forget me. He is king." This simple philosophy formed the basis of modern advertising and marketing. Today, nearly all businesses claim to be "customer-driven" or "consumer-centric." The need for care, as explored in chapter 5, is among the most important vehicles for recognizing others. Wanamaker's hailing of potential and returning customers performed a quite innovative function: attract masses of people to a store that sells thousands of mass-produced products, and still make it about the individual's experience. The customer is king.

The most successful companies that assume this philosophy are able to market and sell their products and services in such a way that the consumer forms a meaningful relationship with the business or the brand. These relationships, like most, require an exchange of care and respect from the business to the consumer. This exchange strengthens customers' positive regard and connection to products and services and fulfills a fundamental human need for care and affection. The timeless concept of consumer care as a staple of business success risks diminishing returns if more leaders don't stop and evaluate what "care" means in the twenty-first century.

With all companies claiming to respect and care for their clients and customers, how do we parse the walk from the talk?

To answer this question, we must first trace the brief history of the science of care and affection. In short, people of all creeds and cultures knew what care entailed long before Wanamaker turned it into a marketing gold mine, but it wasn't until very recently that the subject was studied scientifically. The need for care and affection is so much a natural fact, an essential for personal success and happiness, that it's unfathomable to think that only a few decades ago scientists, including psychologists, denied and outwardly avoided the mounting evidence that supported the importance of the need to human development.

For much of the twentieth century, behaviorists dominated psychology. In this school of thought, it is believed that all learned behavior is a result of rewards and punishments. Translation: humans learn and develop the way your dog learns and develops. John Watson was the leader of the behaviorist school, and the president of the American Psychological Association. Watson was repulsed by emotions, and studied them as if their existence were a human disease to be cured. When it came to human affection, Watson issued many draconian warnings to parents. "When you are tempted to pet your child remember that mother love is a dangerous instrument," he said.[1] Coddling a child would surely produce a weak, dependent, and helpless adult, according to behaviorist logic. Watson wrote that he dreamed of baby farms where mothers never knew their child, so that they could be raised by scientific principles. Yet Watson wasn't some fringe, cultist leader. He was a figurehead of mainstream academic thinking and among the most famous and respected scientists between 1910 and 1930. Ironically, he would go on to become a prominent advertising consultant. As absurd as his views appear now, Watson's contributions to psychology are many. Behavioral psychology teaches us valuable lessons about stimulus-conditioned behavior that remain applicable today. The problem was that, as Abraham Maslow put it, there was a major disconnect between the dry science in the laboratory and the feelings and emotions coloring human experience outside the laboratory. He said: "If you try to treat your children at home in the same way you treat your animals in the lab, your wife will scratch your eyes out."[2]

And really, whose wouldn't?

So in a Watsonian view of child rearing, infants were thought to form attachments to their mothers merely because they were positively reinforced with food when breastfed. The desire for love and human connection are conditioned behaviors.

But American psychologist Harry Harlow's groundbreaking study on "The Nature of Love" changed this view forever. In his famous surrogate-mother experiment, conducted between 1957 and 1963, Harlow studied the effects of separating macaque monkeys from their mothers within a day of their birth. Harlow put the monkeys with two artificial surrogate mothers, one made of cloth and one made of wire mesh, to test the importance of the contact comfort that a mother provides. No matter which mother provided food (an attached milk bottle), the baby monkey spent nearly all of its time clinging to the cloth mother for security and support. The study demonstrated that, for infants, the need for care and comfort trumps even the need for food. For long-term psychological health, affection and physical closeness are paramount during the child's first years.

Harlow was inspired by findings in the same time period from scientist John Bowlby, who developed *attachment theory* to describe child-parent relationships. Bowlby observed what motivates infants to stay close to their caregivers, especially when threats exist in their environment. This behavior was mirrored by the fearful monkeys in Harlow's experiment, and was famously demonstrated by Konrad Lorenz and his gaggle of geese that followed him around. Many species of animals, including humans, have innate mechanisms in infancy to develop close relationships with their adult caregivers. Geese imprint on the first suitable moving stimulus that they see, and follow closely behind it while they are young. Human babies put their arms out to be lifted, smile when they see their caretakers, and cry when they feel abandoned to trigger affection from adults. Bowlby argued that all of these innate actions motivate infants to stay in close proximity to their caregivers. These behaviors are adaptive, because in ancestral environments, it was important to secure close relationships as a means of survival, especially as a child.

In the 1970s, Mary Ainsworth postulated that infants form three basic attachment styles. In longitudinal studies, she found that these attachment styles are shown to be stable throughout a child's life and into adulthood. Psychologists find that children who have insecure attachment styles tend to have difficulties forming social connections later in adulthood. The long-term impact of attachment demonstrates the full impact of care and affection. Care is a fundamental human need at an early age, as is a need for meaningful connection throughout life. Many psychologists argue that those who weren't given enough care as a child unconsciously attempt to fulfill that need in other ways throughout their adult life.

But all the latest research goes back to Harlow's controversial break from a scientific paradigm that shunned affection. As his biographer Deborah Blum claimed in the excellent book *Love at Goon Park: Harry Harlow and the Science of Affection*: "His studies still stand, like bedrock, for psychologists who believe that love matters, that social connection counts, that we are defined as individuals, in part, by our place in the community."[3]

One of Harlow's earliest graduate students was Maslow, who as we know, popularized the focus on meeting higher-order human needs.

Maintaining mutually caring relationships has been shown in countless studies to improve physical health. The benefits of healthy relatedness do not stop at happiness. Strong bonds with friends actually help us live longer. We spend so much time and money in search of the end-all-be-all solution to good health. As it turns out, John Lennon was right: all we need is love. Maintaining close, supportive ties to a group of friends throughout life appears to be among the most effective ways to live longer and happier. An Australian study of approximately fifteen hundred adults aged 70 and over tracked the difference between individuals who maintained an active social circle and those who did not. Over a ten-year period, those who maintained active friendships were 25 percent less likely to die than those who did not. Amazingly, individuals who had relationships with relatives or children, but not with friends, did not see nearly as strong an effect.[4]

The physiological benefits of care are simple. When we're around people who care about our well-being, our stress levels drop, our immune systems are more apt to stay in check, and our bodies thank us for it. A study from Sweden showed that men with close networks of friends had significantly lower blood pressure and were thus faced with a lower risk of heart attack.[5] Even when a person is healing, new evidence suggests that having a caring friend around can lead one to recover faster. In 2004, researchers at Ohio State University discovered that wounded hamsters recovered from minor wounds faster when not isolated from other hamsters.[6]

And speaking of animals, having a pet later in life can produce the same calming, health-friendly effects. Even when walking the dog, we're soothing our need to care.

Ultimately, decades of research on care and affection disprove Watson's belief that love breeds dependence. Care isn't the inhibitor of individuality and independence; it's the source. In the modern marketplace, satisfying a customer's need for care falls somewhere between giving him or her a hug in the check-out aisle and incanting how much the company loves its customers on its website and ads. Over the next few pages, we'll learn of several "care" strategies that are on the right track and of attempts that, while rooted in good thoughts, do more to damage consumer relationships than meet needs. In the Fieldwork discussion, we'll learn about the many ironies of purchasing insurance and how many companies are crafting policies and campaigns used to address the need for care.

Customer Care

Genuinely caring for customers and reflecting that philosophy in practice is complex, but is paramount to creating long-term customers. In the recognition chapter, I detailed my interaction with an Apple Care representative. Apple Care is a service department, but note the deliberate semantic differentiation. They use the word "care" because when one's beloved MacBook, iPhone, or ipad breaks down, it's more than a minor technical impediment—it's a full-blown emotional, life-interrupting event. Functionally, the customer needs technical service, but emotionally, the customer needs caring attention to help in the restoration of their day-to-day, software-assisted lives. This astute recognition of customers' relationship with its products, shows that the personal media giant Apple knows the role their products play.

But care is not at all about marketing semantics. When a partner in a relationship says the magic words, "I love you," he or she had better mean it, because sooner or later, the recipient of romance's most infamous three words will figure out whether or not her or his partner is sincere.

A perfect example of a company making the most of every interaction with its customers is Chick-fil-A, a fast-food company founded by Truett Cathy in 1946. He established the company on the principle that the restaurant should never lose a single customer based on a poor experience, and through several small but effective customer-service touches, Chick-fil-A has grown into a multi-billion-dollar company. Every franchise puts fresh flowers and pepper grinders on every table. Employees are trained to pull out chairs to seat female guests, and when it rains, they are supposed to run outside and greet customers with an umbrella. Every time a customer thanks an employee, he or she responds with, "It's my pleasure." None of these services are costly or time-consuming, but they leave a lasting impression on people, and reviews of Chick-fil-A always mention their extremely friendly and caring service. Customers are left with the impression that employees genuinely care about their dining experience. Chick-fil-A is also famous for giving out free food and coupons to customers who have to wait longer than expected for their food. This is another caring act that serves to strengthen the relationship between business and customer. Businesses need to recognize that the relationships customers have with brands are no different from human relationships. Both types need to be cultivated and maintained during every interaction. A simple demonstration of affection, such as saying "my pleasure," signals to the consumer that the relationship is meaningful. A gift of free food during a long wait resembles a sign of friendship. It sends the message that the business values the customer, and consumers will return these acts of kindness. Simple customer-service touches, like the ones demonstrated by Chick-fil-A, create strong, loyal relationships between businesses and consumers.

The Ben Franklin Effect and Caring for a Company

Satisfying the need for care works two ways. It's important to feel cared for, but instinctively, we also must care for others. But why?

Morality aside, the need for care cuts against the oft prevailing social-Darwinian, every-man-and-woman-for-themselves, doctrine.

At the end of the day, for all the greed, narcissism, and plain evil in the world, we're generally a benevolent species. Altruistic, selfless acts activate pleasure centers of the brain similar to the feelings associated with winning a game or buying a fancy pair of shoes. We fulfill our own needs by helping others. Anyone who has proverbially given him- or herself a pat on the back after "doing the right thing" knows this much.

Care and empathy are inherently linked. Empathy, remember, is the process of feeling the emotions felt by another. A bundle of wires in our brain—called "mirror neurons"—fire madly when we connect to another person's emotions viscerally. In times of crisis, emotions urge onlookers to great selfless acts of heroism. A man who jumps into traffic to push aside a stranger who is seconds away from being struck by an oncoming vehicle doesn't do so because he expects a reward. The human "do good" instinct, which is developed and promoted by many creeds, religions, and philosophies, remains a ray of hope for humanity. From an evolutionary and biological perspective, caring for others insures the growth and endurance of the species.

In his autobiography, Benjamin Franklin observed this peculiar psychological paradox: "He that has once done you a Kindness will be more ready to do you another, than he whom you yourself have obliged."[7] Translation: when someone does a favor for you, she is more likely to pay you another one before you pay her back in kind. Franklin, a founding father, historian, philosopher, and prolific observer of human nature, learned this truth while dealing with a pestering political enemy. Franklin learned that his foe had a book in his library that he wanted to read. Surprised that Franklin would ask a favor of him unrelated to politics, the man lent him the book. Franklin promptly returned it to him when he had finished the book. From that point on, their political relationship turned the corner. They were better able to work together, compromise, and see the other's point of view. His one-time foe paid him another favor by extending his hand across the political aisle.

Today, this is called the "Ben Franklin effect," and a psychological explanation for this is found in cognitive dissonance theory. When we do a favor for a person, we tend to like him or her more as a result because, in order to justify our good deed, we have to know that person is deserving of our attention. To assure ourselves that this person is in fact deserving, we double down, and help him or her again to erase any lingering negative perceptions.

So how does the Ben Franklin effect manifest in the marketplace? Surely a corporation can't ask a favor of its consumer: "Sir, we're wondering if you can pay a little extra today to help us out in these tough times." The likely reaction: "Sorry, I'm hurting too and will gladly take my business across the street." But this hunch isn't entirely true. Companies ask favors of us all the time. We just don't recognize them as favors.

Think for a minute. When we leave a small business, and its owner thanks you politely for supporting his store, we know the "thanks" is also code for: "Thanks for choosing me over my competitor down the street." If we feel we've made a difference and are equally satisfied with their service and the personal attentiveness surrounding the transaction, we build an allegiance that is psychologically no different from the Franklin effect. We return to the store again and again, in part because we "belong" there, but also because we're paying them more favors in exchange for our business. We're even willing to pay a premium price to affirm our caring support. (Think Neiman Marcus, Ritz Carlton, etc.) By caring for the business, we also satisfy the need for care.

Panera Bread recently reopened a suburban St. Louis restaurant as a not-for-profit chain. Customers are told to "take what they need, and pay their fair share." Patrons who don't or can't pay are asked to volunteer their time at the store. The gambit further proves that social consciousness and sound business are not mutually exclusive. The brand association triggered by the flood of goodwill and public relations from the Clayton, Missouri, location is bound to spill over to some of their fourteen hundred for-profit locations around the country. What is more, revenue for the donation model's first weekend was 20 percent more than the restaurant's previous Sunday.

It's a concept that has never been tested by a restaurant chain—and that marks a new career for Ron Shaich, who stepped down as Panera's chief executive officer in 2010. "I'm trying to find out what human nature is all about," says Shaich, 56, who has converted a former Panera-owned restaurant in an urban area of St. Louis into a non-profit restaurant dubbed Saint Louis Bread Company Cares Café. (Similar cafés planned outside of the St. Louis area will be called Panera Cares Cafés. Panera was founded in St. Louis and still brands its restaurants there as St. Louis Bread Company.)[8]

Shaich, now chair of the board for Panera, clearly knows more about human nature than he lets on. The Panera Cares Cafés (he plans on opening hundreds of them) will thrive because it models an attractive way to fulfill multiple needs at one location. On top of the café's functional purpose—food, caffeine—Panera has always presented a comfortable environment in which to work outside the office or connect with friends, family, colleagues, clients, and so forth. But the new model fulfills the altruistic need to express caring, a flood of the pleasure chemical dopamine. Doing good for others is literally a drug—we can't help but give ourselves a pat on the back. At Panera Cares, a donation or payment beyond the suggested retail price connects us positively to a message of caring and corporate responsibility. We feel they care for others—as we do—and we still get our coffee and pastries.

One of the most powerful acts of care and friendship a business can extend to a customer is a free product or service—a gift. If a business is ever in danger of providing a negative experience to a consumer, this will almost surely solidify a positive impression on the part of the consumer. Research shows that after receiving a good gift, people feel a closer connection to the gift-giver and feel that their tastes and interests are more similar to those of the giver. Businesses and brands stand to gain a lot from creating this kind of impression. The more a person identifies with a product or feels that it represents his or her interests and beliefs, the more likely he or she is to be loyal. Based on this research, there is no marketing dollar that could be better spent than a dollar that provides a direct gift to a customer who is in danger of experiencing a poor interaction with a business. Chick-fil-A, as mentioned earlier, offers free food to customers who have a long wait for their food. This is a direct expression of care that will ensure the customer has a positive experience with the business and, according to research, feel that his or her interests are similar to the brand, thus identifying with the brand. This type of relationship can go far beyond any impression an advertisement can produce.

The Consequences of Uncaring: The Nestlé and News of the World Scandals

While many companies have benefited from a positive image of social responsibility for their brand, others have faced a significant backlash against questionable business practices. Nestlé, a Swiss consumer-packaged-goods company violated the trust of its consumers in the late 1970s when, as news outlets reported, the company gave free samples of powdered breast milk formula to poor mothers in hospitals and maternity wards of developing countries. After the mothers and their babies left the hospital, the formula was no longer free, but the mothers' lactation was interrupted and they were forced to buy the formula. It was also discovered that Nestlé sold infant formula products in foreign countries without the correct language on the packaging. Mothers couldn't read the instructions and may have misused the products. In 1977, a consumer boycott of Nestlé gained widespread attention in the United States and expanded to Europe and around the world in the '80s. In this instance, Nestlé had violated the basic trust it had with a special and vulnerable group of consumers—new moms. Those who had a positive relationship and positive attitudes towards the brand lost trust in the company when it appeared that they took advantage of the poor and uneducated in developing countries. In this case, consumers turned vengeful and made efforts to publicly denounce and damage the brand with a boycott. These actions demonstrate the ways that consumers treat brands like relationships—they reward good friends with their loyalty and lash out against the bad ones. If companies maintain trust with their consumers and cultivate a positive relationship, they will be rewarded with equally caring and loyal customers. The friendship will be reciprocated.

One of the most egregious examples of an uncaring corporation is News Corporation and its British tabloid, *News of the World*. The editors at *News of the World*, the United Kingdom's biggest-selling newspaper, allowed activities that shattered even the most basic boundaries of decency. It began in 2006 with the arrest of the newspaper's royal affairs editor and a private investigator who worked for the newspaper, for hacking into the mobile phones of members of the royal family. In 2009, it was revealed that for a number of years, *News of the World* reporters had been illegally accessing messages from the mobile phones of British celebrities and politicians. Continuing investigations in 2010 and early 2011 revealed more details of the widespread illegal hacking into the mobile phones of politicians, other journalists, sports stars, police executives, and entertainers.

But the worst was to come in July 2011, when police informed a lawyer for the family of Milly Dowler, a 13-year-old girl who had been murdered in 2002, that someone, allegedly a *News of the World* investigator, had hacked into Milly's phone. The hackers had deleted voicemails on the phone to make room for more messages, misleading police and her family into believing that the murdered girl was still alive. Police further revealed it was investigating hacking incidents by *News of the World* reporters into the phones of other murder victims, as well as the victims of London's terrorist bombings in 2005. Repeated apologies from Rupert Murdoch and other executives of News Corp, and a series of top editorial firings, could not stem the outrage over the hacking scandal, and on July 7, Murdoch shut down the 168-year-old *News of the World*. Even in a British tabloid industry known for outrageous attitudes and headlines, the *News of the World* could not survive its callous, dishonorable actions. In the mind of the public, the *News of the World*, its reporters, and its editors considered their own needs paramount and simply didn't care— not even about a murdered young girl and her grieving family.

Fieldwork

Forgiveness in the Industry of Irony

Insurance: Healers or Hurters?

Out of perhaps all other products we purchase, insurance is easily the most anomalous. It's probably the only product we buy that we hope we never have to use. Every year, every month, or every six months, we make a payment, and pray that's the last we have to encounter the insurer until the next bill comes through the mail. And yet, we can't go without it.

Try to imagine any other service or product that even borders on this irony. A family who buys a new car just in case the city bus breaks down? A woman who buys an MP3 player, but won't use it until her Walkman finally shorts out? A man who buys a new suit, but won't wear it until the one he bought twenty-five years ago tears? A 401k investor who never intends to cash in at the end of her career? Maybe in the twilight zone there are consumers out there like this, but such behavior is at best a rarity.

But when it comes to insurance, we don't think twice about paying to protect our liabilities, health, automobiles, possessions, and homes. It is essential to satisfying our basic need for security, and in certain cases, we're breaking the law by not purchasing insurance. We buy it. But we never hope to use it.

Why? First, we're afraid of the random, painful life events associated with insurance—a sudden accident or death, for instance. And when the time actually comes to make good on premium payments in the form of a claim, we're typically at our most helpless. We become dependent on the insurance company. We're afraid they won't cover it. We're afraid they'll jack up our rates to a breaking point. We're afraid of the copays and seemingly random increases in premiums. We're terrified to call the 1-800 number to communicate with a representative who has little clue to or interest in our predicament.

Insurance is a vivid reminder of our vulnerability. It's hard to be a fan of a product that on its face is a nagging symbol reminding us that life can be turned upside down without a moment's notice. On the flip side, vulnerability is one reason so many financially strapped individuals choose to go without insurance. It's the "nothing bad will happen to me" mindset that helps people justify not dedicating a huge check toward insurance.

Also lingering in the back of our minds: the countless stories of insurance companies abandoning their customers at crucial moments and cheating or exploiting policy holders by invoking fine print.

This fear isn't based on irrational myths. Time and time again, this industry has shown that it puts profits over consumer care. The most baffling incident occurred after Hurricane Katrina, when thousands of State Farm customers were denied claims for a destroyed home because the insurer categorized catastrophic wind damage as "flood-related," thus voiding coverage on most policies. The homeowners pointed out that it wasn't a flood that knocked over their homes, but the winds from one of the most violent storms in history. However, the customers had no legal recourse. The situation was so shady that even the powerful antiregulation senator Trent Lott, whose home was among the many wrecked in the storm, agreed that Congress needed to reexamine insurance regulatory rules.

Stories like these, extreme or otherwise, feed the idea that it's impossible to know whether or not the insurance company will be there for us when we need them—even when the situation is entirely out of our control. Rightly or wrongly, we see insurance companies as capricious masters of fate, and that, quite frankly, is an unhealthy position for both the consumer and the industry to be in.

Insurance, then, is a perfect storm of conflicting psychological dynamics. We hate to make payments, not only because of the financial burden, but because the idea of filing a claim is associated with terrifying life events—accidents, illness or death, property destruction—yet we make them anyway. We're hesitant to trust an insurance company, because we're afraid of being left vulnerable and abandoned in a crisis.

For many consumers, these feelings breed a behavioral dynamic called inertia. Once we are signed up with an insurer, we're unlikely to switch because it requires us to call to mind all the reasons we fear insurance. Out of sight, out of mind. Many consumers think most insurance companies are the same. *They're all after my money and when the moment of truth comes they may not really be interested in protecting me.*

These dynamics pose a unique challenge for insurance providers trying to differentiate their brand and win new customers. Some marketing campaigns go straight for the rational cost-benefit approach, which is a strong appeal to those who don't see a difference in service quality: *Give us a few minutes of your time, and you can save $X by switching to Brand A.* Other companies recognize the fear of helplessness and try to restore customer agency by appealing to the need for control: *With Brand B, you get to set the price and coverage options!* Some companies still stand by the policy of using actual agents to represent customers, a direct appeal to the need for care: *Snap your fingers, and we will be at your side in a time of need.*

But I want to talk about a marketing and service strategy that is a potential win for brand differentiation and a win for consumer needs satisfaction. It shouldn't even be necessary, as its premise seems to redundantly underscore the concept of insurance. It's a policy centered around "forgiveness," and it tempts us with the idea that the future of insurance might actually center around the need for care (which is what it should have been about all along). To differentiate in the insurance business anymore, it's all about showing you care more.

The Psychology of Accident Forgiveness

In the early 2000s, we consulted with Allstate, one of the largest publicly held insurers in the United States. Currently, Allstate commands nearly one-fifth of the auto insurance market. Since 1950, Allstate has been easily identified by its slogan "You're in good hands" and the accompanying open-palms logo. The message is simple and effective: when bad luck strikes, it's nice to know there is someone present to catch us as we're falling. (For several years, those caring hands have been Dennis Haysbert, the deep-voiced actor made famous by his role as the ever-noble President David Palmer in the counterterrorism drama *24*.) But when it comes to meeting needs, feel-good marketing is not enough. To meet the need for care, we must actually be cared for and feel cared for by the insurer.

As part of their Your Choice Auto campaign, we surveyed non-Allstate customers from small and large competitors to see which new policies would be a point of differentiation strong enough to cause the individual to switch his or her auto insurer. Across all segments, the concept of "accident forgiveness" scored among the top-ranked options. If you've turned on a television once in the last five years, you know that Allstate ran with the idea and ended up strongly promoting the new policy option in major national ads. Many of their competitors matched the effort, each formulating its own forgiveness plans. Such policies obviously come with a price—some forgiveness plans may cost up to 20 percent more than a standard policy. But it's a price many people are willing to pay given the fears of insurance discussed above.

Let's discuss how accident forgiveness policies work. Only then will it be clear how psychologically enticing "forgiveness" is.

For owners of a standard auto insurance policy, accidents are dreaded because it's a default expectation that rates will be hiked for the next pay period. It's just part of the game. The company bumps the driver up a risk tier, and passes off the costs to him or her in the future. But even if consumers expect this, it's hard to get over the notion that the higher premium is punishment. We'll take care of you this time, BUT you cost a lot of money and will now pay the price for your transgression. To most of us, this is unpalatable for a variety of reasons, not the least of which is the fact that accidents are most of the time just that...accidental! Wrecks are not usually conscious acts of negligence or malfeasance.

"Mayhem" (as the compaign notes) just sort of happens—sometimes it's our fault, other times not. But with every accident, the drivers involved undoubtedly wish they could wave a wand and make all the hassle go away. Premiums stay the same. No harm done. No stress of getting the car repaired. At the very least, no matter the culpability, the drivers wish they'd be forgiven—after all, it is what insurance is for.

Most accident forgiveness policies act to ease the stress of an accident, which are emotionally and psychologically wrenching enough to begin with. The most affordable plans typically are offered as rewards for good drivers. Haven't been in an accident for five years? Sign up for this plan, and we'll forgive your first at-fault accident. These plans typically require that the driver has been with the company for a few years before qualifying. Midrange and premium plans, which cost considerably more, will often protect a driver for multiple accidents before a policy is dropped or premiums are hiked. Accident forgiveness is attractive for families with young drivers and heavy commuters who are statistically bound to get into a fender bender at some point.

At their core, these policies are merely insurance for buying insurance, a financial safety net for a product that is in itself a safety net. Let's not be naive. Companies that offer these policies have, of course, figured out ways to profit off of them (in cases where they cannot, the policies aren't available). Financially, accident forgiveness policyholders may possibly end up paying more in the long-run. It's a highly calculated business strategy—perhaps even a gamble. But without the policy, one at-fault accident can make a typically good driver's insurance borderline unaffordable after one slip-up on the road—and with that comes fear of being jettisoned into the "pool".

But for policyholders, the hit to the pocketbook is paid back via emotional satisfaction. This occurs at two levels:

1. **The peace of mind found in knowing we'll be forgiven for something that wasn't necessarily my fault**
2. **The feeling of being cared for and forgiven when we are in a highly vulnerable situation**

What happens to our behavior when someone chooses to forgive us for a wrongdoing? It can be restorative, a cleansing process for both parties.

Grudges in relationships are typically a death knell for that relationship. Harboring ill feelings for past behavior is a cancer to future interactions with that person. The act of forgiveness is one of humanity's strongest virtues, and among the hardest to practice. When forgiven, we're more likely to reciprocate good feelings toward those who have absolved us. It's a sign from the other person that imperfection is inevitable, and that punishment should not eradicate the possibility of a second chance. Forgiveness, plain and simple, is one of the purest forms of care and recognition.

There is no better way for Allstate, or any other insurance company to change its perception as the "Capricious Master of Fate" than to offer policies that truly practice forgiveness and stick to those policies when customers request it. It softens a company's image, changes the balance of power, can be constructed in a way that won't be harmful to revenues, solidifies customer loyalty, and most importantly, satisfies the need for care in an industry that is most feared for its potential to abandon the consumer.

Chapter 8 Summary: How Business Can Empathize with the Core Need of Recognition

Care is one of the most fundamental human needs and a requirement for almost any satisfying relationship, including relationships with other people as well as our relationships with companies or brands. The need for care provides numerous opportunities for businesses to distinguish itself and earn the hearts and loyalty of consumers, but it can also be a double-edged sword. When it is not appropriately addressed, it can have a significant, and sometimes catastrophic, effect on brand perception and sales.

Key Business Success Factors

Below are a few key steps businesses can take to effectively respond to consumers' need for Care:

Suggested Follow-Up Steps

1. **Forget the Talk. Show the Care.** Forget the slogans: "Customers are no. 1." Forget the throwaway phrases: "Your call is important

to us." Customers won't believe you care until you prove it to them concretely. Here are some ways to convey this important need:

a. **Offer rapid, personalized responses to customers' problems and complaints.** This is the baseline for caring in the world of business. Always make a concerted effort to satisfy the dissatisfied customer. In most cases, a problem resolved leads to even greater loyalty.

b. **Prove continuously during interactions with customers that you care.** In addition to dealing quickly, courteously, and effectively with periodic challenges and setbacks, create an atmosphere of caring that permeates customer interactions with the business during the entire length of the relationship, whether it's a special one-off sale in a store or recurring or ongoing discounts for loyalty (based on dollars and/or time). For example, demonstrate an effortless pleasure in serving and satisfying the customer as soon as the customer walks in the door.

c. **Offer unexpected gifts when appropriate.** Gifts work. They display caring and solidify relationships with customers—before a problem surfaces. Even when a problem has been resolved, offer a free gift. This expression of the company's dismay at the original problem is powerful proof that the company is not just talking about care.

d. **Never, ever give the impression that you just don't care.** Don't hide behind "policy" to avoid resolving customer problems. Don't allow employees to be rude or impatient in interactions with customers. Caring begins with courtesy; courtesy must be the standard in your company.

2. **Let customers care for your business.** The need for caring, surprisingly, goes both ways. Customers, often subconsciously, develop an emotional bond with companies for which they have "cared"—specifically by being loyal over a significant period of time. A successful relationship with customers satisfies their own need to care. Don't miss out on opportunities to reward loyalty and foster this emotional bond. For example, companies can provide clear discounts for the number of years a client had been with them, thereby providing their loyal customers with preferential treatment over a new customer.

Epilogue

We live in a time of rapid change and economic unease. Reacting slowly to the new challenges of the marketplace and sticking to business as usual, particularly in regards to how we view consumers, does not help. While many may say the most important issue for any business is to create revenue—we disagree. It is to create and sustain loyal customers. To treat people as mere consumers and transactors is an untenable perspective in this dynamic climate. Despite the cyclical nature of business trends and buzz, there's one constant in the marketplace: the unchanging, core emotional needs of all people. In most every circumstance, from relationships to the grocery store aisle, the needs rise to the forefront of our emotional lives and our motivations.

Control is the reward offered by the iPod. Ceding control helped a small Scandinavian furniture company become one of the world's largest furniture retailers.

Self-expression guided Darryl's varied selections of dinner choices, and it guided which hosiery commercials connected with professional women.

Growth, as Adrianna realized, is not just a matter of changing jobs but of learning new skills. It inspired the United States Army's most successful recruitment campaign to "Be all you can be."

Recognition helped Janet's students feel valued at an age when they were skeptical of authority. Recognition allowed an international company to successfully market and understand the needs of an emerging market in the skin-care industry.

Belonging became Frannie's core motivation to do a job that gave her no satisfaction. The psychology of belonging informed the introduction of a groundbreaking human immunodeficiency virus (HIV) drug to a marginalized community.

As noted in chapter 2, the needs documented in this book are not a complete and exhaustive list of psychological needs in the marketplace. But they are the most crucial ones. And more important, they suggest that a marketplace designed around the psychology of needs will mutually benefit consumers and businesses alike. The Needs must be the nexus of our twenty-first-century economy.

What would a culture whose businesses understand, empathize with, and meet human emotional needs look like? In this vision, we'd most definitely see a leaner, more efficient, more sustainable economy. Consumers would foremost seek to meet their basic needs, but would all the while gravitate toward the most honest, innovative, and emotionally resonant companies to fulfill unmet emotional needs. Service providers that cut corners by pushing its customers around would become extinct. When a company said, "We really care about you" and broke that promise, savvy consumers would seek out and reward a company that had their best interests at heart.

In this culture, people would not be passive reactors and lobotomized drones who picked from a diluted palette of similar products and services, each offering promises of utopian satisfaction. They would be empowered to take control of their own economic decisions, able to choose products and services that are real acts of self-expression, and find themselves reconnected, belonging to like-minded communities, better able to care for their family and loved ones. In short, companies would become partners in meeting human needs rather than adversaries or unintentional impediments to needs satisfaction.

This vision runs against the classic vision illustrated in Aldous Huxley's science-fiction novel *A Brave New World*. The carefully controlled citizens in Huxley's futuristic portrait live carefree lives. They possess the acute impression that their needs are met by its controlling powers through lavish consumption. But this came at the expense of human engagement and meaningful autonomy. Individuals were trumped by willful conformity to an oligarchic overlord; organic human relationships and communities were extinct. We don't want that world!

And fortunately, consumers are becoming reengaged, claiming their stake in reshaping how retail and service industries function in their lives. Consumers are becoming more enlightened and attuned to companies that transgress and companies that deliver. The digital revolution has given us widely used tools like Yelp, Angie's List, twitter, blogs, and other forums that provide savvy consumers a check against corporate power. The examples are many.

When a realty company in Chicago attempted to sue one of its tenants after she lambasted her leased property on Twitter, a public outcry shamed the company and rallied to her defense. When Verizon tried to charge customers an additional $2 fee for certain types of transactions, again an angry public helped abort the surcharge. When a major airline became defensive after breaking a musician's guitar, he created a viral song on YouTube that caused a public relations nightmare for the company. A Texas utility company faced mass outrage when they installed new "smart meters" that seemed to inaccurately measure some consumers' usage. While the meters were in fact mostly accurate, the company's treatment of their "rate-payers" prompted a public relations course correction that resulted in over one hundred open-house style meetings to explain the changes. New mothers banded together online against painkiller brand Motrin in 2008 after an advertisement sardonically depicted baby slings as silly fashion accessories detrimental to the mother's health. The message: sure, wear your baby, but you'll need our product to make it work. Motrin yanked the patronizing ads soon after launch. Poor restaurant reviews on Yelp often drive owners to woo back disgruntled or unimpressed patrons with a revamped experience or free meals. The power and privilege once reserved for professional food critics is being transferred to anyone with a sound opinion and an Internet connection. Google's venture into the cell phone market ultimately proved a profitable venture, as smartphone shoppers were interested in alternatives to the iPhone. But in the early months, Google informed customers who needed service for phones using the Android operating system that it could take up to 48 hours for a response by email. They had taken market share before acquiring the infrastructure to support it. Consumer and media attention to the issue prompted swift action.

This is encouraging for all consumers. Companies that react slowly or underestimate the degree to which people are watching them will fade fast. But my hope is that over the next decade, more companies find it in their best interest to do the psychological heavy lifting that would prevent embarrassing, costly missteps.

Analyzing and listening for human needs on the ground level would help businesses know what their audience needs and how to deliver that message to its audience long before a new product, service, or advertisement finds its way to the market. Motrin would never have launched its ad targeting "baby-wearing" mothers if they'd carefully taken the time to empathize with this audience. Product design would be tailored to the ethnographic work showing how people intuitively use items, when they use them, and why they use them. Services would be crafted based on what we know about the emotions surrounding expectations and promise making in interpersonal relationships.

In other words, harnessing The Needs encourages companies to be proactive in their attempt to satisfy people rather than be reactive.

But Don't Meeting Human Needs and Fostering Consumerism Represent a Paradox?

Critics of consumer culture might argue that if people want to achieve self-realization and satisfaction through meeting The Needs, then looking to the marketplace as the source of their fulfillment is at best misguided and arguably laughable. Although I'm sympathetic to this argument, it misunderstands two critical points worth reiterating here.

First, rarely do we actively and consciously seek to check a need off a list per se. Satisfying needs is embedded in the unconscious, the shadow of our motivation. When we step into a store, sit down with a financial adviser, doctor, or service representative, or engage with a brand or advertisement, our needs are constantly active. While it's true that relationships, careers, and personal endeavors will ultimately become the best source of meeting the balance of individuality and connectedness, the research laid out throughout this book indicates that what we buy has everything to do with meeting needs. At no time would I suggest that a person discover his or her ideal self through the mere accumulation of material goods. But businesses do play a role in facilitating this discovery process at countless junctures.

Linguist, political activist, and philosopher Noam Chomsky considers consumer culture and marketing a grave social ill. Of marketing, he said: "It tries to turn people into something they aren't—individuals focused solely on themselves, maximising their consumption of goods that they don't need."[1] Although certainly overconsumption and detrimental materialism (e.g., adolescents' cell phone/tech addiction) are serious issues, the problem with his critique lies in his implicit definition of "need." He suggests we don't need many of these products and services because we don't *need* them to fulfill basic survival needs. This eschews the inescapable reality that people use services and products to facilitate the fulfillment of deeper psychological needs, which to an individual who already has food, family, and shelter, become the primary impetus underlying much behavior.

Secondly, Chomsky and others might like to see consumer society evaporate over night, but that's a pipe dream, and one our current economy couldn't afford. The consumer-goods-and-services economy will remain the driving force of our economic system for the foreseeable future and very likely forever. Knowing this, a focus on the genuine, emotional needs of the diverse populace becomes essential to maintaining an economy that serves the psychological health of the nation, and in turn, the financial health of its industries. We can't replace the system. But we can change the paradigms by which the system operates. We can have vibrant relationships and communities and thriving individualistic ideals along with a consumer market that takes seriously the facilitation of emotional needs. There's no mutual exclusion. Goods and services should do two things: (1) help us live and survive (fulfill our basic physiological needs) and (2) help us better or enrich our lives by facilitating our dual emotional needs of individuality and connectedness. A marketplace that makes it a priority to empathically understand what contributes to making people psychologically healthy is more desirable through and through (and more sustainable) than one that overpromises, manipulates emotion, or misreads what people need to live better.

But HOW do we get there? What must change in the fabric of business philosophy for this to occur? There's no one simple answer. However, here are a few guiding principles, along with examples of true need-centered change, that should point us in the right direction.

Enabling Demand

Let's take a moment to discuss some of our more basic needs: economic survival. In the still unsettled tide of the 2008 recession, millions of

Americans are struggling to get by. This is not just damaging for the affected households. The continued economic lag and high unemployment rate has a pernicious effect on almost all corners of the economy. And what a vicious cycle it is. Generally speaking, companies are sitting on excess capital and thus not hiring, but primarily because there is not enough marketplace demand. Household incomes are stagnant; the millions out of work have little to no discretionary income, making it difficult for companies to begin expanding their workforce. The options for revival are contentious political and economic topics, but the discussion must be held and solutions acted upon before the slide of middle-class households, which drive sales of goods and services, worsens.

On the ground level, the current climate provides business leaders interested in the psychology of human needs with a real opportunity to empathize with their audience. The Columbia Broadcasting Station (CBS) program, *Undercover Boss* follows executives of major companies as they disguise themselves on the front lines, learning firsthand the reality that their lowest-level employees face daily. In many cases, their experience is jaw-dropping: revelations leading to remarkable organizational change that improves the lives of the often forgotten workers.

By embracing The Needs, perhaps, business leaders can take the root goal of *Undercover Boss* (learning the human reality that is unseen due to the day-to-day stresses of leading large organizations) and apply it to their external audience—their customers and clientele. When we know what a person needs, the fuel of his or her motivation, it is easier to put the pieces in place to satisfy them, making the person's life better and the company or organization stronger. Peeling back the layers of the consumer psyche is as critical now as never before in our history. With limited resources, consumers will be especially attuned to which companies represent what is right for their wallets, right for their communities, and right for their self-ideals. Some companies are reacting to the tough economic times with lip service that merely acknowledges the pain without changing the service (or price.) Others are sincerely allying themselves with the needs of their consumer base in tough times.

Consider a bill that most all Americans dread opening each month: electricity. Power costs are rising, as is the average home's consumption. Thus, a burden is placed on energy companies and households alike.

A strong marketing push toward light-emitting diode (LED) lighting systems and light bulbs on behalf of major appliance companies is a positive development, both ecologically and economically. This mostly affects Americans at Christmas time, many of whom aren't about to skimp on holiday cheer during tough times. LED lights cost a little bit more on the store shelves, but cost households upwards of 1000 percent less to run over five hundred hours of use than standard lights. Pair that with the fact that many utility companies are offering rebates for homes that use LED lights.

Or take, for example, an editorial penned in the *Huffington Post* by Starbucks chief executive officer Howard Schultz in late 2008. Amid the deepest valley of the crisis, he argued that too many business leaders were taking a pure short-term view. "With that mindset comes the false belief that investments in people and training can wait; that corporate social responsibility can be put on the back burner," he said. "I believe passionately that this is precisely what American business leaders should not be doing today. Now is the time for business leaders to step up...and to lead."[2]

The bottom line remains that we cannot continue America's strong economic legacy without the majority of American workers and households being willing and able to spend. Meanwhile, those who do spend will more often than not choose those who respect their pocketbooks as well their communities and emotional needs.

Checking Blind Spots

But let's be honest: an organization cannot change, and meeting emotional needs cannot become a priority if businesses continue to put up a wall to hide their blind spots. This means that learning the dynamic structure and contents of the needs continuum must be paired with an application of the art and sciences of clinical, social, and consumer psychology. Leaders must not forsake emotional insights over analytical problem solving. Both are needed in harmony to recognize needs and organize/act to satisfy them.

The 2009 comedy *The Invention of Lying* is set in a fictional world where people are incapable of lying. Writer, director, and star Ricky Gervais (creator of *The Office*) plays Mark, a downtrodden employee of a documentary film company who turns his life around when he becomes the first human ever to harness the power of dishonesty. People don't question his fiction because they know only the truth. The act of omitting feelings from conversation, in such a world, is a form of lying. Anything the characters feel, they think. And what they think, they say. There is no filter. It's a world where reason rules, where emotion is laid bare.

The alternate universe portrayed in *The Invention of Lying* is jarringly awkward because we would never think of communicating in such a fashion. It underscores just how much we rely on withholding our emotions or denying our emotion to maintain privacy, and in some cases, our sanity.

When it comes to understanding people, which universe do market researchers and business strategists inhabit? Ricky Gervais's, where everybody tells the truth? Or the world where pinpointing and dissecting the true emotional needs and desires take skill, time, and nuance?

Too often, traditional business strategy and research approaches live and die on the assumption that an audience means what they say, and conversely, says what they mean. Psychologists (and *The Invention of Lying* creators) know this idea is simply fantasy. People constantly misinterpret each other's emotions and constantly misinterpret their own. To embrace the needs and interests of an audience, businesses must first recognize that identifying the emotional undercurrent is nothing like Gervais's black-and-white, fictional universe. Inhabiting that world, we will be deceived and led astray by words and actions that don't represent the underlying feelings and emotions that tell the real story.

The Needs coast along next to us, hidden in our blind spot.

Robert Frost wrote, "Something we were withholding made us weak, until we found out that it was ourselves."[3] Too often, business leaders and their employees put a firewall on their emotional brains when clocking in each morning. Doing so denies what makes us, *us*. When we look at how successful leaders and innovators get where they are, it's equal parts intelligence quotient (IQ) and emotional quotient (EQ). Emotional intelligence is an ability to gauge how people think and feel, as well as how emotions affect one's own thinking and perceptions.

Fortunately, more and more leaders over the last few decades have been embracing the value of EQ. However, it can't stop with the individual. Organizational and strategic blind spots can still throw a company off course.

Adopting many of the research approaches described in the Fieldwork sections has proven useful to companies that look for insights beyond the spreadsheet. Psychoethnography, that is, observing people through a clinical, empathic lens, can lead to insights for product designers and marketers that surveys or interviews could never glean. Projective techniques help clinicians access patients' most deeply repressed realities; these techniques can help market researchers decode the enigmatic meaning behind customers' reasoning and behavior. Focus groups have long been part of the market research mix, but their value may potentially be unleashed if analyzed by a business professional trained in psychology. In-depth clinical interviews can bond businesses intimately with the needs of specific audience segments. Social science experiments and behavioral psychology inform the mysteries of how individuals act among groups, a key to influencing customers and understanding the impetus of their desires.

Fearing Failure or Uncertainty Leads Only to Stagnation, More Uncertainty

There's an understandable sentiment rearing its head throughout recent political discourse that says: businesses are afraid to act in light of economic uncertainty. But I wish I heard more of this: *more and more businesses are taking bold risks in an attempt to pull ahead of competition still paralyzed by the great recession.* If there was ever a time to innovate, it is now. Bold innovation, especially on an organizational level, is like moving a boulder up a hill. The rewards for getting the rock to the top are enticing, but the fear of it rolling down on top of us often keeps us from making the first push. Failure has long been a popular topic for psychology studies. Knowing why we are averse to failure also explains how successful companies emerge.

For individuals, stagnation is the result of not responding to our inborn needs. It's impossible to communicate your identity to yourself and others if you have few vehicles for self-expression. It's hard to see where you belong if you don't make an attempt to belong to anything. You can't be recognized for good work or a bold action if you do neither.

Complacency and stagnation are a death knell for the individual, and a harbinger of bad times for an organization, as well.

Fortunately, we see examples of companies taking risks every day. The risks are not new and better ways of concocting financial schemes or shedding employees. They are reorganizing products and services around the evolving needs of their audience. These risks don't always pay off, but without these innovators, the economy would remain stuck in molasses. J. Crew designed a new website in 2010 that forthrightly sold products of other companies alongside their clothing lines. They didn't profit off these third-party sales, but it was a risky attempt to level with and befriend their shoppers that is rarely seen in the retail world.

Oftentimes, the difference between risks that pay off and business as usual is seen in how leaders and organizations approach problem solving. *New York Times* science reporter Benedict Carey documented recent research regarding the apparent effectiveness of sudden insight (a light-bulb moment) solutions. Research suggests that insight and analysis activate different regions of the brain. "Either way, creative problem-solving usually requires both analysis and sudden out-of-the-box insight," writes Carey.[4] The best problem solvers use logic and analysis, but they are also creatively scatterbrained, mentally free and open to try out-of-the-box solutions rather than remaining latched to analyzing patterns. Fortunately, this is not just a natural-born gift. Insight-driven solutions can be induced by changing not just how businesses research challenges, but by changing the mindset of the people tasked with finding the solutions.

Recent research suggests that people with less focused or more open minds before they tackle a challenging puzzle are more prone to coming up with the idea for a winning solution. Sometimes all this takes is a good mood:

> The punch line is that a good joke can move the brain toward just this kind of state. In their humor study, Dr. Beeman and Dr. Subramaniam had college students solve word-association puzzles after watching a short video of a stand-up routine by Robin Williams. The students solved more of the puzzles over all, and significantly more by sudden insight, compared with when they'd seen a scary or boring video beforehand.[5]

When businesses operate on a balanced foundation of strident analysis and whimsical creative spirit, it will become easier to take risks and easier to find solutions.

Commitment to Dialogue

True insights come from a hard, prolonged conversation with an audience. If one mines all the data available in the world, one won't get too much closer to an understanding of the psychology behind human needs than if one commits to speaking with, listening to, and analyzing the emotional lives of a representative portion of an audience.

More and more industries are embracing the importance of two-way communication with their audience. Independent filmmaker John Reiss wrote in *Filmmaker Magazine* about the divide between film artists who want their art to stand alone—those who see branding and marketing as below their ideals as artists—and filmmakers who cultivate their work through traditional branding:

> Branding is a way to create an on-going relationship with an audience. Audience development and connection is hard work. Why reinvent the wheel each time you make a film, why not cultivate those fans who like your work into a core group who can sustain you? Tools exist now like never before to help you do this. Plus talking to like minded people should be a fun thing, feeding off of each other's ideas, contributing to a community of artists, hearing positive feedback on work you have created that means something to someone, touched them in some way.[6]

Reiss cites cult film producer and writer Kevin Smith (*Mall Rats*, *Clerks*, *Dogma*) as a leading example. The Kevin Smith brand thrives on communicating with his fans—iPhone apps, podcasts, live question-and-answer shows, and so forth.

Other celebrities thrive on the day-to-day quest of developing their brand by going viral, playing to the insatiable need of fans to hang onto their every Tweet. Although he did not use dialogue, Shaquille O'Neal invented yet another way to stay in the spotlight by introducing himself to his new market, Boston, by posing motionless for hours—like a street performer statue—while fans literally sat on him, took pictures with him, and so on. Creative or foolish, time will tell.

These are examples of organizations or people sustaining dialogue by forming community, satisfying an audience's need for belonging. It's obvious that service-oriented industries should know the value of staying engaged with their customers because those are more direct interpersonal relationships. But what about consumer retail products? How do companies that sell furniture, soap, blue jeans, or pharmaceuticals, sustain a dialogue when the basis of a consumer relationship is more transactional?

The answer is less glamorous than the solution for sports stars and artists: an ongoing and unique approach to researching their audience. With a marketplace perpetually in motion, a company, large or small, that stops researching its core audience or the conditions of its market will be lapped by a competitor abreast of their needs and the processes of how best to satisfy them. Affordable digital dialog forums and blogs, paid online communities of interest, flexibly allow market researchers to keep an ear on their audience over extended periods of time. Such forums are able to track trends in mood and opinion over the course of a year, and can easily provide compelling evidence to launch larger studies. Moreover, information from public relations departments and customer-service departments must be brought straight to consumer researchers and business leaders.

Force-Fitting a Need and Meeting a Need

Flipping through a *Sky Mall* catalog on a recent trip prompted me to underscore this important, all too common retail pitfall: because a product exists does not mean it can inherently meet an emotional need. Duh!

I admire anyone who wants to make a buck or try his or her hand at crafting the next million-dollar idea, but let's face it, it's often best to not force-fit products and services around a human need. One extreme example: in 1980, a couple from Belmont, California, patented a sound muffler for the human mouth, enabling its wearer to "yell or scream without disturbing others, allowing them to vent built-up anger and frustration." A device to both enable and mute ostentatious self-expression.... That's a bit of an extreme example, but it illustrates a perennial problem facing marketers. Products and services go to great lengths to meet human needs when they just simply aren't a good fit.

Needs can only be met in a particular industry or product category for high-value customers if the need is active in that audience. For example, costly customer recognition/reward programs are only valuable when the customer cares to be recognized and the incentive truly delivers on emotional recognition. Recognizing the most passionate, loyal customers—advocates of a brand—is always worth a company's resources.

Organizational Consistency

From the front lines of customer service, to the tone of a press release, to the copy of a national advertisement, every corner of an organization must be primed on the unique psychology of their audience to recognize needs at all phases of interaction and relationship with a brand.

Normally we think of change and innovation as coming in one of two ways: top down or bottom up. But sometimes we forget what's most important: that the change spreads across the entirety of the group, business, or culture. Consistency is key. A brand manager must be "on emotion" and understand the needs of her audience. But so too must the retail associate on the ground floor. So too must training, sales, research and development teams. So too must the public face of the company. Why? Because as in a relationship, a need can be met or trampled on at any stage of the individual's relationship with a company or brand. Nowhere is this more important than when a company is attempting to satisfy emotional needs.

Think of the importance universities place on training their ambassadors and campus tour guides. The odds of a student choosing a school after a bad tour diminish when comparable options are on the table. When it comes to human needs, organizational inconsistencies are like a hairline crack on a coffee mug. The mug is otherwise 90 percent functional—sharp color, ergonomic handle, perfectly insulated—but that tiny little crack, spreading out from the base, drips the mug's contents onto its user's legs, rendering the item useless. Even if the crack is not noticeable initially, it will spider out over the entire mug. Needs are won and lost at the interpersonal level. Businesses must invest in making sure the entire operation understands what the company stands for and what needs are at stake for its prospective and current customers.

Walking into a Trader Joe's grocery store, whether in Bend, Oregon, or Des Moines, Iowa, one gets the sense that every employee there knows the organization's lineage, principles, and goals. The small, alternative grocery store is a master class in behavioral psychology. Store employees, donned in Hawaiian shirts, are empowered to innovate, share ideas, and satisfy customers' needs as they arise. Towing young, impatient children through grocery aisles is a fear of most all caretakers. Trader Joe's keeps them busy with store treasure hunts and activities. Community is formed with newsletters that put customers on the inside. Products are cheaper than many of the items at Whole Foods, but carry the prestige of originating from one of Trader Joe's many high-quality food makers. Moreover, the company knows that the more choices shoppers have, the less likely they will be to buy an item from that category, so they only carry a few items (or fewer) for each food type. In 1991, the organization purposefully wrote its mission statement in chalk, defying the common precedent set by other corporations: values are static or "set in stone."

Showing versus Telling

Jennifer Aaker and Susan Fournier, in their relationship study detailed in the opening pages, tell us plainly: broken promises do not bode well for companies that claim to stand for more than delivering a functional good/service. There's a classic principle held dear by many contemporary novelists and creative writers that applies here: *Show. Don't Tell.* In other words, it's fine to tell a reader something, but it's better, and usually stronger writing, to show them through a visceral sensory experience.

Compare these two passages:

Meghan was terrified to present to the board of directors. (Telling)

As the presentation inched closer, Meghan searched her bag for a tissue to blot her brow. The air was sucked out of the room. Her throat tightened. Meghan focused what little composure she had on memorizing the data and rehearsing the answers she expected the board to ask. (Showing)

When we're told something, it may not connect with us. When we see something, we feel it. The lesson couldn't be clearer: don't merely tell an audience who you are and what you're about. Show them by following through at each and every opportunity. Relationships aren't won on the first date. The person will tell you who he or she is, but you won't truly know until you spend more time with him or her.

BankSimple, a new bank launched in 2011, claims to take banking back to its roots: where the only way a bank made money was through deposits. Its founders explain on their website: "BankSimple was born out of our frustration with banking. We were fed up with our banks: the fees, the self-serving policies, the constantly changing rules, the horrible customer service. We saw an opportunity to fix these issues by making banking simpler."[7]

BankSimple captures the spirit of frustrated households everywhere. However, the organization was designed not just to bridge a connection to the consumer's frustration (telling), but to construct policies that actually mirror the marketing (showing). There are no fees, and there is personalized customer service, free automated teller machine (ATM) withdrawals, and so forth. But most important, the bank promises to be just a bank, like the nostalgic days before national banks merged with insurance and financial institutions. There's no telling yet how successful BankSimple will be, but the promise and appeal of human-centered services that market empathically will be popularized well beyond BankSimple.

* * *

MEETING NEEDS IN THE MARKETPLACE is like meeting needs in an intimate relationship, sometimes difficult, but always necessary for growth and satisfaction. For individual companies that put needs first and play their part in changing the strategic paradigms, the rewards will be great. Needs sustain our relationships and shape our personalities. Likewise, needs will sustain our economy and shape our commitment to human betterment and innovation.

To conclude, below are a few core guidelines for how companies can take an empathetic approach to marketing.

Follow-up Steps

- **Identify and understand the core emotional needs that drive consumer thinking and behavior.** The list of needs outlined in this book is not by any means complete, but it highlights the most important emotional needs that are hidden behind the purchasing decisions of consumers. Business must make a thorough and sincere effort to uncover and understand those emotions.

- **Don't take consumers at their word.** Traditional market research assumes that consumers or prospects say what they mean and mean what they say. But emotional needs color their decisions and behaviors in ways that might not be apparent even to them. That is why so many products launched on the basis of favorable market research results fail. Consciously, consumers believed they would buy the product, but the hidden emotions made them act otherwise.

- **Dialogue is the key.** A sustained conversation with the customer is the only way to truly uncover the key emotional needs that can significantly impact a person's relationship with a company and its products. Direct and ongoing two-way communication—ongoing because a marketplace is constantly changing—is more vital and, thanks to technology, more possible than ever before. Consumers have choices; they won't stay loyal to a company that doesn't pay attention to them.

- **Stay consistent.** Consumers will have many interactions with the company and often through different channels or departments. At all times, the company must consistently demonstrate an understanding of consumers' needs. If a consumer's experience changes from store to store, or department to department, his or her emotional connection with the company will be lost.

- **Show, Don't Tell.** Words are meaningless if they are contradicted or unsupported by the actions of the company. A well-crafted media campaign may bring the prospective customer to try the product or service, but loyalty is only achieved when the company fully delivers on the public-relations promise. Slogans about caring mean nothing if you don't show clearly how you care.

Notes

1 The Hidden Emotional Needs behind Our Decisions

1. Goleman, Daniel. *Vital Lies, Simple Truths: The Psychology of Self-Deception*. New York: Simon and Schuster, 1985. Print.
2. Abrams, Jeremiah, and Connie Zweig. *Meeting the Shadow: The Hidden Power of the Dark Side of Human Nature*. Los Angeles: J. P. Tarcher, 1991. Print.
3. Damasio, Antonio R. *Descartes' Error: Emotion, Reason, and the Human Brain*. New York: Putnam, 1994. Print.
4. Murphy, Emmett C., and Mark A. Murphy. *Leading on the Edge of Chaos*. New Jersey: Prentice Hall, 2002. Print.
5. Aaker, Jennifer, Susan Fournier, and S. Adam Brasel. *When Good Brands Do Bad: Brand Personalities, Acts of Transgression, and the Evolution of Relationship Strength*. Available at SSRN: http://ssrn.com/abstract=339381.
6. Snyder, Bill. "Highly Trusted Brands Run More Risk of Offending Customers." *Stanford GSB News*. Stanford Business School, Feb.-Mar. 2003. Web. <http://www.gsb.stanford.edu/news/research/mktg_goodbrands.shtml>.
7. Harris, G. E. "Sidney Levy: Challenging the Philosophical Assumptions of Marketing." *Journal of Macromarketing* 27.1 (2007): 7–14. Print.

2 The Needs Continuum

1. *Monty Python: The Meaning of Life*, directed by Terry Jones. (City: Universal Pictures, 1983), DVD.
2. Sheldon, K. M., A. J. Elliot, Y. Kim, and T. Kasser. "What Is Satisfying about Satisfying Events? Testing 10 Candidate Psychological Needs." *Journal of Personality and Social Psychology* 89 (2001): 325–339. Print.

3. *Maslow's Hierarchy of Needs*. Digital image. *Wikipedia.com*. June 18, 2009. Web. Sept. 30, 2011.
4. Gilbert, Daniel, and Jack Youngelson. "This Emotional Life Episode 3." *This Emotional Life*. Prod. Tina Nguyen, Jack Youngelson, and Sabin Streeter. (Arlington, VA: PBS) Jan. 6, 2010. Television.

3 The Need for Control

1. *Encyclopedia of Human Behavior*, ed. V. S. Ramachandran (New York: Academic Press, 1994), s.v. "self-efficacy." Print.
2. Faranda, William. "A Scale to Measure the Cognitive Control Form of Perceived Control: Construction and Preliminary Assessment." *Psychology & Marketing* 18.12 (2001): 1259–81. Print.

4 The Need for Self-Expression

1. Wikipedia, s.v. "Lascaux Painting," accessed Sept. 30, 2011, http://en.wikipedia.org/wiki/File:Lascaux_painting.jpg.
2. Lewis, Jone. "Pearl S. Buck Quotes." *About.com Women's History*. About.com. Web. Dec. 18, 2011.
3. Levy, Sidney J., and Dennis W. Rook. *Brands, Consumers, Symbols, & Research: Sidney J. Levy on Marketing*. Thousand Oaks, CA: Sage, 1999. Print.
4. Mead, Rebecca. "Letter from Tokyo: Shopping Rebellion." *The New Yorker Mar.* 18, 2002. Web.
5. James, William, Frederick Burkhardt, Fredson Bowers, and Ignas K. Skrupskelis. *The Principles of Psychology*. Cambridge, MA: Harvard University Press, 1981. Print.
6. Humphreys, L. (2010). "Historicizing Microblogging." *CHI Workshop on Micro-Blogging 2010*. http://cs.unc.edu/~julia/accepted-papers/Humphreys_HistoricizingTwitter.pdf.
7. Lowery, George. "Dear Diary, I'm Leaving You for Twitter: Researcher Finds Old Diary Entries Are Akin to Tweets." *Chronicle Online*. Cornell University, June-July 2010. Web. Feb.-Mar. 2011.
8. Christine, Rosen. "Virtual Friendship and the New Narcissism," *The New Atlantis*, Summer 2007, 15–31. Print.
9. Jayson, Sharon. "Are Social Networks Making Students More Narcissistic?" *usatoday.com*. USA Today, Aug. 25, 2009. Web. July–Aug. 2011.
10. Harris, Jodi. "MySpace's Gold on Marketing Self-Expression." *MySpace's Gold on Marketing Self Expression*. Imedia Connection, 13 June 2006. Web. 19 Dec. 2011.

11. Murray, H. A. (1938). *Explorations in Personality.* New York: Oxford University Press. Print.

5 The Need for Growth

1. Hensel, Rainer, Frans Meijers, Rien Van Der Leeden, and Joseph Kessel. "The Relation between Personal Growth Needs Concerning the Development of Personal Qualities and the Five Factor Model of Personality." Proceedings of Decowe Conference, Ljubljana, Slovenia. Decowe, Sept. 2009. Web. Oct. 2, 2011. <http://www.decowe.org/static /uploaded/htmlarea/files/The_relation_between_Personal_Growth _Needs.pdf>.
2. Raphaëlle Lambert-Pandraud, and Gilles Laurent (2010). "Why Do Older Consumers Buy Older Brands? The Role of Attachment and Declining Innovativeness." *Journal of Marketing*: 74, no. 5 (2010): 104–121.
3. DePaulo, Bella M. *Singled Out: How Singles Are Stereotyped, Stigmatized, and Ignored and Still Live Happily Ever After.* New York: St. Martin's, 2006. Print.
4. "As Single Becomes New Norm, How to Market without Stigma." *Single Edition.* Web. May-June 2010. <http://singleedition.com/As-Single -Becomes-New-Norm-How-to-Market-Without-Stigma.html>.

6 The Need for Recognition

1. Levinson, Harry. *The Great Jackass Fallacy.* Boston: Division of Research, Graduate School of Business Administration, Harvard University, 1973. Print.
2. Schaffer, Jeff, and Alec Berg. "The Calzone." *Seinfeld.* NBC. New York, Apr. 25, 1996. Television.
3. Honneth, Axel. *The Struggle for Recognition: The Moral Grammar of Social Conflicts.* Cambridge, MA: MIT University Press, 2007. Print.
4. Grant, Adam, and Francesca Gino. "A Little Thanks Goes a Long Way." *Journal of Personality and Social Psychology* 98, no. 6 (2010): 946–55. Web.
5. Johnson, Carolyn. "Hurry Up, the Customer Has a Complaint." *Boston. com.* Boston Globe, July-Aug. 2008. Web. July-Aug. 2009. <http:// www.boston.com/business/technology/articles/2008/07/07 /hurry_up_the_customer_has_a_complaint/?page=full>.
6. "Sami." *Everyculture.com.* Countries and Their Cultures. Web. Sept. 25, 2011. <http://www.everyculture.com/wc/Norway-to-Russia/Sami .html>.

7. Calkins, Tim, and Alice M. Tybout. *Kellogg on Branding: The Marketing Faculty of the Kellogg School of Management*. Hoboken, NJ: Wiley, 2005. Print.
8. The NPD Group. *Men's Prestige Skincare Growth Outpaces Women's*. *NPD.com*. The NPD Group, Oct. 19, 2006. Web.

7 The Need for Belonging

1. Hunt, Morton M. *The Story of Psychology*. New York: Anchor, 2007. Print.
2. Baumeister, Roy, and Mark Leary. "The Need to Belong: Desire for Interpersonal Attachments as a Fundamental Human Motivation." *Psychological Bulletin* 117, no. 3 (1995): 497–529. Print.
3. Gurel-Atay, Eda. "Changes in Social Values in the United States: 1976–2007: Self-Respect Is on the Upswing as 'A Sense of Belonging' Becomes Less Important." *Journal of Advertising Research* 50, no. 1 (2010): 57–67. Print.
4. Baumeister, Roy F., and Mark R. Leary. "The Need to Belong: Desire for Interpersonal Attachments as a Fundamental Human Motivation." *Psychological Bulletin* 117, no. 3 (1995): 497–529. Print.
5. Warhol, Andy. *The Philosophy of Andy Warhol: (From A to B and Back Again)*. Orlando: Harcourt, 2006. Print.
6. Fisher, Don. *Gap.com*. Web.
7. Stephanie W. "Re: There's No Place Like Home…Right?" Web log comment. *Bunje's Ap Langers*. Sept. 20, 2009. Web. Sept. 30, 2011. <http://room204rockssocks.blogspot.com/2009/09/theres-no-place-like-homeright.html>.
8. Gergen, Kenneth J. "Cell Phone Technology and the Realm of Absent Presence," in *Perpetual Contact*, ed. James Katz and Mark Aakhus (New York: Cambridge University Press, 2002): 227–241
9. Heath, Chip, and Dan Heath. *Made to Stick: Why Some Ideas Survive and Others Die*. New York: Random House, 2007. Print.
10. Stannard-Friel, Jessica. "Proving the Win-Win Strategy of Cause Related Marketing." *Changingourworld.com*. Changing Our World Inc., Nov. 5, 2004. Web. Oct. 2, 2011. <http://cwop.convio.net/site/News2?page=NewsArticle&id=5622&security=1&news_iv_ctrl=1043&printer_friendly=1>.
11. Sherif, Muzafer. *The Robbers Cave Experiment: Intergroup Conflict and Cooperation*. Middletown, CT: Wesleyan University Press, 1988. Print.
12. Sherif, Muzafer. *The Robbers Cave Experiment: Intergroup Conflict and Cooperation*. Middletown, CT: Wesleyan University Press, 1988. Print.
13. Schiro, Anne-Marie. "Courting Women Big and Small." *NY Times*. Nov. 24, 1998. Web.

8 The Need for Care

1. Cherry, Kendra. "The Science of Love: Harry Harlow & the Nature of Affection." *About.com Psychology*. About.com. Web. Apr.-May 2009. <http://psychology.about.com/od/historyofpsychology/p/harlow_love.htm>.
2. Blum, Deborah. *Love at Goon Park: Harry Harlow and the Science of Affection*. New York: Berkley, 2004. Print.
3. Blum, Deborah. *Love at Goon Park: Harry Harlow and the Science of Affection*. New York: Berkley, 2004. Print.
4. "Friends 'Help People Live Longer'" *BBC.com*. BBC, 15 June 2005. Web. Oct. 2, 2011. <http://news.bbc.co.uk/2/hi/health/4094632.stm>.
5. Orth-Gomer, K., A. Rosengren, and L. Wilhelmsen. Lack of Social Support and Incidence of Coronary Heart Disease in Middle-Aged Swedish Men. *Psychosom Med*. 55, no. 1 (Jan-Feb. 1993): 37–43. Print.
6. "Study: A Little Help from Friends Makes Wounds Heal Faster." *ScienceDaily.com*. Science Daily, Aug. 4, 2004. Web. Oct. 2, 2011. <http://www.sciencedaily.com/releases/2004/08/040804083847.htm>.
7. Franklin, Benjamin. *The Autobiography of Ben Franklin*. Sioux Falls, SD: Nu Vision Publications, 2009. Print.
8. Horovitz, Bruce. "Non-Profit Panera Café: Take What You Need, Pay What You Can." *usatoday.com*. USA Today, May 18, 2010. Web. Oct. 2, 2011.

Epilogue

1. "On Human Nature." Interview by Kate Soper. *Chomsky.info*. Noam Chomsky Official Website, Aug. 1998. Web. July–Aug. 2011. <http://www.chomsky.info/interviews/199808--.htm>.
2. Schultz, Howard. "Yes Business Can." *HuffingtonPost.com*. Huffington Post, 6 Nov. 2008. Web. Jan.–Feb. 2010.
3. Frost, Robert. "JFK Inaugural Poem - The Gift Outright." *Orwell Today*. Web. 20 Dec. 2011. <http://www.orwelltoday.com/jfkinaugpoem.shtml>.
4. Carey, Benedict. "Tracing the Spark of Creative Problem-Solving." *NYTimes.com*. New York Times, Dec. 6, 2010. Web. 18 Dec. 2011.
5. Carey, Benedict. "Tracing the Spark of Creative Problem-Solving." *NYtimes.com*. New York Times, Dec. 6, 2010. Web. July–Aug. 2011.
6. Reiss, Jon. "Am I a Film Maker or a Brand? Why Not Be Both?" Web log post. *JonReiss.com*. Jon Reiss, Sept. 21, 2010. Web. July–Aug. 2011.
7. *BankSimple.com*. Bank Simple. Web. Sept. 30, 2011.

board—and adding directors with more relevant backgrounds—is part of the solution to this problem, another factor often affects the way the quality of information that board members receive about the company. If your predecessor fed the board a steady diet of financial information and almost nothing relating to the factors that will underlie your strategic analysis—industry trends, competitive landscape, technology change, regulatory/political environment—how can you expect that board to engage in meaningful strategy discussions?

Late last year, I received a call from the Chair of a Philadelphia-based educational organization; she lamented how "useless" her Board of Trustees was. They don't know anything about how this organization works—how we actually make our money and what's going on with our donors that's caused everything to go sideways for us recently. I asked her what kind of orientation program directors received. "Oh, we don't do anything like that," she replied. "People don't have time for it. They just show up at the board meetings." Then I asked about the information board members received—what was in their board packages? "Not much, really. People don't have time to read that stuff. I just throw in some information about our next programs, new faculty—and of course we include the financials and how we're doing against our budget. I have no idea—"I cut in. "Do you see the point of this now? I reminded her. "It's up to you to educate your Trustees about your organization in a way that would enable them to engage in strategic discussions. Yes, you may need some new people at your board table with backgrounds in education—which you don't have now—but that doesn't absolve you from the responsibility to educate the trustees you do have in a meaningful way."

If you're a new CEO and your predecessor abdicated his responsibilities in the same way that this Chair did hers, it means you have some work ahead of you to get your board members up to speed before you engage with them on strategy. Conducting interviews with the board—through the process described earlier—is one way to bring to the surface any "gaps" in their understanding of key issues and ensure that they're addressed. But I'd urge you to go even further. Ask yourself: If you were sitting on the other side of your board table, what kind of information would help you to better understand the business—without getting into a level of detail that would be described as micromanagement? Nearly every board with which I've worked in the past five years has told me that it would prefer more information

Index

Aaker, Jennifer, 18–19, 220
Abbott Nutrition, 117, 120–22
Abrams, Jeremiah, 14
accident forgiveness, 203–5
Ainsworth, Mary, 192
Allstate, 203
Altripla, 175–76, 178, 180–81
American Express, 169–70
American International Group (AIG),
    56–57
American social values, evolution of, 158
Android phones, 209
Apple, 76, 89, 139–40, 176, 194
    see also iPod; iTunes
As You Like It (Shakespeare), 73
Asch, Soloman, 156–57
AT&T, 84
atmosphere, 165–66
attachment theory, 192
autonomy, 21, 28–29, 34, 37, 41, 43, 49,
    57–58, 62, 65, 103, 208
Ax Body Spray, 55–56

bailouts, 56
Bandura, Albert, 58
BankSimple, 221
Baumeister, Roy F., 159
Bayer Aspirin, 169
belonging
    atmosphere and, 165–66
    brands and, 160–61
    bringing groups together and, 160–62
    causes and movements, 167–70

emotional ties and, 164–65
group observation and, 167
HIV and, 175–81
out-groups and, 173–75
overview, 153–56
reference groups and, 163
self-driven culture and, 156–60
targeted marketing and, 166–67
tribalism and, 170–73
Beneath a Marble Sky (Schors), 161–62
Best Buy, 138
Bhaskara Wheel, 102
blind spots, 213–15
Blum, Deborah, 193
brand recognition, 141–45
Branson, Richard, 36
Brave New World, A (Huxley), 208
Bristol-Meyers Squibb, 175, 179
British Airways, 36
British Petroleum (BP), 19–20
Buck, Pearl S., 74

cable news, 91
care
    accident forgiveness and, 203–5
    Ben Franklin effect and, 195–98
    consequences of uncaring, 199–200
    customer care, 194–95
    insurance companies and, 200–5
    overview, 187–90
    science of, 190–94
Carey, Benedict, 216
cause marketing, 168–69

causes and movements, 167–70
Cervantes, Miguel, 35
Changing Our World, Inc., 169
Chapman, C.C., 138
Charles Schwab, 57–59
Charney, Dennis, 38
Chick-fil-A, 195, 198
Chomsky, Noam, 210–11
Cingular Wireless, 81–84, 89
Coca-Cola, 144, 160–61, 169
Coldwell Banker, 115–16
Comcast Cable, 138
communication, 217–18
Conley, Chip, 140
consumerism, human needs and, 210–11
control
    airline travelers and, 60–63
    appealing to control when consumers
        need guidance, 54–55
    vs. choice, 64–65
    cognitive, 59–60
    consumers and, 49–52
    customer service and proxy control,
        52–53
    innovation and, 53–54
    marketing and, 54–59
    overselling, 64
    overview, 47
    psychology of, 48–49
    unpredictability and, 65
Corona, 84–85, 96
creators, 80
customer care, 194–95
customer satisfaction, 20–22, 24, 50–53
customer service, 22, 52–53, 67–68, 137,
    139, 195, 218–19, 221

Daily Kos, 91
Damasio, Antonio, 15
Deci, Edward, 50
demand, enabling, 211–13
DePaulo, Bella, 115
digital identities, 87–88
Disney, 39–41, 111, 166
do-it-yourself (DIY), 58, 90–91
Don Quixote (Cervantes), 35
Doritos, 90

Dowler, Milly, 200
Dunkin' Donuts, 90

Einstein, Albert, 31
emotional needs
    belonging and, 164–65
    branding and, 80–85
    consumerism and, 22–23
    overview, 7–13
    power of trust and, 18–20
    psychology behind, 13–15
    relationships and, 17–18
    satisfaction and, 20–22
    wisdom of, 15–17
E.R.A. (Empathize, Reconcile, Affirm)
    overview, 106–7
    steps to achieve, 107–9
E*Trade, 57, 60
Europe, 40, 54, 145, 147, 170, 199

Facebook, 1–2, 86–88, 90, 92, 148,
    162, 182
false appeals, 114–17
fashion, 10–11, 75–77, 145, 174–75, 209
fear, psychodynamics of, 180–81
Fisher, Doris, 163
Fogel, Adrian, 116
Food and Drug Administration (FDA), 12
force-fitting needs, 218–19
Fournier, Susan, 18–19, 220
Franklin, Benjamin, 195–98
freecreditreport.com, 90
Frost, Robert, 214

Gap, 144–45, 163
Gay, Lesbian, Bisexual, Transgender
    (GLBT) groups, 177
General Electric (GE), 36
General Mills, 167
Gergen, Kenneth, 166
Gervais, Ricky, 213–14
Gilead Pharmaceuticals, 23, 175, 179–80
Gino, Francesca, 135
Giorgio Armani, 76
Glass, Ira, 168
Gold, Shawn, 88
Goleman, Daniel, 14

Google, 1–2, 209
Grameen Bank, 174
Grant, Adam M., 135
Grant, Karen, 147
"Great Jackass Fallacy, The" (Levinson), 129–30
Greenheart Chicago, 169
growth
  affirmation and, 107–9
  disaffirming/misaffirming, 114–17
  E.R.A. and, 106–7
  intellectual expansion, 112–14
  marketing and, 117–22
  milestones, developmental stages, and rites of passage, 109–12
  need for, 103–6
  overview, 101–3
Gurel-Atay, Eda, 158

Hamburger Helper, 167, 182
Harley-Davidson, 165, 173, 183
Harlow, Harry, 192–93
Haysbert, Dennis, 203
Heath, Chip and Dan, 167
Hegel, G.W.F., 133
Hertz, 49
HIV, 175–79, 208
Home Depot, 58, 66
Honneth, Axel, 133, 136
Howard, Darryl, 71–74
Humphreys, Lee, 86
Hunt, Morton, 156
Hurricane Katrina, 201
Huxley, Aldous, 208

IKEA, 53–54, 149
India, 161, 173–74
individuality
  belonging need and, 181
  care need and, 194
  consumerism and, 210–11
  control need and, 45, 48–49, 55
  needs continuum and, 34–39, 41–44
  recognition need and, 125, 128, 132, 134, 148
  self-expression and, 2, 69, 72–73, 75, 88, 92, 95

influencers, 80
Insight Consulting Group (ICG), 111, 117–18, 121
intellectual expansion, 112–14
introverts, 80
Invention of Lying, The, 213–14
iPhone, 194, 209, 217
iPod, 47, 49, 175, 207
  see also Apple
iTunes, 47, 139
  see also Apple

James, William, 78
Japan, 38, 77
Joie de Vivre hotel, 140
Jung, Carl, 13–14, 104
  persona, 13, 104–5
  shadow, 14, 104–5

Kamprad, Ingvar, 53
Kennedy, John F., 95
Keplinger, Dan, 80–84, 89
Kermode, Mark, 91
Kierkegaard, Søren, 167
Kinko's, 54

Leary, Mark, 159
LED lights, 213
Leo Burnett agency, 116
Levinson, Harry, 129
Levy, Sidney, 22, 76
Li, Charlene, 138
linguistics, 142
locus of control, 55–56, 58
logos, 8, 75–76, 132, 144–45, 203
Lorenz, Konrad, 192
Lott, Trent, 201–2
Love at Goon Park: Harry Harlow and the Science of Affection (Blum), 193
Lowe's, 58

Made to Stick (Heath and Heath), 167
Mahler, Margaret, 33
Marina Rinaldi, 174–75
Maslow, Abraham, 30–32, 44, 158, 191, 193
Max Mara, 174

Mayo, Simon, 91
Mead, Rebecca, 77
McDonald's, 54, 149
McEnroe, John, 49
mirrors, 142–43
Morgan, Christina, 94–95
mothers, 3, 33, 41, 117–21, 149, 167, 169, 182, 189–92, 209–10
Motrin, 209–10
Mountain Dew, 90, 160
Murdoch, Rupert, 200
Murray, Henry, 94–95
MySpace, 86, 88

National Public Radio (NPR), 23, 168
NBA (National Basketball Association), 138
needs continuum
  connectedness and, 37–38
  explained, 33–35
  happiness and, 29
  human behavior and, 29
  ignoring, 30
  individuality and, 35–37
  marketplace and, 39–43
  Maslow's hierarchy of needs, 30–32
  needs continuum, 33–35
  overview, 27–28
  relationships and, 17–18
  universality of human needs, 28–30
Nestlé, 199
News Corporation, 199–200
News of the World, 199–200
Nike, 30
Nivea, 23, 145–48
nonprofits, 168–69
Norris, Janet, 127–30

O'Brien, Conan, 144
O'Neal, Shaquille, 217–18
Orfalea, Paul, 54
organizational consistency, 219–20
out-groups, 171, 173–76, 178, 181

Palin, Michael, 27
Panera Bread, 197–98
patterns, 143–45

people living with HIV (PLWHIV), 175–79
Pepsi, 144, 160
personalization, 136–40
pork, 7–10, 12–13
prisoners of war (POWs), 38
proxy control, 52–54

ReadyMade magazine, 90–91
recognition
  brand recognition, 141–45
  marketing and, 145–48
  need for, 131–34
  overview, 127–31
  personalization and, 136–40
  psychology of "thank you" and, 134–36
  rights and privileges and, 140–41
reference groups, 163–64
Reiss, John, 217
retail experience, 67
retirement, 97, 109, 111
rights and privileges, 140–41
Roosevelt, Eleanor, 31
Rorschach test, 94
Rosen, Christine, 87
Rotter, Julian, 54–55
Ryan, Richard, 50

satisfaction, 20–22
Saunders, Clarence, 53
Schultz, Howard, 213
Second Life, 87
Seinfeld, 131
self-efficacy, 58–59, 135
self-expression
  branding and, 92–93
  changing nature of, 79–80
  human nature and, 74–79
  marketing and, 80–85
  overview, 71–74
  technology and, 85–92
Shaich, Ron, 197–98
Shakespeare, William, 73
shame, psychodynamics of, 179
Sharpie, 89, 97
Sheldon, Kennon M., 28–30, 34

Sherif, Muzafer, 171–72
Shors, John, 161–62, 165
showing vs. telling, 220–21
Shumaker, Bob, 38
Six Flags, 111
Skittles, 162
smartphones, 40, 42, 164, 166,
    182, 209
Smith, Kevin, 217
social Darwinism, 195
social learning theory (SLT), 54–55
social media, 1, 86–88, 138, 140, 148,
    162, 182
Sprite, 160
Starbucks, 213
State Farm, 201
Story of Psychology, The (Hunt), 156

T-Mobile, 166
Tata, 174
Taylor, Charles, 131–32
teenagers, 34, 47, 51, 122, 163–64, 181
"thank you," psychology of, 134–36
thematic apperception test (TAT), 94
Town Hall, 91
Trader Joe's, 167, 220
trust, 18–20
Turkle, Sherry, 88
Twenge, Jean, 88

tweens, 166
Twilight, 173
Twitter, 1, 18, 42, 86–88, 91–92, 138,
    148, 182, 209, 217

uncertainty, 215–17
unconscious needs
    psychology behind, 13–15
Undercover Boss, 212
United Airlines, 62, 64, 140
Universal Studios, 23, 39–41, 111

Vaillant, George, 95
Vann, Virginia, 81
Verizon, 209
Virgin Group, 36
Vitamin Water, 90, 92

Wanamaker, John, 190–91
Warhol, Andy, 160–61
Watson, John, 191–92, 194
Wayne, John, 35–36
Welch, Jack, 36
Winfrey, Oprah, 162

YouTube, 91, 209
Yunus, Muhammad, 174

Zweig, Connie, 14

This chapter will discuss some of the key issues for you to consider in working effectively with your board committees. It incorporates the views and advice of collaborators with specialized and practical expertise in Audit Committees and Compensation Committees, where noted.

AUDIT COMMITTEES

The Audit Committee section was coauthored by Beverly Behan and Frank L. Borelli. Mr. Borelli has served as Chairman of the Audit Committees of Express Scripts and Brightcove Financial, and as the Lead Director of the Interpublic Group of Companies. Earlier in his career he served as the Chief Financial Officer of Marsh & McLennan Companies and was formerly an Audit Partner at Deloitte Haskins & Sells.

Directors generally view the Audit Committee as the most important and demanding of the three key board committees, given its responsibilities to ensure that the company's financial statements are accurate and reliable, and that appropriate financial controls are in place. Because the Audit Committee tends to dive into a host of regulatory and financial details in its meetings, many CEOs avoid having much hands-on involvement with this committee—unless they personally come from a finance background—often preferring to delegate the Audit Committee interface to the Chief Financial Officer.

The Audit Committee regularly works with the CFO, controller, head of internal audit, and external auditors. Sarbanes-Oxley requires the Audit Committee to meet alone with the external auditors at least once a quarter; it has increasingly become a best practice for the committee to meet alone with the head of internal audit, the CFO, and the controller once a quarter as well. It would certainly be a mistake for any CEO to try to insert himself between the committee and the company's financial executives. But it is equally a mistake for any CEO to delegate all dealings with the Audit Committee to his financial team unless, or until, some serious financial-reporting problem looms on the horizon.

Since the fall of Enron, Audit Committees have been deluged with a daunting array of regulatory requirements, and most have put in extraordinary efforts and many extra hours to ensure compliance.